ALSO BY GLENN BECK

The 7: Seven Wonders That Will Change Your Life

Broke: The Plan to Restore Our Trust, Truth and Treasure

The Overton Window

Idiots Unplugged: Truth for Those Who Care to Listen (audiobook)

The Christmas Sweater: A Picture Book

Arguing with Idiots:
How to Stop Small Minds and Big Government

Glenn Beck's Common Sense: The Case Against
an Out-of-Control Government, Inspired by Thomas Paine

America's March to Socialism:
Why We're One Step Closer to Giant Missile Parades (audiobook)

The Christmas Sweater

An Inconvenient Book:
Real Solutions to the World's Biggest Problems

The Real America:
Messages from the Heart and Heartland

THE

ORIGINAL

ARGUMENT

The Federalists' Case for the Constitution,
Adapted for the 21st Century

GLENN BECK
WITH JOSHUA CHARLES

CONTRIBUTIONS FROM: KEVIN BALFE,
WYNTON HALL, DAVID HARSANYI, AND
PETER SCHWEIZER

THRESHOLD EDITIONS   MERCURY RADIO ARTS

NEW YORK LONDON TORONTO SYDNEY

A Division of Simon & Schuster, Inc.
1230 Avenue of the Americas
New York, NY 10020

First Threshold Editions trade paperback edition June 2011

THRESHOLD EDITIONS and colophon are trademarks of Simon & Schuster, Inc.

For information about special discounts for bulk purchases, please contact Simon & Schuster Special Sales at 1-866-506-1949 or business@simonandschuster.com.

The Simon & Schuster Speakers Bureau can bring authors to your live event. For more information or to book an event contact the Simon & Schuster Speakers Bureau at 1-866-248-3049 or visit our website at www.simonspeakers.com.

Designed by Ruth Lee-Mui

Manufactured in the United States of America

10 9 8 7 6 5 4 3 2 1

Library of Congress Cataloging-in-Publication Data

Beck, Glenn.
   The original argument : the federalists' case for the Constitution, adapted for the 21st century / Glenn Beck, with Joshua Charles.
     p. cm.
   1st Threshold Editions trade pbk. ed.
   Includes bibliographical references.
   1. Constitutional history—United States.   2. Constitutional law—United States.   3. Federalist.   I. Charles, Joshua.   II. Title.
   KF4541.B37 2011
   342.7302'9—dc22   2011017088

ISBN 978-1-4516-5061-7 (pbk.)
ISBN 978-1-4516-5062-4 (ebk.)

DEDICATIONS

GLENN:

To Joshua Charles and all the other young people in the world who accept the challenge to, as Thomas Jefferson wrote, "question with boldness." They realize that Divine Providence is active in all of our lives and that we are all here for a reason—but they also know that to find that reason and fulfill our potential we must break through the chains of ignorance and fear.

JOSHUA:

To my parents, who unceasingly taught me the one principle from which all other worthwhile principles come: to do good. And to all of those throughout my life who convinced me of the profound uniqueness of this country, along with the responsibility that naturally becomes the burden of all those who live here.

CONTENTS

PART THREE: A REPUBLIC, IF YOU CAN KEEP IT

PART FOUR: THE DELICATE BALANCE OF POWER

PART FIVE: MINIMUM GOVERNMENT, MAXIMUM FREEDOM

PART SIX: TAXATION WITH REPRESENTATION

PART SEVEN: TRUTH, JUSTICE, AND THE AMERICAN WAY

THE BIRTH OF A BOOK ABOUT THE BIRTH OF OUR NATION: HOW THIS BOOK CAME TO BE

by Joshua Charles

CALLER: Do you think that with today's partisan politics on both sides of the aisle the Constitution would ever get signed today?

GLENN: Not today, because there are not people out there making the case for the Constitution. I mean, if you rewrote the Federalist Papers today and there was a real movement to get those Federalist Papers out, to show why the Constitution should be accepted, then yes, people would read it, they would consume it, and they might even renew our country.

—*The Glenn Beck Program*, January 14, 2011

Our Founders strongly believed that Divine Providence played a critical role in the birth of our country. Looking back on the great improbabilities and coincidences that colluded to put this book into your hands, I'm forced to concede that it may have intervened here as well.

But I'm getting ahead of myself. It wasn't long ago that I was majoring in piano performance at the University of Kansas. In other words, I'm not exactly the type of person normally associated with writing a book about the Federalist Papers. But the beginning of this journey had nothing to do with the Federalist Papers, or books, or even America. It all began with a movie.

In the fall of 2009 I saw *Amazing Grace,* a film about the great British abolitionist and humanitarian William Wilberforce. I was inspired by Wilberforce's courageous moral stand, and the sheer grit it took for him to fight for the cause of abolition over almost half a century. What an amazing lesson for someone living in twenty-first-century America, a land where morality is increasingly obscured by euphemism and political correctness.

I decided that I needed to know more about this man. Something about Wilberforce, something very compelling, kindled within me a desire to stand for . . . *something.*

Within a few days of watching the movie, I'd already finished reading two biographies of Wilberforce. Both were excellent, but the one by Eric Metaxas absolutely captivated me. It was in this book that I first learned that Wilberforce had written a book of his own: *A Practical View of Christianity.*

I picked up a copy and devoured it. It was a searing indictment of the religion of his day, yet full of love and grace, insight and brilliance. But I had one major problem with it: The writing style made for a very difficult reading experience. Instead of simply enjoying the book, I found myself spending half my time trying to untangle the elaborate language and Shakespearean vocabulary. I could barely understand, let alone enjoy, the words of my newfound hero. His message was impactful, but the reading experience was difficult.

Not long after I began grappling with Wilberforce, I had completed a second reading of the Federalist Papers and had felt a similar frustration trying to grasp what Publius was saying. Sure, parts of it were understandable, but just as with Wilberforce, the joy in reading them was drained by the archaic vocabulary and sentences that occasionally ran the entire page!

As all of this was going on with me personally, something else entirely was going on with America. Frustrated by decades of an overspending, overreaching, overbearing government, Americans were finally beginning to stand up. Regular people from every walk of life, every background, and every profession began to realize that they had given a pass to our politicians' irresponsibility for far too long. The people asserted their rightful place in determining the course of their country—no matter how much that course diverged from the prevailing "wisdom" of the elites. There was a growing sense, a palpable feeling, that *something* had gone wrong in America, something that went beyond the current president, or the Democrats and Republicans—and it was time to make it right.

With Wilberforce's story fresh in my mind, I decided that *my* something would be to "translate" the Federalist Papers into contemporary English. At a time when so many Americans were reevaluating the nation's fundamental principles, it was unfortunate, and indeed even tragic, I thought, that a work as important as the Federalist Papers was so difficult for most people to read. And when things are difficult, most people don't even attempt them.

During my senior year of college, I "translated" Federalist 1 and sent it to a few family members and friends for their reaction. After reading both the original and my translation, they were shocked at how much better they understood what our Founders were saying. But even more heartening was that they actually *enjoyed* reading it!

I was encouraged, but it was hardly enough to convince me to go any further. So a few friends thought I did a good job on one paper out of eighty-five—big deal. And even if it was good, who else would actually read it? How would it get out to the public?

What possible impact could something like this have, considering that it would be coming from an unknown twenty-two-year-old lacking any special credentials or expertise?

Then it happened.

I'm an enthusiastic viewer of the *Glenn Beck* show. In many ways, I believe Glenn is a great man, a lone voice who isn't afraid to buck popular sentiment for the country he loves. One evening as I watched, I heard him say this:

> You know what the problem is, honestly? We need really smart people that can take the Federalist Papers and rewrite them for the common man . . . If we rewrite these things in common language, people can access them a lot easier.

My jaw dropped to the floor. While I hardly thought of myself as one of the "really smart people" he was talking about, the co-incidence was jarring. Only two days earlier I had seriously con-sidered this idea, and now Glenn Beck was on national television suggesting the very same thing as a way to revive our founding principles, to make right what had gone wrong.

I decided then and there that this project *had* to be completed. I knew that if I could get the finished product into the hands of someone like Glenn Beck, then *he* could do something with it. *He* had the voice, the influence, the visibility, and the trust of many Americans.

That summer, after saving enough money to take a few months off work, I began the project in earnest. Most days, I la-bored over the papers for at least eight hours, though sometimes it was as much as fourteen, as I went sentence by sentence, line by line. But the doubts kept swirling through my mind. *Was it really worth it? Could I really get Glenn Beck to look at it? Even if I could, would he really find any value in some college kid's translations?*

Despite my initial enthusiasm, I was plagued by nearly constant and overwhelming doubts throughout the entire process. Ultimately, it was the sense of Divine Providence, the sense that something bigger than me was at work, that kept me going.

I didn't plan it this way, but I completed the rough draft on July 4, 2010. At that point, I began to edit the manuscript and also started to make numerous calls into Glenn's radio show (sometimes waiting on hold for hours), sending him letters, and writing emails. I even mailed a full manuscript of the book to the Fox News studios in New York City, with his name on it. Nothing seemed to be working. I wasn't getting through.

Meanwhile, I continued to edit the manuscript, and also began looking into smaller publishing houses to see if I could find an outlet for the book. But, truth be told, I was discouraged. At times I felt that what I had done was all for nothing. Sure, I'd learned a lot in the process of translating the papers, but my own education was not the goal. All along I'd held out hope that these papers might one day go beyond me—but now that hope seemed to be nearing a dead end.

Then it happened, again.

Around Christmastime I was again watching Glenn's show, with a fraternity brother and one of my best friends, Derek. That night's show happened to be about Wilmington, Ohio—a town that had been hit hard by the economic downturn. Eight thousand people who worked at the local DHL hub there had been laid off (and the entire town has only twelve thousand residents). Things looked hopeless to outsiders—and likely to some of the residents of Wilmington, as well—but what happened next doesn't happen to hopeless people. This small town banded together and refused to accept defeat. They united around each other, and their families, and around God. As a town, they turned to prayer, and found that the power of prayer is real, it is palpable, and that miracles happen when people fall on their knees before God.

I turned to Derek and said, "Are you thinking what I'm thinking?"

"I think so," he replied with a smirk on his face. "But what are you thinking?"

"I'm thinking we need to go to Wilmington."

"Yes," he responded. And that was that.

Being poor college students, we were concerned about how much a 1,400-mile round-trip by car would cost us. But I remember telling Derek, "You know, somehow I feel we just won't have to worry about lodging and food." Before going to bed that night, I emailed Robyn Morris at the Wilmington House of Prayer, a 24/7 prayer house that had been highlighted on Glenn's show.

A few days later Robyn called me. Without me ever broaching the subject, she offered to find us a host family in Wilmington and have our food covered! Again, I can't really explain it, but it felt like something bigger than me was going on. On the one hand a few college kids were making a road trip—big deal. But on the other hand, this was starting to feel like a trip in which, as I would later say on Glenn's show, we'd get to "see God move."

It turned out I was right.

Unbeknownst to me, Robyn Morris also happened to be the primary contact for the Glenn Beck producers who had organized Glenn's trip to the city. Just days before we were about to leave for Wilmington, Robyn emailed me saying that Glenn's staff had called for updates on the town's situation, during which she mentioned to them that four students from a Christian fraternity at the University of Kansas were coming to serve in Wilmington and that they might make for a good story.

My head was spinning. I had lost all hope that I would ever get in contact with Glenn about my book, and now here I was, closer to my opportunity than I'd ever been before. After all those phone calls and emails, my break had come from the most innocuous of places: me wanting to see God move firsthand in Wilmington. I *knew* then that there was more to this trip than met the eye.

Our trip to Wilmington ended up being one of the most impactful and amazing of my life. I witnessed what happens when individuals, of their own initiative, come together. I saw what happens when people reach out in love to each other—not through an intermediary or some government agency, but in person—face-to-face. Most important, I saw what happens when people pray fervently; when they humble themselves before God and ask for His direction. I saw what happens when it is no longer the stuff in our lives that matters the most, but instead the people in our lives. In a new way, a real way, I had eyes to see and ears to hear. And what was it that I saw and heard? Miracles. It sounds cliché, and I hate clichés, but this was as real as it gets. He is involved.

Just as we were getting onto I-70 to head back to Kansas, my phone rang. It was the Glenn Beck producers. They wanted to know about our trip to Wilmington—why we went, what we did, and what we saw—but they also told me that they'd heard about the book I was working on.

My heart raced as I answered their questions. Then they said, "We'd like you to come out to New York for the January twenty-first show on Wilmington. Would that be something you would be interested in?"

I tried to say yes as nonchalantly as I could. It had now been almost a year since I'd halfheartedly "translated" Federalist 1, and now here I was about to be on a show hosted by the one person whom I'd been trying to get all eighty-five papers in front of ever since.

So, I went to the Fox News studios in New York. Before we started recording the show, I shook Glenn's hand and handed him a bound copy of the translated Papers. He flipped through it and I remember him seeming very moved by it. I was incredibly impressed, both at that moment and in the weeks and months that were to follow, that the man I admired was the same in person as he was on TV.

Glenn told me that he would read more of it later, which was all that I could hope for. But then, without me uttering another word, he told me something else: He said that if this project was really what I'd claimed it was, then he'd like to work with me on creating a book that would not only make the Papers easier to read, but that would also bring them to life by explaining how the central themes that Publius wrote about still apply today.

Things had finally come full circle. Almost a year had passed since I had begun this project for which I had no guarantees of success—and my dream finally seemed to have a chance to come true.

Over the months that followed, Glenn and I spent a lot of time educating ourselves on the Papers. We wanted to go beyond their importance to the events of the 1700s to find the core themes and arguments that would still apply to today's debates. It turned out that those themes weren't difficult to locate—in fact, the hardest part was deciding which Papers wouldn't make the cut.

In the end, we selected thirty-three of the eighty-five Papers for this book. We then asked several people to read the translations to tell us what they were confused by. Based on that feedback we refined the translations further and grouped them according to their central themes (taxation, for example) instead of the straight chronological order they were originally published in. Meanwhile, Glenn and his team were also busy crafting introductions to each section that would provide the historical context and modern relevancy that are so important to understanding the Papers, but is so often missing. They also brought in experts to review the Papers to ensure that our translations were fair and accurate and to lend their insight to his essays.

We believe that *The Original Argument* is part of Glenn's E4 solution: E2 is Education, and E4 is Empowerment. It's meant to educate—but our country doesn't need people who are just educated. It's meant to empower—but our country doesn't need people who are just empowered. Our country needs both. It needs people who *know* the truth, not some vague version of it. It needs people who *know* the Constitution, not just clichés about it. It needs people who *know* what real sacrifice and patriotism are, not just those who can sing the national anthem at a sporting event.

Glenn and I have shared the same basic goal throughout this whole journey: to bring the message of our Founders to as many Americans as possible in a form that people will actually *want* to read. We hope that you come away from it understanding the Constitution, the logic behind its carefully debated principles, and the spirit that makes it much more than just words on paper, but also ready to fight for it and defend it. America needs more Wilberforces and Washingtons, not more Republicans and Democrats.

I believe that we now stand at another moment in history where America is at a crossroads. We all know it, we all feel it, and whatever our political persuasion happens to be, we know that tough decisions will soon have to be made. I can only hope that this book will, in some small way, help those decisions be made by people who have a fuller understanding and appreciation for our founding principles, our Constitution, and the concept of individual freedom itself. With a firm reliance on Divine Providence, I believe with everything in me that this will happen.

I am extraordinarily proud of the finished product, and Glenn and I both hope that it will help reopen the discussion that Alexander Hamilton, James Madison, and John Jay began nearly 225 years ago.

Joshua Charles
Lawrence, Kansas, 2011

INTRODUCTION: THE GREAT AMERICAN EXPERIMENT

A User's Guide

Glenn Beck

It has been frequently remarked that it seems to have been reserved to the people of this country, by their conduct and example, to decide the important question, whether societies of men are really capable or not of establishing good government from reflection and choice, or whether they are forever destined to depend for their political constitutions on accident and force.

—Federalist 1

I t was the central question then just as it's the central question now: *Can man govern himself?* Can individuals peacefully choose to create a government that is good and wise, or must governments always be formed through war—or luck?

We may not yet have the final answer to that question, but before the Constitution was ratified it was unclear whether this historic experiment in individual liberties and limited government would even get off the ground. Distrust was rampant and different groups of people, often forming along state or religious lines, had different ideas on how to move forward.

Those opposed to the new constitution, collectively called the "Anti-Federalists," were generally wary of the power wielded by the larger states and were concerned that the structure being proposed—a true republic—could never work in practice. They believed that it was set up to fail and that the presidency would quickly morph into another monarchy.

Then you had groups like the Puritans, Virginians, and Quakers, who seldom agreed on, well, much of anything. As Virginian William Byrd II said of the Puritans, "A watchful eye must be kept on these foul traders." And both the Puritans and Virginians said things like this about the Quakers: "They pray for their fellow men one day a week, and on them the other six."

How about that for hateful rhetoric?

That kind of disunity and lack of trust made ratifying the Constitution difficult. The young ragtag nation had accomplished the Herculean task of throwing off the British monarchy, but they knew that nature abhors a vacuum. Without a strong central government to replace the initial Articles of Confederation—which did not give the federal government the power to levy taxes, regulate trade, or even enforce laws—they were afraid that the old monarchy might quickly be replaced with a new one, or worse, with anarchy.

So after the drafting of the Constitution in September 1787, all eyes turned to New York, which along with Virginia was considered the eighteenth-century version of a "swing state." If either New York or Virginia rejected the document, the union would have little chance to succeed.

Alexander Hamilton realized right away that this could be a major problem. Back in Philadelphia, Hamilton had witnessed his fellow New Yorkers walk out of the Constitutional Convention. He knew that the citizens of his home state would need to be convinced of the need to abandon the Articles and move forward with a completely new type of government. Interestingly, while Hamilton personally supported a much stronger federal government than what was called for in the Constitution, he understood that the September 1787 document was about as perfect as it would get.

In October 1787, with the public debate in full swing and the proposed constitution hanging by a thread, Hamilton devised a plan to write and publish a series of papers answering the criticisms being lobbied against the Constitution and defending the need for a federal government.

Hamilton attempted to enlist Gouverneur Morris of Pennsylvania, a terrific writer who had added much of the final polish to the language in the Constitution, to help him tackle the writing load, but Morris declined because of business commitments.[1] Hamilton then turned to thirty-six-year-old James Madison, who had served in the Continental Congress and had played a key role in drafting the "Virginia Plan," the document upon which the Constitution was modeled. Madison agreed to join him and, with the help of John Jay, the trio began writing a series of essays, each addressed "To the People of the State of New York."

Despite their noted accomplishments, the men decided to publish their essays anonymously under the pen name "Publius," a reference to Publius Valerius Publicola, a supporter of the Roman Republic. It seems odd to us that they should publish such important ideas under a pseudonym, but almost everyone writing in support of and against the Constitution at this time did the same thing.[2] "Publius" promised to deliver four essays a week, which would have been difficult enough, but when John Jay fell ill after contributing only five papers, Hamilton and Madison were forced to carry an even heavier writing load.

---

1. Richard Beeman, *Plain, Honest Men*, p. 406.
2. Gregory Maggs, "A Concise Guide to the Federalist Papers as a Source of the Original Meaning of the United States Constitution," *Boston University Law Review*, 87:801 (2007).

Hamilton still had his job as a lawyer at the time, so writing time was scarce. When he came home from work he would often drink strong coffee, fire up a lamp for illumination, and write for six hours straight, into the early hours of the morning. He wrote whenever he could, even penning a few of the essays aboard a Hudson River sloop headed upriver to Albany.

The fact that Hamilton and Madison were so prolific while working full-time jobs is astonishing. Between October 1787 and May 1788, more than 175,000 words flowed from their quills. When Hamilton found his writing rhythm, he was able to produce twenty-one essays in just eight weeks. Most of the essays, Madison confessed, were written "in great haste, and without any special allotment of the different parts of the subject to the several writers." He later explained that he used notes from the Constitutional Convention to craft the document.

Given the hardships they were facing, the Federalist Papers should be considered another in a long line of miracles surrounding America's founding. If not for those men coming together at the right moment and anonymously mounting a strong, reasoned, passionate defense, the American Experiment might never have gotten out of the laboratory.

Today, the series of newspaper articles that ran from October 1787 through August 1788 is known as the "Federalist Papers," and, let's be honest, the mere mention of them usually results in most people yawning. They're written in terribly hard-to-read eighteenth-century English, they reference things that most of us have never heard about, and, let's just say it: They seem *irrelevant*. The Federalists won, the Constitution was ratified—end of story.

But the Federalist Papers are more important than that. Yes, they're old. Yes, they're hard to read. And yes, they can be boring. Okay, yes, they can be *excruciatingly* boring. But if the Constitution was like a new electronic gadget in 1787, the Federalist Papers were like its user manual. Sure, you can jump right in and try to use the gadget, but to get the most of it—to really understand how its designers and manufacturers intended for you to use it—you've got to read the manual.

What the Federalist Papers offer to us today is a guide to understanding the Founders' core constitutional principles, the theories behind their words, the why, where, and how of the foundation of America:

- Why smaller government makes better government
- Where federal power ends and state power begins
- How government should be organized and operated to maximize efficiency and minimize the risk of another monarchy

Thomas Jefferson, who supported the Constitution but wanted it to include a Bill of Rights, called the Papers "the best commentary on the principles of government . . . ever written." The British political philosopher John Stuart Mill agreed, adding that the Federalist Papers are "the most instructive treatise we possess on federal government." And Alexis de Tocqueville called the collection "an excellent book, which ought to be familiar to the statesmen of all countries."

But unfortunately, not only are the Papers not "familiar" to most Americans today—a large portion of the country either doesn't know they exist or has no idea what they're about. And that's a shame, because we need the wisdom of these essays now more than ever.

For example, the Papers remind us that our constitutional birthright is a stewardship that must be preserved and protected, not distorted for ideological convenience. Better still, they offer one of the most profound insights available into the human nature of politics: *No matter the century, people are people and politicians are politicians.* Perhaps more than any system designed before or after, our Constitution acknowledges that all men are fallible and that since no man can perfectly rule another, all men must rule themselves.

Yes, the Papers include long arguments about topics that were relevant only to that period or that have changed with the times, but they also include a series of truths that are eternal. Truths that apply to today's world just as much as they did in the eighteenth century.

That is one reason why the Papers' influence has been so far-reaching. There have been more than three hundred editions of the Federalist Papers, including translations in Bulgarian, Chinese, Croatian, French, German, Hebrew, Italian, Japanese, Korean, Russian, Spanish, and others.[1] In fact, leaders in Europe, Latin America, Asia, and Africa have reportedly read the Papers while crafting their own constitutions. Taken together, the Constitution and Federalist Papers have probably done more for individual rights around the world than any other documents in history.

Laurence Silberman, a federal appeals court judge and winner of the Presidential Medal of Freedom, believes that the Federalist Papers are "perhaps even more important as an interpretive aid" than the records from the Constitutional Convention itself. Why? "Because (the Federalist Papers), unlike the records of the Convention, were available to the state ratifying conventions."[2] In other words, since the state delegates were able to read the Papers in advance of their conventions, it's reasonable to assume that they read and implicitly endorsed the arguments made by Publius.

---

1. Quotes from "Explaining the Constitution: The Federalist Papers," www.america.gov, and Wright, *One Nation Under Debt*, p. 92.
2. Quoted in Maggs, "A Concise Guide."

While interest in the Federalist Papers has wavered over the years, their relevance has actually increased. The first citing of the Papers in a Supreme Court decision was in *Calder v. Bull* in 1798—and it was the only citing by the Supreme Court that entire decade. During the nineteenth century, however, the Federalist Papers were cited fifty-eight times. In 1821, Chief Justice of the Supreme Court John Marshall described the Papers as "a complete commentary on our Constitution." In the last half of the twentieth century, they were cited 194 times.

To understand why the Papers have had so much enduring influence, it helps to have a little background on who the people behind "Publius" really were. Alexander Hamilton, then just thirty-two years old, hatched the idea and wrote 51 of the 85 articles. Born out of wedlock, Hamilton was orphaned at an early age and spent the first third of his life growing up in the West Indies on the island of Nevis. As a teenager, he developed a strong interest in commerce and capitalism, which culminated in his governing of a multinational mercantile business. Through these "global" experiences, he cultivated the aristocratic flair for which he later became known.

After immigrating to New York, Hamilton was commissioned as a captain to fight the British. Although just nineteen years old, he quickly gained a reputation for bravery. As one observer put it, Hamilton's unit "drew all eyes by the disciplined appearance of its ranks and the brisk, soldierly stride of its men." George Washington was so impressed with Hamilton's intellect, ambition, and courage that he promoted him to lieutenant colonel and made him his personal assistant. Later, Hamilton would go on to serve as America's first treasury secretary and the chief architect of Washington's economic policies.

James Madison had a different kind of résumé. Madison has the distinction of being the shortest president in U.S. history (five foot, four inches, and just 100 pounds)—but his intellect was inversely proportional to his physical stature. Book-smart and soft-spoken, Madison attended the College of New Jersey (now Princeton University) under the brilliant President Reverend John Witherspoon. It's been said that Madison's public shyness and gentle voice sometimes made him all but inaudible—but of course it was the power of his pen that won him a place in history as the "Father of the Constitution." Madison inked 29 of the 85 Federalist Papers and served on the Committee on Style, which determined the final wording of the Constitution.

Rounding out the group was lawyer, builder, and diplomat John Jay. Tall and thin, Jay had deep-set gray eyes that sat beneath a sweeping bald crown. He was a family man with a deep faith and had served as both president of the Continental Congress and minister to Spain. Once America had severed itself from British rule, Jay gained a reputation as a staunch patriot with a strong command of foreign policy.

Like so much else in American history, the fate of the Federalist Papers hinged on a few ordinary people doing extraordinary things. These three brave, brilliant, and flawed souls understood how fragile the newborn nation was and realized that the ratification process wouldn't be easy. But without a Constitution resulting from the struggle, who knew what would become of America?

In many ways, they were winging it. They had no playbook. Inventing a nation out of thin air like the one they envisioned was an idea without precedent. Yet they knew they had two guiding hands: God, and the miracles He'd already worked to get them this far, and the undeniable lessons of human nature throughout history.

"Experience," James Madison explained, "is the oracle of truth and where its responses are unequivocal, they ought to be conclusive and sacred." The Founders understood that human nature seldom changes, and therefore the importance of history—a record of human nature that serves as a mirror of the human condition—never loses relevance.

The Founders' faith in God meant that they believed our rights came directly from Him. As Alexander Hamilton put it, "The sacred rights of mankind are not to be rummaged for among old parchments or musty records. They are written, as with a sunbeam, in the whole volume of human nature, by the hand of the Divinity itself, and can never be erased or obscured by mortal power."[1] But that same faith made them understand that human sin was here to stay. They were not naïve enough to believe that a government—*any* government—could stop human nature. Therefore, the young upstart nation would need a practical government built on an accurate reading of how flawed creatures think and behave in the real world, not in some idealized utopia.

Hamilton, Madison, and Jay believed that the Constitution offered a workable plan for organizing a federal government. They appreciated the fact that embedded in the Constitution was the commonsense idea that humans are fallible creatures who cannot be trusted with too much power. Greed, ambition, checks and balances, separation of powers—the Federalist Papers addressed and explained it all.

Ultimately, the Federalist Papers were about transparency. Unlike now, when several-thousand-page bills are routinely passed without citizens (and sometimes even legislators) knowing what's in them, our Founders wanted the public to know exactly what they would be getting. The Papers gave citizens a chance to hear the best arguments in support of the Constitution and

---

1. Quoted in John Eidsmoe, *Christianity and the Constitution*, p. 145.

understand how the new government would actually function. They outlined what a balanced government would look like and explained why certain powers belonged to the federal government while others should remain with the states. Best of all, the Papers were written in a clear voice that lacked pretense and was easy for most Americans (well, at least most eighteenth-century Americans) to understand.

In terms of the actual writing of the Papers, the authors worked separately and didn't consult with each other much, yet they found a natural division of labor. Madison tended to focus on general issues of government, republicanism, and representation. Hamilton covered issues such as taxes and the judiciary. And Jay, the diplomat who was older and a virtual reservoir of foreign-policy knowledge, had been brought aboard to cover international affairs.

At the time of their publication, New York City had seven newspapers, most of which were just a few pages long and primarily contained advertisements, printed on heavy paper with small type that made them hard to read. For this reason, many speculate that more citizens likely heard the Federalist Papers read aloud in taverns and homes than actually read them for themselves.[1] Four of New York City's seven newspapers decided to publish some or all of the Federalist Papers. The first one appeared in the *Independent Journal* on October 27, 1787.

No sooner was that initial essay printed than the barrage of attacks began. One critic, also anonymous and just called "Centinel," said that Publius suffered an "imbecility of judgment" and that his "deranged brain" produced "myriads of unmeaning sentences."[2]

---

1. Wright, *One Nation Under Debt*, p. 93.
2. Quoted in ibid., p. 95.

Even today, some people would prefer that you not read the Federalist Papers. Instead they would rather contort Publius's words to serve their own narrow ideological ends. Some people have tried to rewrite history and the intent behind the Federalist Papers to create a false portrait of our Founding Fathers as the "New Dealers" of their day.[1] Others have attempted to diminish the Papers' importance by labeling them as outdated and irrelevant. It's probably no surprise, however, that many of the people who make those claims have a very different vision for America than the one Publius outlined. After all, those who are honest in their love for America should have no issue with anyone reading our founding documents and drawing their own conclusions. It's people who want to speak in place of those documents that we should be wary of.

Today, once again, we find ourselves in a country embroiled in a heated debate about its future. Is big government or small government the answer? Should more power be in Washington, or with the states? Is power really able to be shared among the three branches? And, of course, that eternal question that has yet to be answered: *Is man really capable of ruling himself?*

Our Founders understood that history could be their guide to the future, and now we must realize that as well. Yes, some of the specific issues we face today are different from those contemplated in the eighteenth century (believe it or not, they weren't worried so much about "trans fats" back then), but the fundamental questions remain the same.

The Federalist Papers are perhaps the most complete attempt ever made at outlining specifically how a government should operate to ensure maximum freedom without anarchy. And therein lies the problem: Very few people care to read them. It's much eas-

---

1. Edward Millican, *One United People: The Federalist Papers and the National Idea*, p. 5.

ier to pick up some modern-day book with great packaging and a clear, concise, contemporary writing style than it is to go onto the Internet, print out all of the Federalist Papers, and attempt to struggle through reading and understanding them.

That's where the idea for this book came from. By translating a selected number of the original Federalist Papers into a more readable and relatable format, we hope to expose their wisdom to a far wider audience. It's not about ideology, it's about history. It's about understanding the case for the Constitution as it was made in the eighteenth century, not the case that is being made today by political parties hoping to push forward their own agendas.

Great care was taken in the translation process to update Publius's words in the most accurate, nonideological way possible. When interpretation was necessary we erred on the side of caution. We also try to explain some of the historical references that may not be familiar to modern-day readers. These are often important to understand, since they explain the world that our Founders lived in and provide the context necessary to understand their ideas. My hope is that readers will make up their own minds and form their own opinions on Publius's arguments and how they apply to the issues we face today.

Alexander Hamilton, James Madison, and John Jay translated the genius of our founding charter in ways that average citizens could understand and appreciate. In so doing, they won over the hearts and minds of not only New Yorkers but Americans across the confederacy and tipped the balance toward ratification.

The Federalist Papers breathed new life into the Constitution back then.

I believe they can do the same thing now.

Glenn Beck
New York City, 2011

PART ONE

NOVUS ORDO SECLORUM:
A NEW ORDER
FOR THE AGES

If you have a one-dollar bill handy, go ahead and pull it out. Turn it over to the back and look at the pyramid on the left. Beneath it you'll find the Latin phrase Novus Ordo Seclo-rum. It means "A New Order for the Ages" and it's a permanent part of the Great Seal of the United States.

That concept—that America was creating something entirely new and historic—can also be found woven throughout the Federalist Papers. Read, for example, the words Alexander Hamilton chose for the introduction in Federalist 1:

"After an unequivocal experience of the inefficacy of the subsisting federal government," he began, "you are called upon to deliberate on a new Constitution for the United States of America. The subject speaks its own importance; comprehending in its consequences nothing less than the existence of the UNION, the safety and welfare of the parts of which it is composed, the fate of an empire in many respects the most interesting in the world."

It's easy to forget that Americans were expecting the delegates they'd sent to Philadelphia to come back with a plan for how to amend the Articles of Confederation. Instead, they came back with a bold new vision for government—and a new constitution to match. But that didn't make it an easy sell. People were justifiably concerned about the need to take such a dramatic step, and they were duly confused about exactly what the Constitution would mean for them personally.

Federalist 1 was Hamilton's first chance to make the case that not only was a completely new document necessary, but also that the specifics of the document would make America, as he wrote later in Federalist 11, "the envy of the world." He wanted readers to understand that the vision articulated in the Constitution wasn't meek or timid but rather one that could point the world toward freedom.

History has proven that he was right.

Making the Case for Change

There are over 175,000 words in the Federalist Papers but perhaps none of them sum up the documents' purpose as clearly and succinctly as these 46:

> Nothing remains as obvious as the fact that either the new Constitution will be adopted, or the Union will be torn apart. It is therefore necessary to examine the advantages of the Union, as well as the evils and dangers that would result from its disbanding.

For Hamilton, it was do or die: Either the Constitution would be ratified or the young nation would die a premature death. For New Yorkers, the choice was even starker: ratify and join with the rest of the union, or stand aside even as the document was likely ratified without them, an event that might have resulted in the country's being torn apart.

Yet instead of trying to frighten people with the dire consequences they might face should they not accept the Constitution, Publius calmly took on each of the legitimate objections being raised by critics.

First, they addressed the objections of the New Yorkers who were wondering what was wrong with the Articles of Confederation. These citizens claimed that the Constitutional Convention overstepped its boundaries by creating an additional document that wasn't even necessary. These critics believed that the Articles themselves could simply be amended to strengthen the rule of law—as was the original plan. Publius would have to explain how the Constitution itself was necessary.

Next, Hamilton knew that he needed to explain why a national government over the states was preferable to one over individuals—and why a combination of states into a Union made sense. For citizens who were blindingly loyal to their individual states, this was a big mental hurdle to get past.

Then Hamilton wanted to paint a clear-eyed, panoramic picture of America's economic peril. The states were awash in war debt and their use of paper money had spun out of control. Congress remained in gridlock and state administrations were woefully inefficient. And, as if all that weren't enough, there was no consensus on trade policies and foreign affairs. To put it simply, America was in utter disarray. Hamilton wanted readers to come to grips with the reality and gravity of their situation as a means to understanding why such drastic change was necessary.

Additionally, Hamilton wanted his fellow New Yorkers to understand that the constitution under consideration represented something truly original: a pathway to the liberty they desired—one that empowered individuals to have a voice without threat of violence. This was a sharp break from the history of governments around the world. It was, after all, not just a minor tweaking of a government that had been tried before; it was a brand-new concept, an experiment in individual freedom that would allow man to govern himself.

Finally, Hamilton sought to explain how the Constitution would ensure a "firm and efficient" form of government. By "firm" he meant a government that had the strength to execute the duties and powers prescribed to it. But "efficient" was Hamilton's driving focus. The theme of efficiency echoes throughout the Federalist Papers, and for good reason: Absent a common currency or standard federal tax policy, state governments struggled to maintain a semblance of effectiveness and, at times, even basic order.

Hamilton let readers know from the beginning that all of Publius's arguments would be made in a civil tone, one worthy of the government they envisioned. Sure, the papers would call out the critics who were opposing the plan without even reading it, but Publius would avoid personal attacks. In fact, Publius could be the poster child for reasoned, rationale debate—a fact that is easy to overlook 225 years later but one that may have been key in bringing the country together. After all, it's easy to point to all of the crises, wars, and revolutions throughout history that have been started by people looking to divide, attack, and marginalize. It's much harder to find the instances of peace and unity brought on by those people who decided to do exactly the opposite. The Federalist Papers helped bring the country together.

One Nation, Under God

John Jay, who ended up contributing the fewest papers, wrote the next four opening papers (Federalist 2 through Federalist 5). While this set of essays eventually went into discussing the potential threat from foreign countries to the states, Jay started by picking up where Hamilton left off: with a pep talk.

The Constitution that was being debated, Jay reminded readers, was just that—a document that was being *debated*. It was being recommended to them, not forced on them, which he felt already made the process fairly unique in world history. People were having a real say as to whether some autocrat would have to be brought in, whether some title of nobility would be bestowed, or whether it was time to see if man was really capable of ruling himself.

Jay, of course, believed it was the latter—and he didn't believe that the country had come to that moment in history through luck. He mentioned the word *Providence* three separate times in Federalist 2 alone, including this paragraph, which shows that Jay did not believe that the concepts "one nation" and "under God" were separate from each other.

> This country and this people seem to have been made for each other, and it appears as if it was the design of Providence, that an inheritance so proper and convenient for a band of brethren, united to each other by the strongest ties, should never be split into a number of unsocial, jealous, and alien sovereignties.

It was God's plan that the colonists eventually throw off a tyrant and experience freedom. Splitting apart would not only be foolish, Jay argued, but it would also be against God's will.

Peace Through Strength

The Founders understood that prosperity and national security depended on each other. Profits produce taxes, and taxes fund the military. It's probably no coincidence, then, that America's rise to prosperity coincided with the rise of our national strength and unity. But back then this wasn't quite so obvious. Anti-Federalists believed that state sovereignty was paramount and that each state should be in charge of its own economy and security. In Federalist 11, Alexander Hamilton explained why that would never work.

Hamilton argued that a federal navy was necessary not only

to ensure that business could run smoothly and grow quickly, but also to ensure that the world would take the country seriously. Thirteen independent navies each patrolling the waters off their own borders would be chaotic, to put it mildly.

In order for a national navy to be founded, however, the federal government first had to be given sovereign authority over commerce. Otherwise, there would be thirteen states making thirteen sets of commercial laws—all of which would be unenforceable by some centralized military force.

Think about it: The U.S. Navy protects the ports and passageways where large commercial ships voyage. This makes those waterways less vulnerable to attack or piracy, thereby giving consumers and merchants the confidence they need to buy, hire, and invest.

But what if each individual state had to create its own state navy to protect all the transoceanic commerce for businesses headquartered in that state only? Pennsylvania had to form a navy to protect Hershey's chocolate-distribution channels, or Georgia had to forge a navy to guard Coca-Cola's international shipping. What then?

In words that made some bristle, Hamilton compelled readers to "refuse, as Americans, to be the tools of European arrogance!" by unifying the states' commercial interests so that the nation could "erect one great American system superior to all transatlantic force and influence" that is "capable of dictating the terms of connection between the Old and the New World!"

No King's Speech

Americans have never been unified by our politicians (that's why approval ratings over 50 percent are considered high!), but rather by our common values and virtues. These principles, many of which are enshrined in the Declaration of Independence and the Constitution, make up the core of who we are.

This was in sharp contrast to Europe, where unity often sprang from royalty. The British were united because they all bowed before the same king. The Founders were decidedly anti-monarchical, and they wanted a Constitution that reflected this belief. Slogging through a bloody Revolutionary War only intensified their disdain for power based on privilege.

As a result, the Constitution bans titles of nobility. No kings and queens—only presidents, senators, representatives, and judges. To the greatest extent possible, the Founders sought to make family name and wealth irrelevant to one day being put in a position to lead. While the system isn't perfect—the Kennedy and Bush families come to mind—it has resulted in many people being able to rise up through the system to reach a level of office that would have been virtually impossible in any other nation. Our current president comes to mind as an example of how well that imperfect system still works today.

Concerns about the imperfection of the Constitution almost led to its demise. Critics were out in force asking people why they would possibly approve a document that was, by everyone's admission (even its most ardent supporters), imperfect. In Federalist 85, the last paper published, Hamilton confronted those people directly. Far from being a weakness, he explained, disagreements among the Constitution's supporters merely demonstrate that unity and consensus on core principles take precedence over petty partisan squabbles.

And besides, Hamilton argued, the sinful nature of mankind naturally meant that a perfect system could never arise from imperfect men. As such, the best we could do was to craft the best document possible—and then amend it in the future as experience warranted.

A New Idea Is Born

Embedded throughout the Papers was a core belief that seemed to be manifesting itself publicly for the very first time: American exceptionalism. Since then, this belief has been at the center of America's standing in the world, and stands at the center of how we carry ourselves as a nation.

American exceptionalism is the idea that America is not merely different from other nations and governments on earth—but exceptional among them. More specifically, it's the belief that the hand of Providence brought together peoples of all colors and creeds to unite around a core set of universally shared values such as the rule of law, natural rights, and equality of opportunity to create a nation unlike any other across the arc of human history.

To some, American exceptionalism amounts to cheering for one's own team, a puffed-up sense of superiority, or misplaced national pride. Alexander Hamilton, James Madison, John Jay, and the rest of the Founders could not have disagreed more. They believed that, far from being about ego, American exceptionalism was the axis on which human freedom spins. If you don't believe you are exceptional then who else will? If you don't hold yourself up to the highest possible standards, then how can you expect to accomplish anything great? If you are unexceptional then you deserve to be ruled by others.

Unfortunately, some now believe that this concept is out of date. We may believe we are exceptional, they say, but other countries believe the same about themselves. That is simply not true. No other country has ever taken such a leap of faith with their future as our Founders did in the eighteenth century. A representative democracy, governing centrally over independent states to ensure the individual rights of man, wasn't simply original, it was *exceptional*.

And it still is.

But perhaps even more exceptional was the idea that all of these concepts—many of them as foreign as they were complex—could be explained to average citizens in a way that provided them with the confidence they needed to move forward. Accomplishing that feat required someone with an outstanding grasp of history, civics, and human nature; someone who could be both logical and academic; someone who could speak to the elites and the working class simultaneously without upsetting either side; and someone who could take on the opposing arguments with a degree of civility that was virtually unprecedented. That someone was Publius: Hamilton, Madison, and Jay.

Without the three of them, it is possible, perhaps even likely, that New Yorkers would have rejected the Constitution and, with it, the proposed Union. Fortunately, Providence had other plans—and a *Novus Ordo Seclorum,* a new order for the ages, was soon to be set in motion.

FEDERALIST NO. 1

The Message: America is special because our rights come from God, but those rights must be protected by a central government that serves the people.

Original Quote: "The subject speaks its own importance; comprehending in its consequences nothing less than the existence of the UNION, the safety and welfare of the parts of which it is composed, the fate of an empire in many respects the most interesting in the world."

Relevance to Today: The Founders believed America to be exception, but some students are now being taught "multiculturalism," the idea that no culture or country is superior to or better than another. For example, Howard Zinn, a historian and author of *A People's History of the United States,* which is widely used in classrooms, has argued that America is so morally flawed that it cannot possibly be exceptional. Even President Obama seems to have mixed feelings about American exceptionalism. "I believe in American exceptionalism," he said, "just as I suspect that the Brits believe in British exceptionalism and the Greeks believe in Greek exceptionalism."

Original Quote: ". . . a dangerous ambition more often lurks behind the specious mask of zeal for the rights of the people than under the forbidden appearance of zeal for the firmness and efficiency of government."

Relevance to Today: Zealots for individual rights (which back then could be translated as anarchists) are more dangerous that those who believe that an efficient government is a good thing. But would anyone today refer to the federal government as "efficient"? After all, it took a 1,924-page bill to lay out the budget of the United States and another 359 pages simply to cut $38 billion in spending.

NUMBER 1

Introduction

For the Independent Journal
The Importance of a Strong Union to Our Safety and Prosperity

After experiencing the ineffectiveness of the current federal government we are called upon to take part in a discussion about a new Constitution for the United States of America. The importance of this discussion is clear—nothing less than the Union itself, the safety and welfare of all of the states, and the fate of a nation, one which is in many ways the most interesting in the world, is at stake.

Many have observed that, because of their conduct and the example they've set, the People of this country have been put in the position of deciding a very important question: Are societies capable of freely choosing to establish good government for themselves, or will such things forever be determined by accident and force? If that observation is true, then we find ourselves at a time in history in which this question will be answered. If we are to falter now, it would be, in my opinion, to the detriment of all mankind.

To frame this debate another way, it is not simply about patriotism, it's also about philanthropy for the world. Given the stakes, we should all take this process very seriously. I will be happy if our decision is made through a sensible debate that ignores issues not having to do with the public good. That, however, is something more to be wished for than expected. Our undertaking, after all, affects so many people, so many local institutions, and so many varied interests, that it would be impossible for it not to be influenced by issues having little to do with the truth we are trying to discover.

Among the greatest challenges the new Constitution will face will come from local politicians who fear that they might lose some of their current power, along with those who might seek to profit from the division of this nation into several confederacies, as opposed to its Union under a single government.

It is not my intention to focus on such obstacles, since it really isn't fair to raise suspicions about a certain class of people simply because of the power they currently hold. An honest man can only acknowledge that such people can have good intentions and that opposition will no doubt come from good and honest people who have their own preconceived ideas and opinions. Since the motives behind each of the opinions surrounding this discussion are so strong, it is certain that wise and good people will be found on both sides of the issues. This fact should remind us all to remain modest in our opinion—no matter how right we might think we are.

It should also be remembered that those on the side of the truth are not always led by more honest motives than those who oppose it. Ambition, greed, personal animosity, party opposition, and many other motives that are just as impure, are guaranteed to be at work on both sides of the debate. Even if these motives didn't exist, we must still remember that intolerance has always characterized political parties. In politics, just as in religion, it is absurd to try to win converts by fire and sword. Dissent, after all, can rarely be cured by persecution.

And yet, despite the fact that honest men agree with all of these opinions, we have already seen indications that a torrent of angry and hateful rhetoric will be unleashed during this discussion—just as it has in every great national discussion of the past. Judging by their conduct so far, those who are opposed to this plan will attempt to grow their numbers and prove their point by being loud and bitter. Those who are enthusiastic about this plan will be stigmatized as lovers of despotic rule and haters of liberty. Those who fear for the rights of the People—a fear that most often comes from the head rather than the heart—will be exposed as being more interested in popularity than in the public good.

On one hand, it will be forgotten that excessive jealousy for one's own rights is often the sister of violence, and that the enthusiastic desire for liberty is often infected with a spirit of distrust. On the other hand, it will also be forgotten that a strong government is essential to the security of liberty and that those two things can never be separated. Dangerous ambition often lurks more in those who have excessive enthusiasm for the rights of the People than those who believe in a firm and efficient government. History proves that the former more often leads to tyranny than the latter, and that the people who have trampled on the liberties of a republic often began their campaigns by being overly concerned with the rights of the People and helping to end tyranny.

Fellow citizens, throughout these papers it is my intent to put you on guard against all those who might seek to influence your opinion on this important subject through arguments that have no basis in truth. You will find that I am convinced that this Constitution will protect your liberty, dignity, and happiness and, therefore, believe that it is in your interests to adopt it. I will not express any feelings to you other than my own, nor waste your time by debating what I have already decided for myself, since I will freely acknowledge my convictions and the reasoning behind them. I will be concise and to the point, and my motives are mine alone; my arguments will be available to all, may be judged by all, and will be nothing but truthful.

The subjects I will discuss in these papers are:

A. The extent to which the Union will promote your political prosperity;

B. The inability of the current Confederation to preserve the Union;

C. The necessity of a government that is at least as strong as the one proposed in the Constitution;

D. The ways in which the Constitution conforms to the principles of a truly republican government;

E. The Constitution's similarity to New York's state constitution;

F. The additional security which the Constitution will provide not only to the republican form of government, but also to liberty and property.

Throughout this discussion, I will attempt to provide good answers to all of the objections that appear worthy of our attention. It may seem like a waste of time to justify the usefulness of the Union, since it is so obvious to so many, but, in private circles, it is already being argued against those who oppose the new Constitution that the Thirteen States are too large for any one General government, and must, therefore, remain separate confederacies. I have no doubt that this view will be expressed in the dark until it finds enough support to come into the light—meaning that either the new Constitution will be adopted, or the Union will be torn apart. Therefore, it's necessary to closely examine the advantages of the Union, as well as the evils and dangers that would result if it were to fall apart. And that is what we will now do.

—Publius

FEDERALIST NO. 2

The Message: Divine Providence brought the country to this point, but America's future prosperity is dependent on a union.

Original Quote: "This country and this people seem to have been made for each other, and it appears as if it was the design of Providence, that an inheritance so proper and convenient for a band of brethren, united to each other by the strongest ties, should never be split into a number of unsocial, jealous, and alien sovereignties."

Relevance to Today: The constant fighting over elections, policies, and legislation makes it hard to remember that in the beginning, it was God who brought us all together. Restoring His place in the country is the first step toward restoring the union.

Original Quote: "the prosperity of America depend[s] on its Union . . ."

Relevance to Today: There has been a concerted effort to divide Americans along arbitrary lines like ethnicity, religion, or tax rates. The NAACP, for example, has attacked the Tea Party movement for giving a "platform to anti-Semites, racists, and bigots" and some politicians, along with activists like Michael Moore, have declared a "class war" on the wealthy.

The last thing we need to do is to be tearing each other apart. Too often we focus our attacks on each other, as though alienating one group somehow makes us better, when the truth is that without the union and the freedoms it secures, we have nothing.

NUMBER 2

The Dangers of Foreign Force and Influence

JOHN JAY

For the Independent Journal

The Importance of a Strong Union to Our Safety and Prosperity

Upon reflection, the People of America must realize that one of the most important questions of their lifetimes is now upon them. They must, therefore, give it their complete and undivided attention.

It's clear that government is an absolute necessity, and that the People must cede some of their natural rights in order to give it its essential powers. Therefore, it's worth our time to consider whether the interests of the American People will be better protected if they remain one nation under a single Federal government, or as separate confederacies, each of which would have the same types of powers that are now being suggested for the single National government.

Until recently, it has been undeniable that the prosperity of the American People depended on them remaining united, and that the prayers and efforts of our greatest citizens have been continuously exerted in pursuit of that goal. But it now appears that there are some politicians who believe that we shouldn't look for safety and happiness in the Union, but instead in dividing ourselves into several distinct and sovereign confederacies. However extraordinary that idea may seem, it does have its advocates—including some who were once opposed to it. Whatever the reasons behind their change of opinion, it wouldn't be wise for the American People to follow along without being fully convinced that such an idea is based on sound policy.

It gives me great pleasure to sit back and realize that this now independent America of ours was not made up of distant and detached territories, but that our western Sons of Liberty were blessed with a connected and fertile country. We have been blessed by Providence with many different types of soils, industries, and waterways for the benefit of our people—waterways that surround our borders, act as highways for easy communication amongst friends, foster our commerce, and bind us together as one.

It has also given me great joy to realize that Providence has given such a connected country to a united people who descended from the same ancestors, speak the same language, profess the same religion, embrace a similar culture and similar notions of government, and who fought for their liberty and independence as one. Providence seems not only to have destined this country and this people for each other, but also that such a country, united by the strongest ties, should never be divided.

Similar feelings have been expressed by every part of our society—and for good reason: We have been, for all intents and purposes, a single people, and we've each enjoyed the same national rights, privileges, and protections. As a single nation we have made peace and war, defeated our common enemies, and formed alliances and negotiated treaties with foreign nations.

An understanding of the blessings and advantages of the

Union convinced us from very early on to establish a federal government.[1] We did this almost from the start of our political existence, even though our country was in flames, our citizens were dying on the battlefield, and the progress of the war left us very little room for the type of calm, mature decisions that have always preceded the founding of a wise and well-balanced government for a free people. Therefore, we shouldn't be surprised that a government founded during such chaotic times is now incapable of fulfilling its original purpose.

The intelligent people of this country understood these problems and regretted their existence. During the war, when we were equally in love with both our Union and our liberties, we recognized the imminent danger to our Union more easily than the threat to our liberties. And now, since we have been persuaded that a more thoughtfully constructed National government would provide the best security for both, we spoke with one voice and convened the Convention in Philadelphia.[2] That Convention, which was composed of men who, because of their patriotism, virtue, and wisdom, had the confidence of the People, was tasked with debating this difficult subject. In this time of profound peace, with their minds not distracted by power or influence but instead focused only by their love of country, these men went through months of honest, civil conversations, and, as a result, presented the People with a Constitution that they unanimously agreed on.

I have to emphasize that while this Plan is being recom-

---

1. This was initially done via the Articles of Confederation, ratified in 1781. (Referenced in detail in Federalist 7.)

2. *Convention:* This was the convention that was called in order to revise the Articles of Confederation. It took place from May 25 to September 17, 1787. Instead of revising the Articles, however, the Convention ended up forming a completely new charter of government for the United States of America: the U.S. Constitution, which was ratified in full on June 21, 1788.

mended and not imposed by the Convention upon the People, the importance of this decision and the gravity of our situation demand that we should nonetheless calmly and honestly consider it. However, as I mentioned earlier, our experience has taught us that we shouldn't be too optimistic that such consideration and thoughtful examination will actually happen. The People remember, in order to address their legitimate fears of imminent danger, they formed the memorable Congress of 1774.[1] While that Congress did make wise recommendations to its constituents, we will no doubt remember that it was immediately attacked by numerous pamphlets and weekly papers in the press. Many self-

---

1. *Congress of 1774:* The First Continental Congress was held from September 5 to October 26, 1774, in Carpenters' Hall in Philadelphia. It was attended by fifty-six delegates appointed by the legislatures of twelve of the Thirteen Colonies (not including Georgia) in response to the "Coercive Acts" (known as the "Intolerable Acts" throughout the colonies), which were instituted by Parliament after they became aware of the Boston Tea Party, which occurred on December 16, 1773, and which was itself a response to the *Tea Act,* which imposed a tax on tea in the Colonies. They included the *Boston Port Act* (closed the port of Boston until the British East India Company was compensated for the damages which were incurred because of the Boston Tea Party), the *Massachusetts Government Act* (unilaterally transferred control over the government of Massachusetts to the British government, making it so that nearly every single position in the colonial government had to be appointed by either the governor or the King, while also severely limiting the holding of town meetings in Massachusetts), the *Administration of Justice Act* (allowed the governor of Massachusetts to transfer the trial of any accused royal officials to either another colony or to Great Britain itself if he believed that they could not receive a fair trial in Massachusetts), the *Quartering Act* (this law was applied to all of the colonies, and was an update of the Quartering Act of 1765; the first act required that colonists provide housing for soldiers if called upon to do so, but the colonial legislatures were largely uncooperative; the Quartering Act of 1774 allowed the governor of each colony to find suitable housing for soldiers if none could be found), and the *Quebec Act* (this act enlarged the boundaries of what was then the colony of Canada, while also removing references to the Protestant faith in the oath of allegiance, while guaranteeing the free practice of the Catholic faith; many objected to the transfer of land which was once part of the Thirteen Colonies to a nonrepresentative government, in addition to the general feeling that French Canadians were being courted in order to oppress British Americans, although this act had no relation to the events in Boston).

interested politicians, as well as those who were unduly influenced
by former attachments, feared the consequences of that Congress's
decisions and were therefore tireless in their attempts to convince
the People not to accept its advice. Many were deceived and mis-
led, but the majority wisely decided to follow the Congress, and
are today happy they did so.

The People decided that that Congress included many wise,
experienced men from all over the country, who brought with
them and shared with each other a great amount of useful information. They also knew that in the course of their discussions
concerning the true interests of the country, the Congress no
doubt had at its disposal a great deal of knowledge, and therefore
recommended only those things they felt were the wisest and
most necessary for the sake of public liberty and prosperity.

Despite the many attempts to convince them otherwise, these
facts persuaded most people to follow the advice of the Congress. So, if the People placed their confidence in the men of that
Congress, many of whom were neither widely known nor highly
experienced, they must certainly place their confidence in this
Convention, since it included many of the most distinguished
and patriotic members of that 1774 Congress,[1] who now have the
added benefit of knowledge and experience.

It is important to realize that every Congress (including the
Convention) has joined with the people to insist that the prosperity of America depends on its Union. The People formed the Convention to maintain the Union, and the Convention has drawn
up a Plan to accomplish that purpose, a Plan that must now be
considered by the People. Why, then, are some people now trying

---

1. William Livingston (New Jersey), Thomas Mifflin (Pennsylvania), George Read (Delaware), John Rutledge (South Carolina), Roger Sherman (Connecticut), and George Washington (Virginia).

to argue that the Union is not as important as previously thought, or to somehow suggest that we would be better off as three or four separate confederacies? I am convinced that the People have always been correct, and that they have many important and good reasons to believe in the Union. Those who support dividing up America have no doubt assumed that if the Plan of the Convention were to fail, it would bring an end to the Union. I agree with them, and I sincerely hope that every good citizen will see that the end of the Union would force America to exclaim, in the words of the poet, "FAREWELL! A LONG FAREWELL, TO ALL MY GREATNESS."[1]

—Publius

---

1. Cardinal Wolsey's speech in Shakespeare's *Henry VIII* (Act III, scene 2). In this scene, Cardinal Wolsey suddenly recognizes his imminent downfall. The historical Cardinal Wolsey (1475–1530) was appointed to the position of lord chancellor of England in December 1515, stripped of the title in October 1529, and arrested for high treason in November 1530.

NUMBER 11

How the Union Will Foster Commerce and a Navy

ALEXANDER HAMILTON

For the Independent Journal

The Importance of a Strong Union to Our Safety and Prosperity

Constitutional References:
Article I: §8/3, 13

There are many opinions regarding the importance of the Union to commerce,[1] but most people who understand the subject have already come to the same conclusion. This applies not only to our internal commerce, but also to our trade with foreign nations.

There are indications that several of the powerful maritime nations are nervous about what they see in the adventurous spirit that makes America's commercial character so unique. They seem to fear that we might possibly interfere with their commercial maritime trade—trade that supports their navigation of the seas and forms the foundation of their naval strength. Those nations

---

1. United States Constitution: Article I, Section 8, clause 3.

FEDERALIST NO. 11

The Message: American economic prosperity depends on our union's ability to trade domestically and internationally and to defend itself with a strong navy.

Original Quote: "Let Americans disdain to be the instruments of European greatness! Let the thirteen States, bound together in a strict and indissoluble Union, concur in erecting one great American system, superior to the control of all transatlantic force or influence, and able to dictate the terms of the connection between the old and the new world!"

Relevance to Today: The Founders wanted the American union to be strong and independent from foreign influence so that we could control our own destiny. But as our debt continues to skyrocket, the owners of that debt, including China, are able to exert more and more influence over us. In addition, efforts are afoot to make the United States accountable to the United Nations and subject to an International Criminal Court, and to curtail what some call American "unilateralism" in the world.

Original Quote: "The rights of neutrality will only be respected when they are defended by an adequate power. A nation, despicable by its weakness, forfeits even the privilege of being neutral."

Relevance to Today: One key benefit of military strength seems to have been lost: it allows you to not only *win* wars, but also to stay out of them. You cannot be neutral unless you maintain a credible threat of force. As the debate over major budget cuts heats up, it's important that we all keep that lesson in mind.

that have colonies in the Americas realize, with great anxiety and concern, what this country is capable of becoming. They can see the danger that America, possessing the desire and ability to create a powerful navy, would pose to their colonies.

Given that attitude, these nations will no doubt attempt to divide us as much as possible, while at the same time depriving us of any sort of active commerce for ourselves. By doing so, they would achieve their three goals of taking our commercial profits for themselves, preventing us from interfering with their commerce, and clipping the wings on which we might one day soar to dangerous greatness. If it was worth our time to go into detail, it wouldn't be difficult to show that these policies originated at the highest levels of their governments.

If we remain united, it would be possible for us to counteract these policies, which are clearly at odds with our prosperity in a variety of ways. By putting in place appropriate regulations at the same time and throughout all of the states, we could require all foreign countries to bid against each other for the privilege of accessing our markets. This claim will not be seen as unrealistic by those who can appreciate the importance that an industrial nation (such as Great Britain) would place on having access to the markets of a rapidly growing population of three million people, the majority of whom are exclusively dependent on agriculture (and who are likely to remain that way because of their local circumstances). It would be immensely beneficial to any industrial nation to have its products transported directly to and from America on its own ships, rather than on the ships of another country.

Suppose, for example, that we had a government in America capable of excluding Great Britain (with whom we currently have no treaty of commerce) from all of our ports. What would be the most likely effect of this on the policies of Great Britain? Wouldn't it allow us to negotiate, likely successfully, for extensive and valuable commercial privileges within the territories of that nation?

These questions have been asked on other occasions, but they have only received plausible answers, not satisfactory ones. Some have said that such an action would produce no change in the policies of Great Britain, since she would just continue her trade with us via the Dutch, who are much closer, are customers of her goods, and who could act as the middleman for products which were needed to supply our markets. But wouldn't Great Britain's commerce be significantly damaged if she lost the ability to be her own carrier in that trade? Since the Dutch would be facilitating and taking upon themselves the risks of that trade, wouldn't a large portion of the profits go to them? Wouldn't the mere presence of cargo be considerably expensive? Wouldn't such an inconvenient arrangement make it easier for other nations to compete with Great Britain by raising the price of their goods in our markets, let alone the fact that Great Britain would be placing effective control over this entire aspect of their commerce into the hands of others?

Any honest look at this subject makes it clear that the disadvantages Great Britain would suffer in this situation, combined with the demands of her West Indian islands and the positive opinion that the majority of Great Britain's people have of the American trade, would persuade her to compromise and allow us the privilege to access her markets and the markets of her territories—all of which would greatly benefit our commerce. Such a concession by the British government (which would of course include concessions, exemptions, and immunities for them on our part as well) would most likely be repeated by other nations, who would see that they are not completely barred from trading with us either.

The establishment of a Federal navy would also be an excellent asset to use in influencing our commercial relations with other European nations. There is no doubt that the continuation of the Union under an efficient government would give us the power to create, in the not so distant future, a navy[1] that, if not equal to those of the great maritime powers, would be powerful and respectable enough to go up against the navy of any other nation in a two-party conflict. This would especially be true as far as military operations in the West Indies are concerned. A few ships of the line[2] sent in at the right time to reinforce either side is usually enough to decide the outcome of any campaign which is important to our interests. If we take into account how useful military supplies from this country would be for military operations in the West Indies, it's obvious that we would be in a very strong position that would give us an advantage in bargaining for commercial privileges. Our friendship and our neutrality would both become greatly desired. By maintaining a long-term and steady commitment to the Union, we could become the authority in the Americas that Europe would have to deal with, and we would also be able to direct Europe's competitors in this part of the world in whatever direction our interests may dictate.[3]

By abandoning the Union, the rivalries between the states would hinder them and prevent them from exploiting the advan-

---

1. United States Constitution: Article I, Section 8, clause 13.

2. *ships of the line:* This refers to a type of naval warship that was constructed from the seventeenth century through the mid-nineteenth century. They were built so that they could engage in a tactic known as the "line of battle," in which two columns of opposing warships would maneuver themselves in such a way that they could fire ("broadside") the greatest number of guns at the opposing side.

3. This idea eventually came true in terms of policy with the advent of the "Monroe Doctrine" under President James Monroe, which was introduced on December 2, 1823. It declared that any further efforts on the part of European powers to colonize or interfere with states in the Americas would be viewed by the United States as an act of aggression that would require U.S. intervention.

tages that nature has kindly placed within our grasp. If we went down this path, we would become so weak and insignificant that all nations at war with each other would, without any doubt, hesitation, or remorse, interfere with our commerce and destroy our property as often as they wanted for the sake of their own selfish desires.

Being neutral is only respected when that neutrality can be defended by adequate power. A nation shamed by its weakness would surrender even the privilege of being neutral.

A vigorous National government that could direct the natural strength and resources of the country toward our common interest would baffle all the jealous European leaders as to how to restrain our growth. In that situation even the motives for plotting and scheming against us would be removed since the likelihood that they would succeed would be so low that it wouldn't make sense for them to even try. An active commerce, extensive shipping/transportation, and a flourishing navy should therefore be the inevitable result of moral and physical necessity. We must defy the petty schemes of petty politicians who try to control or direct the irresistible and unchangeable course of nature.

However, if not united, malicious plans against us would not only be concocted, but they might even succeed. Because of our universal weakness, maritime powers would have the ability to not only set the conditions by which we could exist as a nation, but would also attempt to decrease our shipping and commerce to the point of basically destroying it. This would restrict us to merely passive commerce so that we would not transport their goods, but they would likely transport ours (as is in their common interest). We would therefore be forced to accept their prices for our own commodities, while seeing our profits stolen from us and used to enrich our enemies and those who would persecute us. The unparalleled spirit of enterprise which so characterizes the genius of American merchants and navigators, and which is itself a source of inexhaustible national wealth, would be extinguished and lost, leaving in its path poverty and disgrace across this country—a country which, if it were wise, could realistically become the source of the admiration and envy of the world.

There are rights of the Union that are of great importance to America's commerce, including the fisheries, the trade of the Great Lakes, and along the Mississippi River. Should the Confederacy be dissolved, delicate questions regarding the future of these rights would no doubt be answered by more powerful nations than us, and to our disadvantage. The attitude of Spain toward the Mississippi, for example, requires no comment. Both Britain and France are concerned about the fisheries, which they view as essential to their commerce. And no one can blame them for their concern, for our mastery of the fishing industry has allowed us to offer better prices than those nations, even in their own markets. What could be more natural than for them to want to get rid of such dangerous competitors?

The benefits of this type of trade should not be underestimated since all the states that engage in maritime commerce may take advantage of it in one way or another—especially if they increased their commercial capacity. Also, since this trade produces many excellent seamen, it is now, and will continue to become, a universal resource as the principles of commerce continue to develop throughout the states. These things will all be absolutely essential for the establishment of a navy.

The Union will contribute to the great national goal of a navy in several other ways as well. For example, every institution involved in creating and supporting the navy will grow and flourish relative to how much support it provides. A United States navy supported by the resources of all of the states would be much more likely to exist than a navy of any single state or partial confederacy, which would be able to leverage the resources of only part of the country. It just so happens that each part of the current Confederacy of America has unique advantages that would be helpful in achieving this essential goal. The southern states, for example, produce greater amounts of certain naval necessities, such as tar, pitch, and turpentine, and also wood that is more solid and long-lasting, and therefore better for the construction of ships. If the ships of the navy were constructed of wood from the south then their greater durability and lifespan would not only help our naval strength, but also our national economy. Also, some of the southern and middle states produce great amounts of higher quality of iron. Seamen, of course, must be recruited mostly from the northern states.

A navy is required to protect all external and maritime commerce, but such commerce also naturally supports the success of such a navy. Both maritime commerce and a navy mutually benefit and support each other, a point that is too obvious for me to prove with any further explanation.

Unrestrained trade between the states will also advance the trade of each individual state through the exchange of each other's goods, the satisfaction of their reciprocal desires, and also the greater ability they will have to export their products to foreign markets. The veins of commerce will be replenished and reinvigorated in every part of the country by the free movement of goods.

The variety of goods produced throughout the different states bring greater possibilities to commercial enterprise. If, because of economic circumstances, one state experienced a drop in the production of their goods or their staple crops (because of a bad harvest or an unproductive crop), that state would be able to call on the products and staple crops of another state.

The value of the products involved in foreign commerce is just as important as the variety of those products. Because of competition and market fluctuations, commerce can be carried out more efficiently with a large number of products of a given value, rather than a small number of products of the same value. Some products may be in high demand at some times, but impossible to sell at other times. However, if there are a great variety of products to sell, it would be nearly impossible for all of them to be un-sellable at the same time, which makes it less likely that any given merchant would either be obstructed or forced to watch his business stagnate. Investors will surely recognize the strength of these arguments, and will acknowledge that the combined stability of the commerce of the United States would be much better for our commerce than the commerce of thirteen disunited states, or several unconnected confederacies.

Some may respond that, whether or not the states remain united, they will still maintain intimate commercial relations with each other and that will have the same effect as if they existed under the Union. However, trade like this would face many obstacles and would be interrupted and decreased for many reasons that have been examined in detail throughout these papers. A unity of commercial and political interests can only result from a unity of government.

This subject can be viewed in other interesting ways, but to do so would require me to look too far into the future and would involve topics that are not appropriate for a newspaper discussion. However, I will briefly say that our situation calls for us to seek a unified system of American affairs.

The world can be politically and geographically divided into four parts, with each having their own unique interests. Unhappily for the other three, in one way or another, Europe has extended her power over all of them by force, negotiation, and fraud. Africa, Asia, and America have all felt her supremacy for a while, which has caused Europe to imagine herself as the Mistress of the World, while considering the rest of mankind as created merely for her benefit. Men who are admired and regarded as "profound philosophers" in Europe have explicitly said that Europeans are physically superior to everyone else in the rest of the world, while all animals, and even the human species itself, degenerates in America; they even say that dogs stop barking once they have breathed the air in our atmosphere![1]

For too long, facts have supported these arrogant European pretensions. It is therefore our duty to vindicate the honor of the human race and teach this pompous brother some humility, and only the Union will allow us to do that. Disunion would only add yet another victim to this brother's list of victories. As Americans, let us refuse to be the tools of European arrogance! Let the Thirteen States, bound together as one in a strong and indestructible Union, agree to erect one great American system that is superior to all transatlantic force and influence, and capable of dictating the terms of connection between the Old and the New World!

—Publius

---

1. A reference to *Recherches philosophiques sur les Américains* (Philosophical Studies of the Americans), by Dutch philosopher Cornelius de Pauw (1739–99), who was part of the group of "profound philosophers" that Hamilton refers to sarcastically, a group that also included Georges-Louis Leclerc, Comte de Buffon (1707–88) who wrote the multivolume *Histoire naturelle, générale et particulière* (Natural History, General and Particular). At the time, many eighteenth-century European scientists were arguing that nature produced inferior species in the New World. Americans resented this because of its implications with regard to the American mind, and those such as Thomas Jefferson and Benjamin Franklin spent a great deal of time and energy refuting the theory.

NUMBER 85

Conclusion

ALEXANDER HAMILTON

Miscellaneous Objections and Conclusion

Constitutional References:
Article I: §9/8—Article IV: §4—Article V

According to my own list of the subjects to be discussed in these papers, there are two points remaining: "The Constitution's similarity to your own state constitution" and "The additional security which the Constitution will provide not only to the republican form of government, but also to liberty and property." These subjects, however, have been covered so thoroughly that I would basically only be able to repeat what has already been said.

It's remarkable that the Plan of the Convention has more in common with the defects of the constitution of New York state than its strengths. For example, among the supposed defects of the Constitution is that it allows the President to be elected more than once, it lacks an executive council, and it does not include a formal Bill of Rights (including a provision respecting the freedom of the press). These supposed defects, along with several others

FEDERALIST NO. 85

The Message: People are imperfect, as is our Constitution. But through debate, reason, experience, and the tenets of the enlightenment, we've come up with the best document man can possibly devise.

Original Quote: "A NATION, without a NATIONAL GOVERNMENT, is, in my view, an awful spectacle . . . "

Relevance to Today: Living under framework of the Constitution, America has been blessed with a more prosperity and liberty than any nation in world history. And though imperfect, we have been able to rectify its failures—slavery and women's suffrage, for instance—as time goes on. While some people (both today and back at our founding) believe that no federal government is better than the one we have, there's no way to secure our rights and freedom without it. The solution isn't to destroy the government; it's to restore the proper balance of power.

Original Quote: "The constant favors and special treatment which have been common for the wealthy, the well-born, and the great, must surely disgust all reasonable men, just as the numerous misrepresentations and concealments of the truth from the public eye deserve the disapproval of all honest men."

Relevance to Today: We should have equal protection before the law, but Congress continues to pass legislation and get special treatment. Senior government officials, for example, are exempt from TSA pat-downs at the airport. And some government officials don't have to comply with all elements of the Health Care Reform Act.

Original Quote: "The establishment of a Constitution during both a time of profound peace, and with a voluntary consent of the People is an absolute wonder, one which I look forward to with trembling anxiety."

Relevance to Today: While it's far easier to make sweeping changes to laws in the midst of a crisis (the Patriot Act comes to mind), changes made during times of peace and with the full support of the people are far more effective.

that we have examined throughout these papers, also occur in the constitution of this New York, making it difficult to accept one and not the other and pretend to remain consistent. There can be no better proof that some of the most forceful critics of the Constitution are completely insincere than that they attack the Plan's defects while ignoring the exact same defects in their own state's constitution.

In regards to the additional security that will be provided to republican government, liberty, and property by adopting the new Constitution, it will be the result of the following:

1. The restraints that the Union will impose on local factions and rebellions, along with the ambitions of powerful people in individual states who might otherwise become tyrants over the People as a result of their own fame and influence;

2. Greater protection against foreign conspiracies and plots, which disunion would not only invite, but also facilitate;

3. The prevention of a permanent and extensive military establishment, which would be the natural result of wars between the states—something that would surely happen if they do not unite;

4. A guarantee of the republican form of government to each state;[1]

5. An absolute and universal ban on any and all titles of nobility;[2]

6. Additional protections that are intended to prevent the states from engaging in policies that have undermined the foundations of property and credit, have fostered mutual

---

1. United States Constitution: Article IV, Section 4.
2. United States Constitution: Article I, Section 9, clause 8.

distrust between every group of citizens, and have brought about nearly universal moral decay.

Therefore, I have completed the task that I assigned myself at the beginning of these papers. Only you can determine whether I have succeeded. I trust that you've seen that I conducted myself in the spirit that I claimed I would. My arguments appealed to your reason and good sense only, rather than to your emotions, and I carefully avoided engaging in the harsh rhetoric that typically disgraces political opponents—which is exactly what has happened to the Constitution's opponents.

The accusation that the supporters of the new Constitution are engaged in some sort of conspiracy against the liberties of the People is so shameless and malicious that those who know it is a lie must now be ashamed that it was ever made in the first place. The continual favors and special treatment that are common for the wealthy, the well-born, and the great must disgust all reasonable men, in the same way that all the misrepresentations and lies that have been made to the public deserve the disapproval of all honest men. I admit that these circumstances may have caused me to occasionally and unintentionally use harsh language—my only excuse is that it did not happen often, nor was it extreme when it did.

Let's now take a break to consider whether or not these papers have vindicated the Constitution from all the criticism it has received, and whether or not they have shown that it is necessary to both our public safety and prosperity, and therefore deserves to be ratified. We are all responsible for deciding the answer to that question for ourselves based on our own conscience and understanding. It is essential that this responsibility be carried out sincerely and honestly. We are responsible to ourselves, our country, and our children to not allow our own personal interests, pride, or anger to get in the way of carrying out this duty. No one should remain stubbornly attached to any political party, but rather realize that the question at hand not only involves the very existence of the nation (not merely the interests of a particular community or state), but has also already been approved of by a majority of America.

I won't lie, I am completely confident in the arguments made in support of the proposed Constitution, and I find the arguments against it to be unreasonable. I'm convinced that it is the best system that can be created given our politics, habits, and opinions and is far better than the Articles of Confederation.

Those who oppose the Constitution have gloated over the fact that its supporters admit that it is not perfect. "Why," they ask, "should we adopt something that is imperfect? Why not make it perfect before we make it permanent?" That may sound plausible enough, but it is only plausible—not practical.

In the first place, the admissions regarding the Constitution's imperfections have been greatly exaggerated, even to the point that "not perfect" has been interpreted as some sort of admission that the Constitution is fundamentally defective, and that without substantial revisions it will place the rights and interests of the nation at risk. That, of course, was not what the Constitution's supporters intended when they admitted that it was imperfect. Every advocate of this Plan, while admitting it is not perfect, would say that it is still a good one, and the best that can be formed in our current situation, since it provides every type of security desired by a reasonable people.

It would be extremely unwise to prolong our dangerous national situation in the naïve hope that by constantly experimenting we will eventually have a perfect system, since a perfect system will never arise from an imperfect humanity. The results of any discussion of any group of men will always end up being a combination of wise judgment, along with the errors and prejudices of its members. Any agreement that involves thirteen different states with different interests will always include compromises. How can such an agreement ever be perfect?

A recent pamphlet[1] excellently explained how the circumstances surrounding the recent Convention and its deliberations will most likely not improve, and that it is highly unlikely that we will ever be able to call for another Convention under conditions as good as we have now. Since it was widely circulated, I will not repeat its arguments here, but it would be worthwhile for all patriots to read.

Before I conclude these papers, I want to discuss one other point that has not yet been examined thoroughly enough: the subject of amendments to the Constitution.

It's easy to demonstrate that subsequent amendments to the Constitution will be easier to make than previous ones. If anything is changed in the Constitution before it is ratified it essentially becomes a new document and must be approved by each state. However, if the Constitution as it exists right now is ratified by all thirteen states, then, in the future, amendments can be approved with the consent of just nine states. Based on this fact, the chances are thirteen to nine[2] of subsequent amendment rather than the original adoption of the entire Constitution.

That's not the only reason it will be easier in the future. Any new Constitution for the United States must inevitably include many specific details so that, in one way or another, all thirteen states can be accommodated. It is no surprise, of course, that there ended up being many varied interests amongst the men who

---

1. *An Address to the People of the State of New York* (1788) by John Jay (1745–1829), who was also another Publius who worked on *The Federalist* along with Hamilton and Madison (he wrote Federalist 2–5, and 64). Contained in the Appendix of this work.
2. It may as well be said "thirteen to ten," because while only two-thirds of the states are required to propose an amendment, three-fourths of them are necessary to ratify it.

were put in charge of drawing it up. The majority on one issue was the minority on the second, and another group of a different size ended up being the majority on a third issue. Therefore, it was necessary to arrange all of the specific details and provisions in a way that all of the various groups and parties could agree to it. That, no doubt, was an extremely difficult and timeconsuming task, especially given not just the number of interests, but also the number of different groups involved.

Any future amendment to the Constitution will be in the form of a single proposal that is debated as a single amendment. There would be no need for political maneuvering or compromise concerning any other point—no giving or taking. If the required number of states agree to the amendment then that amendment would without a doubt be added to the Constitution.[1] It is therefore impossible to compare the process of establishing an entirely new Constitution with that of adding an amendment to an already existing one.

Some people have claimed that it is not likely that future amendments will ever be added since those in charge of the Federal government will most likely be unwilling to give up any authority they might have. It is my personal belief that any thoughtfully considered amendment will be more related to the organization of the government rather than to its powers, and for this reason alone I find that this claim lacks merit. I also find that idea to be wrong on another count: Public spirit and integrity aside, the difficulty of governing thirteen states will make it necessary that our National leaders compromise in order to comply with the reasonable demands of their constituents.

There is one last argument I have to make on this point. Whenever nine states concur, the National rulers will have no

---

1. United States Constitution: Article V.

choice but to take action on any proposed amendments. Article V of the Constitution says that the Congress shall be required:

> ... on the application of the legislatures of two-thirds of the states, to call a convention for proposing amendments, which shall be valid to all intents and purposes as part of the Constitution, when ratified by the legislatures of three-fourths of the states or by conventions in three-fourths thereof.

The words of this Article are absolute, since the Constitution says that Congress "shall call a convention." Nothing is left open to interpretation in this provision. It is also not difficult to see how any amendments that are important to the general liberty or security of the People, and which might also affect local interests, will earn the confidence of two-thirds or three-fourths of the state legislatures. We'll be able to rely on the state legislatures to obstruct any violations on the part of the Federal government in this regard.

If that argument is mistaken then I have been deceived by it myself, for it's one of those rare political questions that can be tested with mathematical precision. Those who see the question in the same light, no matter how passionate they are about the subject of amendments, have no choice but to agree that this is the best and most sensible path toward their desired goal.

The enthusiasm of those who wish to amend the Constitution before it has even been ratified will surely disappear if they agree with the following observation by an ingenious writer:

> To balance a large state or society, whether monarchical or republican, on general laws, is a work of so great difficulty, that no human genius, however comprehensive, is able by the mere dint of reason and reflection, to affect it. The judgments

of many must unite in the work; experience must guide their labor, time must bring it to perfection, and the feeling of inconveniences must correct the mistakes which they inevitably fall into, in their first trials and experiments.[1]

These insightful thoughts teach us the lesson of moderation, a lesson that is incredibly important to all sincere lovers of the Union, and ought to very seriously remind them of the dangers involved in risking anarchy, civil war, the continual alienation of the states from one another, and perhaps even the military dictatorship of some rabble rouser, all while they are busy pursuing some imagined idea of perfection that we are incapable of obtaining except through time and experience.

Perhaps I am completely wrong, but I just can't understand those who seem to believe that the dangers of continuing our current situation are merely imaginary. A nation without a National Government is an awful sight indeed. The establishment of a Constitution during a time of profound peace, and with the voluntary consent of the People, is an absolute miracle—one that I look forward to witnessing with trembling anxiety. Given the difficulty of such a task, I see no reason to let go of the hold we now have on seven of the thirteen states,[2] and, having come this far already, beginning all over again. I dread the consequences of starting over, since I know that powerful individuals in this state and others are enemies of a general National Government, no matter what form it takes.

—Publius

---

1. *Essays, Moral and Political*, Volume I, by Scottish political philosopher David Hume (1711–76).
2. The first seven states to ratify the Constitution were (in order): Delaware, Pennsylvania, New Jersey, Georgia, Connecticut, Massachusetts, and Maryland.

PART TWO

THE GREAT COMPROMISE

In framing a government which is to be administered by men over men, the great difficulty lies in this: you must first enable the government to control the governed; and in the next place oblige it to control itself.

—James Madison, Federalist 51

F reedom is not the natural state of man. Without a shield in place to protect individual rights and the force to hold that shield strong, freedom becomes fleeting. Tyranny, the natural state of government, inevitably returns.

In America, that shield is our Constitution, and the force that allows us to hold it strong is God. The purpose of the Constitution was simply to provide a structure that would protect us from anyone who thought they were greater than God. That, of course, includes the federal government itself. "The Constitution is not an instrument for the government to restrain the people," Patrick Henry wrote. "It is an instrument for the people to restrain the government—lest it come to dominate our lives and interests." The government, as you'll clearly see explained later in the Papers, is not a protector of anything—it is simply an agent of our collective will.

While the Federalists believed strongly in this concept, they were also pragmatic. As a governing document, The Articles of Confederation had proven to be far too weak and they worried that a foreign power would sense an opportunity to come in and take their hard-won freedom. The Founders understood that the rights they fought so hard for would mean nothing if they were not defended. The result was the belief that a Union had to be formed, and, along with it, a central government strong enough to defend it.

That was not an easy sell to a public that was wary about handing any power back over to leaders—especially those who would be located a great distance away. Part III of the Federalist Papers, titled "Explanation and Justification of the New Powers of the Union," was Publius's attempt to bridge the gap and explain why this was necessary.

In Federalist 23, the first paper of Part III, Alexander Hamilton laid out the four primary purposes of the union: national security, protection from domestic disturbances, regulation of commerce (domestically between states and internationally between countries), and diplomatic relations.

We will take a look at the specific rationale Hamilton offered for each purpose in other sections of the book, but it was national security that was weighing on his mind in No. 23, since without it, none of the other goals of the republic could be met.

Hamilton wrote: "The authorities essential to the common defense are these: to raise armies; to build and equip fleets; to prescribe rules for the government of both; to direct their operations; to provide for their support." But a key for the new government was not only obtaining those powers, but in actually being able to *exercise* them without constraints. "These powers ought to exist without limitation," Hamilton wrote, "because it is impossible to foresee or define the extent and variety of national exigencies, or the correspondent extent and variety of the means which may be necessary to satisfy them. The circumstances that endanger the safety of nations are infinite, and for this reason no constitutional shackles can wisely be imposed on the power to which the care of it is committed."

I can't say that I agree with all of that, but my opinion is beside the point—Hamilton was clearly making the case that the federal government needed to have every tool possible with which to protect and defend the country.

Part of the reason he was so passionate about this issue was that the Articles of Confederation weren't binding on the states. The Confederacy had several duties assigned to it but lacked the power to carry them out. In essence, states were sovereign entities that were all looking out for themselves. That can be a good thing for some issues, but not being invested in the success of the Confederacy itself left it vulnerable. That wouldn't be the case under the Constitution. "If we are in earnest about giving the Union energy and duration," Hamilton wrote, "we must abandon the vain project of legislating upon the States in their collective capacities; we must extend the laws of the federal government to the individual citizens of America . . . The result from all this is that the Union ought to be invested with full power to levy troops; to build and equip fleets; and to raise the revenues which will be required for the formation and support of an army and navy, in the customary and ordinary modes practiced in other governments."

It was asking a lot of people, but Hamilton argued that providing the government with that much power in the area of defense would help ensure that citizens would get a Constitution and country as good as its people and would provide the security necessary to shield the individual liberties that everyone cherished. That sounds straightforward, but it's easy to see one of the problems that could develop over time: how you define "national security."

These days the federal government pushes not only the boundaries of its power, but also the very definition of the terms our Founders used. We are told that poor academic performance is a threat to our national security, that global warming could leave us susceptible, and that certain crops are critical to our national survival. In other words, politicians have figured out that it's easier to change the meaning of the language than it is to change the Constitution itself.

The Almighty's Finger

It wasn't just the idea of a central government being empowered to use force that concerned people; they were also rightfully confused about the Constitution itself. True federalism, after all, wasn't exactly common around the world. People had legitimate questions about how this new structure would work.

In Federalist 37, James Madison, who may have understood the Constitution's workings better than anyone else, began a series of papers devoted to explaining the work of the Convention and this whole idea of "new federalism." But, before getting into the details of things like the Electoral College system and presidential terms (see Part Three: "A Republic, If You Can Keep It" for these items), he first tried to impress upon people how difficult the debate had been and just how much compromise was required to draft something that not only provided liberty *and* security, but met the approval of all the various groups and parties who had special agendas. Yes, special interests existed back then—and not only along business or religious lines. The larger states, for example, desired to have power and influence equal to their wealth and population, while the smaller states believed that equal representation was the only fair solution. It was not easy to strike a compromise that would be acceptable to everyone.

It's also important to remember the historical context surrounding the argument that was taking place while this series of papers was published. There was a wistful sense of drama and uncertainty in the air as to whether this Constitution, and the republic it created, would really work. Not because our Founders didn't believe in the theoretical underpinnings of it all—they did—but because they knew that the devil was in the details. Quite honestly, they didn't know if they were getting those details right.

In No. 37, Madison admitted: "Experience has instructed us that no skill in the science of government has yet been able to discriminate and define, with sufficient certainty, its three great provinces—the legislative, executive, and judiciary; or even the privileges and powers of the different legislative branches. Questions daily occur in the course of practice, which prove the obscurity which reins in these subjects, and which puzzle the greatest adepts in political science."

Consider how amazing that is (and how unlikely it is that a similar degree of candor would happen today). Here was the primary author of the Constitution admitting to people that some political decisions simply have no right answer. The Convention debated, they negotiated, and, eventually, they compromised—but they weren't sure they were *right*, only that they did their best.

It was an amazing process and Madison (who isn't known as the most religious of the Founders) wanted readers to understand that God's hand had clearly been at work during that hot Philadelphia summer:

> The real wonder is that so many difficulties should have been surmounted, and surmounted with a unanimity almost as unprecedented as it must have been unexpected. It is impossible for any man of candor to reflect on this circumstance without partaking of the astonishment. It is impossible for the man of

pious reflection not to perceive in it a finger of that Almighty hand which has been so frequently and signally extended to our relief in the critical stages of the revolution.

With the debates put into the proper context it was time for Madison to begin explaining how new federalism would work, and why it was necessary that the people lend a new central government their power. For Publius, that meant starting at the beginning with a discussion of why government exists in the first place.

The Happiness Equation

While monarchies are predicated on the idea of a perfect, wise ruler and utopias are based on the notion of the perfectibility of man, the Founding Fathers based our government on neither. They were students of history and understood that no man—ruler or otherwise—can ever be perfect. That's one reason why power is shared and balanced so delicately throughout the government: The government would watch over the people, but the people would watch over the government.

For Publius, the primary goal of government was simple: to protect our liberties and rights so that the people can pursue happiness. As Madison explained in Federalists 41 through 44—a series of Papers focusing on the specific powers being given to the new federal government—the "power to advance the public happiness involves a discretion which may be misapplied and abused." In other words, if you give someone a sword and ask them to protect you, there's a chance they may one day stab you with it.

So why, then, were the Founders asking people to hand over so many of their swords to the federal government? Their rationale, while counterintuitive, is pretty ingenious and can easily be applied to the issues we face today. As Madison wrote, "It is in vain to oppose constitutional barriers to the impulse of self-preservation. It is worse than in vain; because it plants in the Constitution itself necessary usurpations of power . . ." Translation? A republic needs a government with certain specific powers in order to operate effectively. Denying those powers on the basis of wanting to maintain your freedom is foolish because it means that someone will eventually have to violate the Constitution to obtain them. It was exactly what had happened with the Articles of Confederation: Necessary powers were held back in the name of sovereignty, but now that very sovereignty was in jeopardy.

Before moving on, Madison wanted to make one other point extremely clear: There was a big difference in the powers being given to the government in the name of national defense and those given in the name of, say, collecting taxes. Madison mocked critics (deferentially, of course) who claimed the opposite by accusing them of intentionally obscuring the punctuation and language used in this clause to create fear among the people. (I wonder what he would say about the arguments made by gun control advocates over the placement of the comma in the Second Amendment.) And, if that weren't enough, Madison pointed out that the language of the clause that was causing so much concern was actually copied right from the Articles of Confederation.

The Commerce Clause

In Federalist 42, Madison explained why the federal government needed to have the power to regulate commerce with foreign countries and between states, and the power of international diplomacy. He argued that chaos would inevitably result if each state were to be in charge of these.

One interesting side note of No. 42 is Madison's references to the importation of slaves, which, as an issue dealing with foreign commerce, would be regulated by the new federal government. Contrary to what is being taught in some schools today, many of the Founding Fathers wrestled with the issue of slavery—not simply as a moral issue, but as a political one. "It were doubtless to be wished," Madison, who was a slave owner himself, wrote, "that the power of prohibiting the importation of slaves had not been postponed until the year 1808, or rather that it had been suffered to have immediate operation."

Madison, the Father of the Constitution, wanted the importation of slaves to be outlawed much earlier, but he also recognized something that most of us have seen firsthand: The machinery of government moves slowly. Political will can't be created overnight. He knew that this act was barbaric and inhumane, but he also knew that the political and economic realities of the day were such that it would be impossible to forge a union with that issue on the table. So, once again, they compromised.

We face similarly divisive issues today—abortion being a great example. I am pro-life and I believe it's an important issue—but I don't believe it's an issue that would merit breaking up the country into "pro-life" and "pro-choice" America. Our Founders had the same mind-set. They knew that there were a wide variety of issues that would never be solved in the short term, but those debates shouldn't preclude the greater good from being served.

With a compromise on the importation of slaves reached, Madison turned toward the states. The Founders were strong believers in letting the individual states be laboratories of representative government and make decisions based on local preferences. But there were limits. Madison noted how important it was for the federal government to have the ability to intervene in the affairs of the states when necessary. As someone who is a strong believer in states' rights, that's hard to swallow. So what was his rationale? It went back to national defense. If a state was not bound to a greater, stronger union, it could fall under the "influence of foreign powers." If New York, say, fell under the influence of Spain and was turned into an autocratic state—how could the states around it survive? The key, of course, was outlining specifically when that federal intervention would be allowed, and the language defaulted to the idea of a republican form of government. So long as a state continued with a republican form of government, the federal government could not interfere. But if they attempted to change that—say, to a monarchy—then the federal government would have the right to step in.

Today we once again see that the language has been played with to promote an agenda. The meaning of clauses like "general welfare," "necessary and proper," and the commerce clause have purposefully been changed and paired together to make implications of intent that were stated neither in the Constitution itself nor in any of the Federalist Papers. As a result, the federal government has been able to manipulate, bully, and dictate to the states policies and regulations that it has no authority over. Washington creates unfunded mandates (laws that require state governments to spend money, without Washington actually providing the money to pay for the programs), a pile of regulations, and a whole host of laws that push the states in one direction or another. This is a clear abuse of power that we've grown accustomed to over the years—but one that we should nonetheless be outraged over. Publius believed that the federal government has power over the states to *protect our liberties and our nation*, not to force the states to carry out policies that the federal government believes threaten those liberties.

Paper Money, Paper Tiger

In handing the federal government the power to regulate commerce between the states, the principle of sound money was a major factor. After the Revolutionary War, the states, many of which were heavily in debt, printed their own money—much of which was not backed by anything other than the faith and credit of that particular state government.

Publius believed that this system was not sustainable and that the union needed a common currency to inspire confidence, both domestically and internationally. As a result, he pushed for a ban on both the printing of paper money by states and on the states being able to set the value of their coins. The "pestilent effects of paper money," Madison wrote in Federalist 44, was preventing America from moving forward. "The power to make anything but gold and silver a tender in payment of debts, is withdrawn from the States, on the same principle with that of issuing a paper currency."

Over two hundred years later, we've maintained the principle of a national currency—but we've long since gone away from concerns that paper money backed by nothing but faith might eventually break the trust of those we do business with. Only time will tell if Publius was right in believing that all currency should be backed by precious metals, or if the academics and economists who eventually overruled our Founders were as smart as they led everyone to believe.

Of Angels and Men

"If men were angels, no government would be necessary. If angels were to govern men, neither external nor internal controls on government would be necessary."

That line, written by James Madison in Federalist 51, illustrates at a very basic level the Founders' view on republican government. Some political ideologies believe that it's possible to create "heaven on earth," usually by seizing control of individual freedoms and then putting a more enlightened group of bureaucrats in charge of reorganizing and reengineering society—but our Founders were smarter than that. They understood, through their experiences or religious beliefs, that all humans are self-interested, fallible, and sinful and that salvation can be found only at the hands of a holy and loving God, not a government. America's Founders sought neither to "fix" human nature nor to deny its predictable ends. Instead, by devising a republican government based on checks and balances and an economy functioning as a free market with commonsense regulation, the Founders turned the weakness of human nature into a strength of its government.

One key to that strength was in ensuring that the people were the ultimate source of power—but that they, too, would be watched and guarded. A true majority-rule democracy, the Founders knew, could not survive in the long run. As Madison wrote, "A dependence on the people is, no doubt, the primary control on the government; but experience has taught mankind the necessity of auxiliary precautions."

Auxiliary precautions . . . a nicer way of saying that a safety net would be put in place so that every level of power in the country would be checked by another. That was the essence of new federalism: Trust, but verify.

The unique part of the system being proposed, however, was in the fact that power was not simply handed over by the people to some central authority. Instead, Madison explained, "the power surrendered by the people is first divided between two distinct governments, and then the portion allotted to each subdivided among distinct and separate departments. Hence a double security arises to the rights of the people. The different governments will control each other at the same time that each will be controlled by itself."

It was an elegant solution to a complicated problem: How do you hand over power without it being used against you? But the Founders still worried about creating those "auxiliary precautions," mainly to prevent special majorities of people from being able to bond together to the disadvantage of minority groups. They wanted to ensure that the will of the people was the true will of society, not simply a temporary majority who had come together along some kind of specific line (like, for example, religion) in order to effect change across the entire population.

That created quite a problem: If a majority of people come together and use their power as prescribed in the Constitution, how can they be prevented from enacting the "wrong" kind of change? Madison believed the answer would be found in the size of the country. "The society itself," he wrote, "will be broken into so many parts, interests, and classes of citizens, that the rights of individuals, or of the minority, will be in little danger from interested combinations of the majority."

Has that prediction held up? In many respects, yes—a national religion was never established, for instance. And, in terms of the ability of a simple majority to enact their will in the Constitution itself—there's no doubt it's difficult. Recent polls, for example, show that a majority of Americans now support gay marriage—but a constitutional amendment to that effect is nowhere to be found. And what about something even more basic like term limits for senators and representatives? Polls show that upwards of 80 percent of Americans favor them—but is that even close to passing? Same goes for a balanced budget amendment (61 percent favor).

The truth, and many of us have experienced this firsthand, is that living in a republic is equal parts awe-inspiring and frustrating. We are so ingrained to believe that majorities rule that it's hard to comprehend why the will of the people sometimes does not—especially when you are personally part of that majority.

But when our system has you so mad over some issue that you're ready to shred the whole thing and start over, just take a deep breath and think back to the original argument over the Constitution itself. As Hamilton, Madison, and Jay tried to impress upon their readers, they were involved in an experiment seldom seen across the arc of history. The vast majority of the world's constitutions are, after all, *imposed* upon their people. But not America's. Our constitution was crafted through open, peaceful debates propelled by the will of the people channeling their wishes through the representatives they sent to Philadelphia. "The novelty of the undertaking," Madison wrote in No. 37, "immediately strikes us."

And that novelty should strike us again today. Just as often as it frustrates us.

FEDERALIST NO. 23

The Message: The federal government should do only a few things, but it must have the power and force to do them well.

———————————

Original Quote: "The principal purposes to be answered by union are these—the common defense of the members; the preservation of the public peace as well against internal convulsions as external attacks; the regulation of commerce with other nations and between the States; the superintendence of our intercourse, political and commercial, with foreign countries."

Relevance to Today: The Founders were clear about the extremely limited scope of powers being given to the federal government. But now it's commonplace to hear national politicians pressing for legislation that deals with local issues, like what food to serve in public school. The "Healthy, Hunger-Free Kids Act," for example, has a great-sounding name, but, according to *USA Today*, it, "gives the USDA the authority to set nutritional standards for all foods regularly sold in schools during the school day, including vending machines . . ."

———————————

Original Quote: "The essential point which will remain to be adjusted will be to discriminate the OBJECTS, as far as it can be done, which shall appertain to the different provinces or departments of power; allowing to each the most ample authority for fulfilling the objects committed to its charge."

Relevance to Today: The Founders wanted the responsibilities of the federal, state, and local governments to be well defined so that each would be held accountable for what they had done. Today, with the federal government encroaching on state and local authority, this has become much more difficult. The Endangered Species Act, for example, is enforced by federal agencies that are unaccountable to local citizens—sometimes leaving those citizens with little recourse in protecting their property rights.

The Necessity of a Government at Least as Energetic as the One Proposed in the Constitution

ALEXANDER HAMILTON

For the New York Packet: Tuesday, December 17, 1787

Explanation and Justification of the New Powers of the Union

Constitutional References:
Article I: §8/12–16—Article II: §2/1

The next point we will examine is the necessity of a Constitution capable of preserving a Union that is at least as strong and energetic as the one proposed. This examination will fall into three categories:

1. The goals of the federal government;
2. The amount of power the federal government will need to achieve these goals;
3. Those to whom this power will be delegated.

The distribution and organization of the federal government will be discussed at a later time. The primary purposes of the Union will be:

A. The common defense of all the states;
B. The preservation of peace and tranquility both between the states, and against foreign attacks;
C. The regulation of commerce with other nations, as well as between the states themselves;
D. The supervision of all of our diplomatic relations with foreign countries, both political and commercial.

The authorities that federal government will need in order to provide a common defense are: the ability to raise armies and to build and equip fleets and regulate both, to direct their operations, and to provide support to them (financial and otherwise).[1] Since it is impossible to predict, let alone define, the host of national emergencies that we may face in the future, these powers should have no limit. There are an infinite number of things that can jeopardize the safety of a nation, and for this reason, we should not place any constitutional shackles on the government's ability to maintain our safety. This power should be as broad as every possible combination of future emergencies may require, and ought to be directed by the same powers appointed to command our common defense.

This is one of those unbiased truths that clear-thinking people will see as obvious and, although it may be unclear from time to time, it cannot be made any simpler by argument or reasoning. It rests upon principles that are as simple as they are universal: The *means* should be proportional to the *end*; anyone who is expected to achieve a certain *end* or goal should have the *means* or ability to achieve it.

Whether or not the federal government should be given the

---

1. United States Constitution: Article I, Section 8, clauses 12–16; Article II, Section 2, clause 1.

responsibility of providing for the common defense is a question that is still open to some discussion. But the moment we decide that it should have this power, then the government ought to be given all the powers required to fulfill that duty. Unless we can know for sure, and in advance, all of the issues that will affect public safety in the future, we must admit that there should be no limits placed on the authority provided for the defense and protection of the rest of the community. These limits could hinder the effectiveness of carrying out this responsibility. In other words, anything essential to the *formation*, *direction*, or *support* of the NATIONAL FORCES should not be loaded with constitutional burdens.

Congress currently has unlimited freedom to require both men and money from the states (via the requisition and quota system) to regulate the army and the navy. It also directs their operations. Since these requirements are constitutionally binding on the states, who are solemnly sworn to provide the supplies Congress requires of them, the intention was that the United States would command whatever resources were needed for the "common defense and general welfare." It was assumed that the states would recognize their true interests, and show good faith in their agreements, both of which, it was hoped, would guarantee that they would make good on whatever was required of them by the federal government.

In reality, this expectation was both mistaken and misleading. I am hoping that our discussion in these Papers has proven how misleading this idea has been. I'm also hoping that our discussion has convinced both wise and objective people that it is necessary to change the basic foundations of the system. If we are serious about making our Union strong and enduring, we must abandon the idea of legislating for states, which are basically considered nearly sovereign political entities, and we must extend the laws of the federal government to the individual citizens of America. Additionally, we must throw out the mistaken idea of Congressional quotas and requisitions being forced upon the states as they are both impractical and unfair. The conclusion we must reach is that that Union should be given full power to levy troops, to build and equip fleets, and to collect the revenue required for the formation and support of these things in the same way that other governments do.

If the circumstances of our country continue to demand that we have a compound rather than simple government [meaning one central government with smaller state governments, versus just a single, all-controlling central government], then we must figure out what powers we should give to the central and state governments, making sure that each is afforded all the power they need in order to carry out their respective responsibilities.

Should the Union be made the guardian of our common safety? Aren't fleets, armies, and revenue required for this purpose? If so, then the government of the Union must be empowered to pass all the laws and make all the regulations necessary to do these things. The same must be true for commerce, and any other matter the federal government is charged with. Isn't the administration of justice between citizens of the same state best left to local governments? Of course, and the states must have authority to carry out this duty. To fail to provide it with the powers necessary to achieve their goal would be a violation of the most basic rules of common sense. Not to mention, it would carelessly place our most important national interests in the hands of those who are unable to manage them successfully.

Who is more suitable to provide for the public defense than those who already guard our public safety, especially when they are already the center of information and would be in the best position to understand the magnitude and urgency of the dangers to the country? Who, as representatives of the whole country, would be the most deeply concerned about the preservation of every part of it and, because of the serious nature of this duty, will always be mindful of the necessity of carrying it out? And who, by having its authority extended over all of the states, is capable of ensuring uniformity in our defense plans? Isn't it inconsistent to give the federal government the responsibility of providing for the common defense, but leave the state governments with the power necessary to carry it out? Wouldn't the main problem with such a system be a lack of cooperation, as well as general weakness, disorder, an unequal sharing of the burdens of war, and an unnecessary and ultimately unsustainable increase in our financial expenses? Haven't we just experienced those very things throughout the Revolution?

Since we are in search of the truth, we must acknowledge that no matter how we look at this issue, it is both unwise and dangerous to deny the federal government the powers necessary to carry out its duties. Making sure that the federal government is endowed with all of the powers it requires deserves the careful attention of the People. If any plan is proposed to us that we cannot objectively say meets this requirement, then we should reject it. Any government unfit because of its constitution to be entrusted with the powers that a free people *ought to delegate to any government* is also an unsafe and improper guardian of the NATIONAL INTERESTS. Once we decide where it would be most appropriate to place the responsibility for these interests, then whatever power is necessary in order to protect them should follow.

The opponents of the Constitution would have seemed more sincere in their criticism if they had kept it focused on the internal workings of the proposed government and proved that government did not deserve the confidence of the People. Instead, they chose to use harsh rhetoric and offer distracting arguments about the extent of this new government's powers. The Constitution does not give the Federal government too much power to manage our NATIONAL INTERESTS, nor has any convincing argument been offered to show that it has. If that were true, as has been suggested by some critics, then the enormous size of our country will make it unsafe to give any government enough power to rule it. That would also mean that the very nature of the Constitution is flawed and would prove that we should divide ourselves into separate confederacies capable of ruling over countries of a more practical size.

Obviously, it would be absurd for us to delegate the management of our most essential national concerns to a government of our own making without daring to also trust it with the authority necessary to properly and efficiently manage those concerns. Let's stop embracing contradictions, but firmly decide upon a rational alternative.

I believe it's impossible to argue that a single central government (with no state governments) would be practical. I trust that the ideas I have written about in these papers have made an argument that argues the exact opposite side of that notion in as clear a way as possible, given how little time and experience we've had with this issue. In fact, of all the things that may convince us a strong central government is necessary, the strongest argument is actually (and surprisingly for the opponents of the Constitution) the large size of our country. No other government could preserve the Union of such a large empire. However, if we began to believe in the political doctrines of the opponents of the proposed Constitution, then we would simply do nothing but confirm the beliefs of those who gloomily predict that it is completely unrealistic to forge a national system that extends to every corner of the current Confederacy.

—Publius

The Difficulties the Convention Must Have Experienced in Forming the Constitution

JAMES MADISON

For the Daily Advertiser: Friday, January 11, 1788
The Constitutional Convention and the New Federalism

Constitutional References:
Article I: §10—Article V

During our review of the defects of the current Confederation we also reviewed the most important principles of that Confederacy and argued that they couldn't possibly be fixed by a government that would be any *less* energetic than the one proposed in the Constitution.

But since the ultimate goal of these papers is to clearly and fully determine the merits of the Constitution, as well as the wisdom of adopting it, we must do a more critical and thorough overview of the work of the Convention itself—including examining it from all sides, comparing all of its parts, and determining what effects it will likely have. To do this while also being just and fair, we must also think about things that we've previously reflected on.

FEDERALIST NO. 37

The Message: The work of the Convention was difficult and required a lot of comprise, but unity means finding common ground and putting the interests of the nation, not one small group or political party, first.

Original Quote: "Among the difficulties encountered by the convention, a very important one must have lain in combining the requisite stability and energy in government, with the inviolable attention due to liberty and to the republican form."

Relevance to Today: A compromise has to made between having a government strong enough to keep the country together and one that allows for complete and total liberty. But that line has moved quite a bit over time and these days it seems that the federal government passes laws that are not about liberty *or* order, but instead amount to social engineering. Whether it's HOV lanes, subsidies for buying certain kinds of cars, or taxes on foods they don't like, the federal government is trying to guide our preferences.

Original Quote: "The [Constitutional] convention must have enjoyed, in a very singular degree, an exemption from the pestilential influence of party animosities the disease most incident to deliberative bodies, and most apt to contaminate their proceedings."

Relevance to Today: The Founders had strong and differing views about the Constitution, but they were guided by a spirit of unity. That spirit isn't present quite as much in today's Washington. As former senator Evan Bayh said when he retired in 2010, "There is too much partisanship and not enough progress; too much narrow ideology and not enough practical problem-solving. Even at a time of enormous national challenge, the people's business is not getting done."

A problem, inseparable from human affairs, is that public policy is rarely examined with a calm, moderate spirit, both of which are required in order to determine whether those policies advance or obstruct the public good. The more unusual or extraordinary the events are, the harder that spirit is to find. To those who have experienced this firsthand, it certainly isn't surprising that the act of the Convention, an act that recommends so many important changes and innovations, has aroused unfriendly comments on both sides of the debate—comments that get in the way of fair discussion and accurate assessment of the Constitution's qualities. In addition, the important changes and innovations that are included in the Constitution can be viewed from different angles and perspectives, and affect so many different aspects that are connected with people's passions and interests, that none of this should really be surprising.

In some of these debates, it is obvious from their own publications, that many of the Constitution's critics have only scanned the document with a predetermined bias and a predetermined decision to condemn it. In fact, the language of some of those who support the Constitution shows that they have the exact opposite bias—which ultimately means their opinions aren't all valid either. By mentioning these two groups together on the basis of their opinions, I don't mean to imply that there isn't a material difference in the purity of their motives. It is only fair to say, that since our national situation is universally acknowledged to be serious, and since it absolutely requires us to do something to fix it, those who've read the document with preconceived notions and yet support it may have based their decision on the graveness of our situation, as well as on considerations of a sinister nature. On the other hand, those who chose to oppose the Constitution in advance could not have possibly had any justifiable motives whatsoever. The intentions of the first group could be good ones, or they may also be sinister. The views of the second group, however, must be sinister. But, the truth is that these papers are not addressed to anyone who falls into either of these categories. They are intended for those who possess a sincere passion for the happiness of their country, as well as for those capable of discerning the best way to promote this happiness.

These types of people will examine the Plan of the Convention with a desire to uncover or magnify its faults, but they are also aware that it would be unreasonable to expect a perfect Plan in the first place. They will not stubbornly anticipate a Plan with no errors, as they realize that the results of the Convention were written by men who are, by their nature, not infallible. They will keep in mind that they themselves are also just human beings, and they ought not to assume that they will perfectly judge the imperfect opinions of others.

While these may, in and of themselves, be strong reasons to engage in a candid discussion, we must always remember how many difficulties are inherent in the Convention's undertaking in the first place. We should be immediately struck by the novelty of this undertaking. It has been shown throughout the course of these papers that the existing Confederation is founded on erroneous principles, and therefore, we must change this first foundation, and with it, the superstructure that rests upon it. It has been shown that the other confederacies that could be used as historical examples are plagued by the same erroneous principles, and while these examples act as a beacon that shows us the wrong path, they don't point out the path that we should follow. The most that the Convention could do in such a situation was to avoid the mistakes that have occurred at different times and in different nations, including our own, and also provide a convenient method so that their errors could be corrected as needed according to experience.[1]

Among the difficulties faced by the Convention, a very significant one must have been forming a Constitution that combines the necessary stability and energy of government with the inviolable attention that is due to liberty and a republican form of government. If they had not substantially accomplished this part of their undertaking then they would not have lived up to either the purpose of their appointment, or to the public's expectations. And yet, no one (at least no one who wants to betray their ignorance) would deny that this task would be very difficult to accomplish in the first place. Energy in government is essential to providing security against external and internal dangers, as well as a quick and beneficial execution of the laws, all of which form the very definition of good government. Stability in government is essential to national character as well as to the peace and confidence of the People, and is among the chief blessings of civil society. An irregular and constantly changing legislature is not so much evil as it is disconcerting to the People. And it may be confidently declared that the People of this country, enlightened about the nature of good government and interested in its effects, will in fact never be satisfied until a solution is applied to the constant changes and uncertainties that presently characterize state governments.

When we compare these valuable ingredients of good government with the vital principles of liberty, we will instantly see the difficulty involved in mixing them together in just the right proportions. The genius of republican liberty seems to demand that all power should be derived from the People, but also that those entrusted with power should be entirely dependent on the People

---

1. *For the amendment process, see* United States Constitution: Article V.

via short terms in office. And even during these short periods, the trust given to them should not be placed in the hands of the few, but in the hands of the many.

On the opposite end of the spectrum, stability requires that those who have been given power by the People should hold that power for a longer period of time. A frequent change of men will result from frequent elections, and a frequent change in government measures results from a frequent change of men. While energy in government requires a certain length of time for men to hold power, it also calls for the execution of that power by a single hand. Once we have more accurately examined their work, we will be able to see just how much the Convention succeeded in combining these two opposites. From a cursory review, nevertheless, it appears that this part of their work was difficult to accomplish.

The task of marking out appropriate boundaries between the authority of the Federal and state governments must also have been difficult. Every person, depending on how accustomed they are to thinking about and differentiating between vast, complicated things, can understand this problem. Even the most intelligent and metaphysical philosophers have not yet been able to identify or precisely define the faculties of the mind. Sense, perception, judgment, desire, volition, memory, and imagination have been found to be separated by such delicate boundaries and subtle nuances that their actual borders have eluded the most detailed and delicate investigations, and remain a topic that has resulted in the writing of ingenious treatises and controversy. The boundaries between the great kingdoms of nature, and even more the various categories and classes into which they can be subdivided, afford another illustration of this important truth. Even the most intelligent and diligent naturalists have not yet succeeded in identifying with any certainty the line between plants and unorganized matter, or that which marks the end of the plant kingdom and the beginning of the animal empire. There are even more mysteries surrounding the various characteristics that have been used in order to organize and classify each of these great departments of nature.

When we go from the works of nature, in which everything can be described objectively, to the institutions of man, where there is even more uncertainty—not just because of what is being observed, but because of what observes it—we must realize that it is even more important for us to not get our hopes and expectations up concerning those undertakings that flow from human wisdom. Experience has shown us that no amount of skill in the science of government has allowed anyone to define and differentiate with adequate certainty the three great departments of government: the Legislative, Executive, and Judiciary, or even the privileges and powers of the different Houses of the Legislature. Every single day, new questions are asked about this subject, which proves both just how obscure and theoretical it is, as well as how much it puzzles even the greatest political scientists.

Ages of experience, along with the combined efforts of the most enlightened legislators and jurists, have been unsuccessful in describing things to which different codes of law apply. Even in Great Britain, where legal subjects such as these have been more diligently pursued than in any other part of the world, the precise extent of the Common Law,[1] Statute Law,[2] the Maritime

---

1. *Common Law:* A system of law that is unwritten (especially in England) and is based on custom or court decisions and precedent. The basic principle of the system is that it would be unfair to treat similar facts differently on different occasions, which is why great weight is given to court "precedent," which are the previous decisions made by courts, and which make up what is known as "common law." (Referenced in Federalist 29, 42, 65, 83–84.)

2. *Statute Law:* "The written law established by enactments expressing the will of the legislature, as distinguished from the unwritten law, or 'Common Law.'" (Referenced in Federalist 84.)

Law,[1] the Ecclesiastical Law,[2] the Law of Corporations,[3] and other local laws and customs has yet to be clearly and conclusively established. The jurisdictions of both her general and local courts of law, of equity,[4] of admiralty,[5] etc., are frequently the sources of detailed and complex discussions, discussions that have only been able to describe the undefined limits within which each of them is confined adequately, but not with any certainty. All new laws, crafted with the greatest technical skill, and passed only after a great deal of discussion and deliberation, are considered as more or less obscure and uncertain until their full meaning is ascertained by a series of discussions and adjudications in the courts.

Besides the complexity of the laws themselves, and the fallibility of man in interpreting them, the medium through which men convey ideas to each other—namely, the words—adds yet another obstacle. The purpose of words is to express ideas. Therefore, for the sake of clarity, not only should ideas be distinctly formed, but they should be expressed by words uniquely and exclusively suit-

---

1. *The Maritime Law:* The laws that relate to maritime commerce and navigation and to maritime matters generally. Maritime Law is judged in admiralty courts. (Referenced in Federalist 83.)

2. *Ecclesiastical Law:* Commonly known as "canon law," these laws are those that are adopted by and regulate the government of a Christian organization and its members. Those Christian churches that use canon law are the Roman Catholic Church, the Eastern and Oriental Orthodox churches, and the Anglican Communion (association of Anglican churches; there is no central Anglican authority). (Referenced in Federalist 83.)

3. *Law of Corporations:* The collection of laws that govern the most dominant types of businesses and enterprises (i.e., corporations).

4. A court of equity was specifically authorized to apply principles of equity, rather than law (as in Courts of Law) to the cases brought before it where the application of the law might be considered overly harsh. A modern-day example of a court which could be considered a "Court of Equity" are U.S. Bankruptcy Courts. (Referenced in Federalist No. 83 under the footnote "Court of Chancery.")

5. Also known as "maritime courts," these courts have jurisdiction over all maritime contracts, torts (from the French word for "wrong"; a non-contractual, non-criminal wrongdoing), injuries, and offenses.

able to them. But no language has enough words and phrases to express every complex idea, and none has been so perfect that the words and phrases it does have are not at times ambiguous. None are capable of describing different ideas at the same time. Therefore, it must always be the case that, no matter how accurately certain things may be differentiated from each other, and no matter how accurately such differentiation may have been conceived in someone's mind, the definition may turn out to be inaccurate simply because of the inaccuracy in the terms used to describe them. This unavoidable imprecision will tend to vary, depending on the complexity and uniqueness of the things being defined. When the Almighty Himself comes down to address mankind in their own language, His meaning, as luminous as it must be, will be rendered dim and doubtful by virtue of the cloudy medium through which it is communicated.

There are three main sources of inaccurate or vague definitions:

1. Obscurity in the words;
2. Imperfections in those who perceive the words;
3. An inadequate medium in which to express ideas.

Any one of these can result in a lack of clarity. The Convention almost certainly experienced the effects of all of them when defining the boundaries between the jurisdictions of the Federal and state governments.[1] In addition to the difficulties mentioned, we could add to the mix the opposing interests and pretensions of the larger and smaller states. The larger states would obviously fight for participation and representation in the Federal government fully in line with their superior wealth and importance,

---

1. United States Constitution: Article I, Section 10.

while the smaller states were no doubt just as stubborn in defending the equality of representation that they currently enjoy under the Articles of Confederation. We can assume that neither side entirely yielded to the other, so the struggle could only be concluded by a compromise.[1] It is also extremely likely that, after the ratio of representation had been adjusted, this very compromise probably ignited an entirely new struggle between the very same states, with each trying to organize the government and arrange the distribution of its powers in such a way as to provide them with the greatest share of influence. These assumptions about the process are proven by the various features in the Constitution and, insofar as they are reasonable, it shows that the Convention was forced to sacrifice theoretical ideals to more practical realities and concerns.

The battle lines over different issues could not have always pitted large and small states against each other. Depending on the varying local interests and policies that were represented at the Convention, there must have been additional difficulties created by different combinations of those interests. Just as every state can be divided into different districts, and its citizens into different classes—which then gives rise to competing interests and local rivalries—the different parts of the United States also have diverse circumstances that result in the same rivalries—just on a larger scale. Even though this variety of interests may have a beneficial influence on the administration of the government once it is formed, everyone must still be aware that the existence of so

---

1. This refers to the Connecticut Compromise, which was proposed by Roger Sherman from Connecticut and called for a bicameral National Legislature (Congress), in which representation in one of the Houses (the House of Representatives) would be according to population (to the advantage of the larger states), and in the other House (the Senate) it would be equal for each state (to assuage the concerns of the smaller states).

many interests probably resulted in just the opposite effect while the Convention was actually forming the government.

Given the pressure of all of these competing interests, was it actually a good thing that the Convention was forced to deviate from the artificial and theoretically perfect government that may have been created in the imagination of some ingenious theorist locked away in his closet? In fact, the true miracle is that so many difficulties were overcome in the first place, and overcome with unity of agreement that was almost as unprecedented as it must have been unexpected. It is impossible for any honest person not to be astonished. It is impossible for the religious man not to once again perceive the finger of that Almighty Hand that so frequently and notably extended relief to us during the critical stages of the Revolution.

In a previous paper we discussed the unsuccessful struggles by the United Netherlands to reform the destructive errors of its constitution. The history of almost all great councils that have ever been convened by mankind in order to resolve their opposing opinions, defuse their rivalries, and reconcile their respective interests, represents a history of factions, disputes, and disappointments. Those incidents have provided us with some of the darkest and most degrading evidence of the weaknesses and evils of the human character. If we see scattered examples of a happier picture, they are only exceptions to the rule that serve to remind us of the truth—which in turn makes such things appear even darker and gloomier when compared with those exceptions.

Once we have discovered what leads to these much happier exceptions to the rule, and then apply those discoveries to our own circumstances, we are forced to conclude two things. The first is that the Convention must have been blessed with an utterly unique exemption from the deadly influence of party hostilities, the disease that most often affects any human assembly, and that was most likely to contaminate their discussions. The second conclusion is that all the representatives of the Convention were either sufficiently pleased with the final result, or were persuaded to accept it by the deep conviction that it was absolutely necessary to sacrifice their own private opinions and personal interests for the sake of the public good, in addition to their great fear that if our national dilemma was not confronted immediately, then our national situation would become even worse by any further delays and new experiments.

—Publius

NUMBER 41

A General Overview of the Powers to Be Vested in the Union by the Proposed Constitution

JAMES MADISON

For the Independent Journal

The Constitutional Convention and the New Federalism

Constitutional References:

Article I: §2/1 | §8/1–2, 11–13, 16 | §10

The Constitution proposed by the Convention can be examined in two fundamental ways. The FIRST is the sum, or quantity of power vested in government, including the restraints imposed on the states.[1] The SECOND is how the government is structured and how its power is distributed between the three branches. As to the first, there are two important questions that arise:

A. Are any of the powers which are transferred to the Federal government unnecessary or improper?

---

1. United States Constitution: Article I, Section 10.

FEDERALIST NO. 41

The Message: The powers being conferred to the national government are necessary, but many precautions have been taken to ensure that these powers are never abused.

———————

Original Quote: "The clearest marks of this prudence are stamped on the proposed Constitution. The Union itself, which it cements and secures, destroys every pretext for a military establishment which could be dangerous. America united, with a handful of troops, or without a single soldier, exhibits a more forbidding posture to foreign ambition than America disunited, with a hundred thousand veterans ready for combat."

Relevance to Today: A united America is more powerful than any army. But too many actions by the federal government now serve to divide us rather than to bring us together. We need a common language, a common national identity, and common equality before the law—and a government that clearly celebrates our diversity while facilitating our unity.

———————

Original Quote: "Every man who loves peace, every man who loves his country, every man who loves liberty, ought to have it ever before his eyes, that he may cherish in his heart a due attachment to the Union of America, and be able to set a due value on the means of preserving it."

Relevance to Today: Love of our country should not be scorned, but embraced. Patriotism and nationalism have almost become clichés, but they are *essential* to our liberty. Love does not spring from compulsion but from true attachment to a common cause. It should not take a terrorist event or natural disaster to bring us all together.

B. Do all of these powers, taken as a whole, threaten the
sovereignty left to the states?

Is the total, aggregate power vested in the Federal government
greater than it ought to be? That is the first question. Those who
support the Constitution have responded to the arguments made
against the extensive powers it gives the government. The supporters no doubt realize, that their opponents did not consider
how necessary these powers were. Critics have chosen to focus
on the inevitable inconveniencies. Naturally, the other side takes
political advantage and focuses on possible abuses bound to occur
whenever a power can be abused.

This type of response to an objection is probably not the best
way to convince the People of America. It may display the subtlety
of the writer, it may allow him to boundlessly exhibit his rhetorical
prowess and eloquence, it may inflame the passions of the unthink-
ing, and it may even confirm the prejudices of the *mis*thinking.

But levelheaded and candid people will realize that even the
purest of human beings are not perfect. They realize that the
choice is not always between the lesser of two evils but sometimes
it is between the GREATER instead of the PERFECT good. And
that in every political institution, the power to advance the public
good will always run the risk of being misapplied and abused.
Therefore, they will see that in all cases where power is conferred,
the first thing to decide is whether the power is necessary for the
public good. If we answer "yes" to that question, then the next
thing to decide is how best to guard against that power being
used against the public good. So that we can arrive at the correct
conclusion, it would be appropriate to review all of the powers to
be given to the government of the Union. This is far easier to accomplish if you divide the powers into different categories based
on the following goals:

1. Defense against foreign danger;
2. The regulation of commerce and diplomacy with foreign nations;
3. Maintaining harmony and proper interaction between the states;
4. Various things that are generally useful;
5. Restraining the states from certain harmful actions;
6. Making sure that all of these powers are employed effectively.

The powers that fall under "Security against foreign danger" include those of declaring war and granting letters of marquee,[1] creating armies and fleets,[2] regulating and calling forth the militia,[3] and collecting and borrowing money.[4] Security against foreign danger is one of the most basic goals of civil society, and an avowed and essential goal of the American Union.

The powers required to achieve this goal must be given to the Federal government. Is the power of declaring war necessary? No one would answer "no" to this, so it would be a waste of time to prove it is a necessary power. The existing Confederation distinctly establishes this power. Is the power of raising armies and equipping fleets necessary? This is related to the previous power, as well as the power of self-defense. But was it necessary to give an indefinite power to raise troops, as well as providing fleets, and maintaining both in peace, as well as in war?

---

1. United States Constitution: Article I, Section 8, clause 11; *letters of marquee*: a legal authorization to cross an international border for the purpose of reprisal (an action that is directed against an attack or injury). Letters of marquee issued jurisdiction to the party in question to conduct "reprisal operations" outside the borders of its respective nation.
2. United States Constitution: Article I, Section 8, clauses 12–13.
3. United States Constitution: Article I, Section 8, clause 16.
4. United States Constitution: Article I, Section 8, clauses 1–2.

The answers to these questions have been sufficiently provided in another place so we do not need to extensively discuss them here. The answers seem so obvious and conclusive that a discussion is hardly even required in the first place. How on earth can the force necessary for defense be limited by those who cannot limit the force of offense? If a Federal Constitution can foil the ambitions and set boundaries on the actions of other nations, then indeed it can also properly control the discretion of its own government and set boundaries on the actions it takes for its own safety.

How could we safely prohibit preparing for war in time of peace if we can't control the very same preparations and establishments of other hostile nations? How we go about protecting our security can only be done according to the ways we can be attacked, and the amount of danger we face of actually being attacked. We can only decide how to go about protecting ourselves in this way, and in no other.

It would be senseless to support constitutional barriers to the impulse of self-defense. In fact, it is worse than senseless, because it would plant in the Constitution itself the necessity of violating the Constitution, and every violation would act as a precedent for unnecessary or dangerous violations to be repeated in the future. If one nation constantly maintained a disciplined army capable of serving the ambitions and vengeful desires of that nation, it would require even the most peaceful nations who were within its reach to engage in similar actions.

The 15th century was an unhappy time period when military establishments were created in times of peace. They were first introduced by Charles VII of France,[1] and all of Europe eventually

---

1. Charles VII (1403–61) reigned from 1422 to 1461 and was called "The Victorious." He was crowned in Reims in 1429 as a result of the efforts of Joan of Arc to free France from the English.

followed his example. If other nations had not followed, Europe would have long ago worn the chains of a single, universal monarch. If every nation except France were to disband its peacetime military forces today, the same thing might happen. As mistress of the world, the Roman Empire and her veteran legions were more than a match for the undisciplined courage of all other nations.

It is equally true that the liberties of Rome finally fell victim to her military triumphs, just as the liberties of Europe (insofar as they have existed) have, with few exceptions, been the victims of military establishments. A standing army is therefore a dangerous, albeit a sometimes necessary feature of a nation. On a micro-level, they can be inconvenient. On a macro-level, their consequences can be fatal. On any level, they must be approached with foresight and caution. A wise nation will take into consideration all of these things. While it should not rashly prevent itself from using any resource that may become essential to its safety, it should be as wise as possible in making it less necessary and dangerous to resort to standing armies as they threaten its liberties.

The Constitution bears the clearest signs of this wisdom. The Union itself, which the Constitution cements and secures, destroys every pretext for a dangerous military establishment. A united America with few troops, or even none at all, appears much more threatening to foreign ambitions than a disunited America with a hundred thousand veterans ready for combat. It was previously remarked that a similar situation in one of the nations of Europe had actually saved its liberties.

Because it is an island and also has a powerful navy, Great Britain has been rendered virtually unbeatable against the armies of her neighbors. As a result, her rulers have never been able to fool the public into believing in real or artificial dangers that would require the establishment of a large military force in peacetime. The great distance between the United States and the powerful nations of the world provides us with the same happy security. As long as we remain a united people, a dangerous military establishment will never be needed, let alone plausible. But let it never be forgotten that it is only because of UNION that we have this advantage. The moment the Union is disbanded will be the moment a new order of things begins.

The fears of the weaker states, as well as the ambitions of the stronger states (or confederacies) will set the same example in the New World as Charles VII did in the Old World. The same motives that led to the situation over there will be the same motives that lead to them here. Instead of reaping the benefits from our situation as Great Britain has from hers, we will become a mere copy of continental Europe. Liberty everywhere will be crushed by standing armies and never-ending taxes. In fact, the fortunes of a disunited America will be even more disastrous than those in Europe. In Europe, however, the sources of her evils can all be found within Europe, as there are no other powerful nations from another part of the globe able to make them their puppets by stirring up trouble amongst them. In America, all the miseries and problems that would come from her own internal jealousies, arguments, and wars would only be the beginning of her troubles. Because Europe is more powerful than us, and continues to have influence on this part of the globe, this would cause problems for us that Europe does not have to deal with, especially since there is no other part of the globe that relates to her as she relates to us.

The consequences of disunion cannot be made clearer or shown too often. Every person who loves peace, who loves their country, and who loves liberty should have this picture always before their eyes so that their heart can cherish the Union of America, and thereby make every effort to preserve it.

Besides the Union, the best possible way to avoid the peril of standing armies is to limit the amount of time in which revenue can be appropriated for their support. The Constitution has prudently added this requirement.[1] I will not repeat my previous points that I believe fully justify this requirement in the Constitution. But it may not be improper to address an argument against this part of the Constitution based on the policies and practices of Great Britain.

Part of the critics' argument is that, in Great Britain, maintaining an army has to be voted on annually by Parliament, whereas the American Constitution has lengthened this critical time period to two years. This is how the case is usually presented to the public. Is it a fair comparison? Does the British constitution require Parliament to vote on this once every year? Does the American Constitution force Congress to appropriate money for a standing army for at least two years?

No. As those who make this erroneous argument must surely know, the British constitution does not put any limit on the discretion of Parliament, and the American Constitution actually makes two years the maximum time, rather than the minimum amount of time money can be appropriated to a standing army (before requiring another vote). Had the argument been stated correctly, it would have stated that while Parliament is not required to vote on supplying the military establishment on a regular basis, it has typically, *in practice,* voted for it once a year. Here is the situation in Great Britain: Members of the House of Commons are elected for seven years and a great number of them are elected by a very small proportion of the people. The electors are corrupted by the representatives, and the representatives are in turn corrupted by the crown. Now, if Parliament has unlimited discretion to appropriate money for a military establishment, but did not desire or dare to go beyond a year in voting for such an establishment, is it reason-

---

1. United States Constitution: Article I, Section 8, clause 12.

able to presume that the Representatives of the United States, who are elected freely by the whole body of the people every two years,[1] cannot be safely entrusted with the power to appropriate money for a military establishment, while being explicitly limited to the short period of two years for doing so?

A faulty argument seldom fails to betray itself. Those who oppose the new Federal government have provided an excellent example of this. But among all of the blunders made by the opposition, none has been more striking than their attempt to get the People on their side by taking advantage of this fear of standing armies. This attempt has fully engaged the public in a discussion of an important topic, and has led to debates that prove once and for all that not only does the Constitution provide effective safeguards against the dangers of standing armies, but that nothing short of a Constitution fully capable of uniting and defending the Union can save America from the multiple standing armies that would result from her splitting into many different states or confederacies. In addition, the standing armies of each of these confederacies would become progressively large enough to eventually become more financially burdensome to maintain, as well as more dangerous to the liberties of the People, than any such establishment would ever be if it was under a single, united, and efficient government.

The obvious necessity of creating and maintaining a navy has been less open to criticism. We must count this as one of our greatest blessings since the Union will be the primary source of our naval strength. This strength will be one of our primary sources of security against dangers from abroad.

We are in a situation very similar to Great Britain's in this respect. Happily, that which will be our most effective defense against foreign danger, namely our navy, won't be able to be used

---

1. United States Constitution: Article I, Section 2, clause 1.

by a deceitful government against the liberties of the People. All of the citizens on the Atlantic seaboard are deeply interested in naval protection. If they have been able to sleep quietly in their beds, if their property has remained safe from danger, and if their seaside towns have not yet had to pay any ransoms to invaders, then this is only because of temporary good fortune and random circumstance—the credit for which should not be given to the current government to whom they all owe allegiance.

Not including Virginia or Maryland, particularly vulnerable on their eastern Atlantic seaboards, no state in the Union ought to be as worried about this danger as much as New York. She has a long coast, and a very important part of the state is an island. The state itself has a river that penetrates inland more than fifty leagues [172.62 miles]. Its greatest commercial center, and the great source of its wealth [New York City], is always at the mercy of events, and can almost be regarded as a hostage of the humiliating threats of foreign powers, as well as the predatory demands of pirates and barbarians. Should the unstable situation in Europe result in a war whose destruction extended into the Atlantic Ocean, it would be a miracle if it were not affected by outrages and plunder.

With America in its current condition, the states that have the most to fear from these dangers cannot rely on our present phantom government. If their resources were indeed enough to protect them, then the things that needed to be protected would be swallowed up by the amount of resources required to protect them in the first place! The power in the Constitution to regulate and call up the militia has already been sufficiently justified and explained.

Since the power to collect and borrow money is a necessity for the national defense, it is appropriate to put it in the same category. This power has already been clearly examined and given so much attention that I trust that everyone understands why it is necessary, both in its scope and form. I only want to address one other aspect that has been brought up by those who believe this power should have been limited to external taxation, by which they mean taxes on goods imported from other countries [tariffs].

It is beyond doubt that this taxation will always be a valuable source of income; that it will be our primary source of income for a long time; and that, right now, it is an essential source of income. But we draw many incorrect conclusions about this subject if we do not take into account that the amount of revenue derived from foreign commerce will be proportional to the changes in the amount and variety of our imports. In addition, such changes will not correspond with our population growth, which is the most general way to determine the desires of the public.

As long as agriculture remains the largest sector of our economy, then the amount of manufactured goods will have to be increased to meet demand. As soon as there are people who are no longer needed in the agricultural sector, and who begin to manufacture goods domestically, then the amount of imported manufactured goods will decrease as the number of people increases. Further into the future, a great amount of what we import may turn out to be raw materials that we will manufacture into exportable goods. That will then require the encouragement of government rewards rather than the discouragement of higher taxes. A system of government that is meant to last must be able to anticipate these changes and accommodate itself to them.

Those who have not denied the necessity of the power of taxation have, however, engaged in a fierce attack against the language used in the Constitution. It has often been said that the power "to lay and collect taxes, duties, imposts, and excises, to pay the debts, and provide for the common defense and general welfare of the United States,"[1] amounts to unlimited permission to utilize every

---

1. United States Constitution: Article I, Section 8, clause 1.

power that is allegedly required for the common defense or general welfare. The detractors who have stooped to make this misinterpretation have not provided more proof, searching to make any objections they possibly can, no matter how true or false they are.

If the only definition of the powers of Congress in the Constitution had been the general one quoted above, then those who came up with this objection might have had good reasons to, even if they could've expressed their objection less awkwardly. Surely "to raise money for the general welfare" cannot be construed to mean the power to destroy the freedom of the press, the trial by jury, or even to regulate the Course of Descents[1] or the Forms of Conveyances.[2]

But how much weight can this objection have when all of the things that these general terms apply to are specified, and not even separated by a longer pause than a semicolon?[3] If we were to interpret everything like this and attach meaning to whatever part we wished, then should we simply remove and exclude any part of a sentence we desire, or should the more ambiguous and unclear terms be fully retained, while the clear and precise terms are denied any significance whatsoever? What would be the point of even listing specific powers if these and all others were merely meant to be part of the general powers?

Nothing is more common and natural than first using a general phrase and then explaining and qualifying it by listing specifics. Thus, the idea of including specifics that neither explain nor qualify the wide-ranging phrases and do nothing more than confuse and mislead is absurd. So, we are left with a dilemma: Either

---

1. *Course of Descents:* This refers to the legal pathway by which property/inheritance/estate/ etc. was passed on. (Referenced in Federalist 33 as "Law of Descents.")

2. *Forms of Conveyances:* This refers to the legal method by which the title for property is legally transferred from one party to another.

3. United States Constitution: Article I, Section 8.

we accuse those who made this objection, or those who authored the Constitution, of absurdity. The facts tell us we must give the benefit of the doubt to the authors of the Constitution.

This objection is even more incredible given that the language being objected to is actually copied from the Articles of Confederation! The duties of the Union to the states, as described in Article III of the Articles of Confederation, are "their common defense, security of their liberties, and mutual and general welfare." The terms of Article VIII are even more identical: "All charges of war, and all other expenses, that shall be incurred for the common defense or general welfare, and allowed by the United States in congress, shall be defrayed out of the common treasury, etc." Similar language occurs in Article IX. If we decided to misinterpret these old clauses in the same way that the new Constitution is being purposely misinterpreted, then they would give the current congress the power to legislature over absolutely anything! But what would everyone have thought of congress if they had only listened to the general phrases and disregarded the specific ones that determine and limit their powers? What if instead they had exercised unlimited power over the common defense and the general welfare? I appeal directly to opponents of the Constitution, and I ask whether they would have used similar reasoning that they have used to criticize the Convention to justify and make excuses for the current congress. Oh how difficult it is for an error to not condemn itself!

—Publius

FEDERALIST NO. 42

The Message: It is imperative that the world see us and treat us as one nation. That is why the federal government must be empowered to regulate international trade and make treaties with foreign nations with one voice.

Original Quote: "The regulation of foreign commerce, having fallen within several views which have been taken of this subject, has been too fully discussed to need additional proofs here of its being properly submitted to the federal administration."

Relevance to Today: A major sticking point between the North and South during the Civil War era, trade policy has always been a contentious issue. Especially in the midst of economic downturns, a debate over trade rages between those who support restrictive agreements and those who support free-market ones. In recent years, trade deals with China, North Korea, and Columbia have sparked debate. But, either way, a united nation has much more leverage than fifty individual ones—it's just a matter of using that leverage in the best way possible.

Original Quote: "The authority of the existing Congress is restrained to the regulation of coin struck by their own authority, or that of the respective States. It must be seen at once that the proposed uniformity in the value of the current coin might be destroyed by subjecting that of foreign coin to the different regulations of the different States."

Relevance to Today: The true value of currency has always been on the minds of Americans. Today, as the nation faces possible inflation and a stagnant economy, the role and power of the Federal Reserve and its handling of United States currency is becoming an increasingly important issue.

A General Overview of the Powers to Be Vested in the Union by the Proposed Constitution (Continued)

JAMES MADISON

For the New York Packet: Tuesday, January 22, 1788
The Constitutional Convention and the New Federalism

Constitutional References:
Article I: §8/3–7, 10 | §9/1—Article II: §2/2—Article IV: §1

The second group of powers that will belong to the new Federal government are related to regulating our relationships with foreign nations and include:

1. *"The regulation of commerce and diplomacy with foreign nations"*
   a. Making treaties;[1]
   b. Sending and receiving ambassadors, other public officials, and consuls;[2]
   c. Defining and punishing piracy and other felonies

---

1. United States Constitution: Article II, Section 2, clause 2.
2. Ibid.

      committed on the high seas, including those against
      international law;[1]

d. Regulating commerce with foreign nations, including
   the power to prohibit the importation into the United
   States of slaves after the year 1808, and in the meantime
   to immediately enact a tax of $10 on every slave
   imported into the United States.[2]

This group of powers is obvious and essential to the administration of the federal government. If there is an arena where we should be one nation, it is in respect to other nations. The power to make treaties and send/receive ambassadors is a clear necessity. While the Articles of Confederation authorize both of these powers, they also differ from the new Constitution in two important ways.

First, the Constitution does not allow treaties to be regulated by the states, and it also appropriately includes the power to appoint and receive "other public ministers and consuls," rather than just ambassadors. The technical meaning of the term "ambassador" (as it appears in Article II of the Articles of Confederation) means simply the highest-ranking public official representing a country in another country, and it does not include anyone of lower rank whom the United States may wish to appoint where foreign embassies are necessary. In no way can the term "ambassador," as it appears in the Articles of Confederation, be interpreted to also include consuls, even though congress has found it convenient to disregard this and appoint lower-ranking diplomatic officials anyway.

It is true that the power of appointing consuls may come from

---

1. United States Constitution: Article I, Section 8, clause 10.
2. United States Constitution: Article I, Section 9, clause 1.

certain stipulations in commercial treaties that require them by both sides when those duties are connected with commerce; thus the power of appointing consuls under the Articles of Confederation might fall under the power of making treaties. Where no such treaty exists, the power to appoint consuls under the Articles of Confederation could *perhaps* be covered by Article IX, which allows congress to appoint all government officials that are necessary in managing the general affairs of the United States. But it seems that appointing and receiving consuls where there was no treaty requirement has been overlooked. Making up for this omission in the Articles of Confederation is one of the small examples of how the Constitution has improved upon them. Even the smallest provisions become important when their inadequacy makes it likely that they will be violated in some way. If I were to list all of the examples of how congress has inadvertently (as with appointing consuls), or been forced, to violate the powers explicitly given to it by the Articles of Confederation, it would surprise many people. These examples alone would provide an excellent argument in favor of the new Constitution, a document that carefully improves on the smaller errors, as well as the glaring defects, of the Articles of Confederation.

It is equally appropriate, and a great improvement on the Articles of Confederation, for the Federal government to have the power to punish both piracy and other felonies on the high seas, as well as enforce international law. The Articles of Confederation contain no provisions related to violations of international law, so some indiscreet state can possibly get the whole Confederacy into trouble with foreign nations. The provision that allows the Federal government to define and punish piracy and other felonies on the high seas extends only to establishing courts in order to try these crimes. It might be more convenient to leave the definition of piracy up to international law, although it is legally defined in most municipal (internal affairs, as opposed to international) codes. It is obvious that a definition of what constitutes a felony on the high seas is required.

Under Common Law[1] in England, and even to a certain degree under Statute Law,[2] this term is somewhat loosely defined. But we shouldn't use the Common or Statute Law of any nation as a standard for defining a felony unless it has actually been a law adopted by a legislature. The definitions given for this term in the laws of the states would be just as impractical an example for the Federal government as the Common and Statute Laws of England would be a dishonorable and illegitimate one. Not only is the definition not precisely the same in any two states, but it changes in each state after each revision of its criminal laws. Therefore, for the sake of uniformity and certainty, it was necessary to give the new Federal government the power to define felony cases on the high seas.

The power to regulate foreign commerce has already been so thoroughly discussed and defended that no more proof is required in order to prove that it is an appropriate power for the new Federal government.

It is extremely regrettable that the power to abolish the slave trade will not exist until the year 1808, and even more so that it cannot be stopped at this very moment. Even so, it is not difficult to see why this restriction was put in place, or why it was worded the way it was. It ought to be considered a great human triumph that this barbaric modern practice can be forever eradicated in these states within twenty years. During that twenty-year time frame, the Federal government will be able to greatly discourage this trade, and it may even be totally abolished (with

1. *Common Law:* Referenced and defined in Federalist 37.
2. *Statute Law:* Referenced and defined in Federalist 37.

the agreement of the very few states who continue to engage in it) in accordance with the example of the great majority of the states of the Union who have already abolished it. How incredible it would be if the poor Africans who are the victims of this trade had the same hopes of being redeemed from it by their European brethren!

Some have attempted to pervert this clause in the Constitution by either representing it as a criminal tolerance of an evil trade, or as a deliberate attempt to prevent voluntary and perhaps beneficial emigration from Europe to America. I mention these deliberate misrepresentations not to give an answer to them (for they deserve none), but to provide an example of the type of objections that some have shamelessly made against the new Constitution.

The third group of powers that will belong to the Federal government are related to maintaining peace and proper relations between the states. Also included in this group will be the specific restraints that will be placed on state authority, as well as certain powers of the Judicial Branch. The restraints placed on the states belong in a specific group, however, while those placed on the Judicial Branch will be examined when we arrive at our examination of the structure and organization of that Branch of the new government. I will quickly review the powers that fall under this category:

2. *"Maintaining harmony and proper interaction between the states"*
    a. To regulate commerce among the several states and the Indian tribes;[1]

---

1. United States Constitution: Article I, Section 8, clause 3.

b. To coin money and regulate both its value and the value of foreign coin;[1]

c. To provide for the punishment of counterfeiting the current coin and securities[2] of the United States;[3]

d. To fix the standard of weights and measures;[4]

e. To establish a uniform rule of naturalization, and uniform laws of bankruptcy;[5]

f. To prescribe the manner in which the public acts, records, and judicial proceedings of each state, shall be recorded, and the effect they shall have in other states;[6]

g. To establish post offices and post roads.[7]

Our own experience has uncovered the Articles of Confederation as defective in regard to the regulation of interstate commerce. In addition to all the observations and arguments made in previous papers on this subject, it may be added that without the supplemental powers that the new Constitution provides, the great and essential power of regulating foreign commerce would be rendered incomplete and ineffective. One of the vital purposes of this power is to provide relief for states that import and export products via other states, and, as such, have to pay exorbitant amounts of money to do so. If such states were at liberty to regulate the commerce between one state and another, they would be able to pile taxes on imported and exported goods, all of which

---

1. United States Constitution: Article I, Section 8, clause 5.
2. "Bonds issued by the government; negotiable U.S. Treasury securities."
3. United States Constitution; Article I, Section 8, clause 6.
4. United States Constitution: Article I, Section 8, clause 5.
5. United States Constitution: Article I, Section 8, clause 4.
6. United States Constitution: Article IV, Section 1.
7. United States Constitution: Article I, Section 8, clause 7.

would fall on the consumers of imported goods, and the manufacturers of exported goods.

From our own past experience, we can be assured that such practices will be used in the future, and that these practices, along with human nature, will facilitate constant hostility between the states, and could very well lead to serious disruptions of the public peace. To those who are able to view this situation calmly and rationally, the attempt by some of the commercial states to collect indirect revenue from their noncommercial neighbors appears not only tactless, but unfair. It stirs up the resentment of the noncommercial states and it provides them with an incentive to pursue their own commercial interests with foreign nations through some other channel. Sadly, however, the reasonable voices that defend the large and permanent interests of such commercial states, both to political bodies (i.e., governments) and individuals, are all too often drowned out by those voices that clamor for immediate and enormous profits.

Our examples, along with the examples of others, have shown that overall authority is necessary to manage the mutual trade between states. Even in Switzerland, where the union between the Cantons is very weak, each Canton is required to allow the goods and merchandise of the other Cantons through its territory without raising the tolls (taxes) on them. In Germany, it is the law of the empire that the princes and states shall not impose tolls or taxes on bridges, rivers, or passages without the consent of the Emperor and the Diet. A quotation from a previous paper makes it appear that, as in so many other cases related to Germany, this law has not been followed in practice, and has produced all the same types of problems there that we have only begun to experience for ourselves. Among the restraints placed on the members of the United Netherlands by their central union government is that none of the members can implement taxes which might be disadvantageous to their neighbors unless they receive the permission of the central government.

Appropriately, the new Constitution does not include two obscure and contradictory limitations that exist in the Articles of Confederation related to the regulation of commerce with the Indian tribes. The power in the Articles of Confederation is entirely confined to the Indians, and not anyone within the states, so it is not able to violate or infringe upon the legislative rights of a state within its own boundaries. It has not yet been determined what type of Indian can be a member of a state, causing this to be a frequently perplexing and frustrating question within the current federal government. Also, it is not known how an external authority can regulate trade with Indians who, though not citizens of a state, lie within its legislative jurisdiction, without infringing on the right of a state to have its own laws.

Unfortunately, this has not been the only case where the Articles of Confederation have haphazardly attempted to accomplish the impossible by reconciling a partial sovereignty in the Union with complete sovereignty in the states, to try to maintain the integrity of a mathematical equation by removing a part of it and acting as if the whole remains.

There is little that needs to be said regarding the power to coin money and regulate both its value and the value of foreign coin. The authority of the current congress is limited to regulating coins *struck* by their own authority, or that of the respective states. It must be clearly obvious that the proposed uniformity in the *value* of our current coins would be destroyed by allowing the states to individually regulate the value of foreign coin.

The power to punish the counterfeiting of public securities as well as the current coin is, of course, given to the authority which will secure the value of both.

The power to regulate weights and measures is taken directly from the Articles of Confederation and is based on the same reasons which support the power to regulate coin.

The many differences that exist between the states with regard to the rules of naturalization have not only been a frequently noticed fault within our system, but have also spurred several intricate and delicate questions. Article IV of the Articles of Confederation declares "that the *free inhabitants* of each of these states, paupers, vagabonds, and fugitives from justice excepted, shall be entitled to all privileges and immunities of *free citizens* in the several states, and *the people* of each state, shall in every other, enjoy all the privileges of trade and commerce, etc." There is remarkable confusion about the language here. It is difficult to determine why the term *free inhabitants* was used in one part of the Article, *free citizens* in another, and *people* in another, or what was meant by "... to all privileges and immunities of free citizens ... all the privileges of trade and commerce."

It seems to be the case that those who are called *free inhabitants* of a particular state, although not citizens of that state, are entitled in every other state to all the privileges of *free citizens* as defined by those other states. In other words, they seem to be entitled to more privileges in other states than they may be entitled to in their own state. This surely requires that State A not only confer the rights of State B on any people considered free citizens of State A, but also anybody who State A allows to live within its boundaries. Even if the term "inhabitants" was changed so that the listed privileges applied to citizens only, the difficulties are only diminished, not removed. It would still be the case that each state would have the very inappropriate power to naturalize aliens in every other state. In some states, living in the state for a short time would confer all the rights of citizenship, while in others the requirements are much greater. Therefore, an alien who does not possess the rights of a citizen in one state may have access to that state simply by living in another for a short time. Thus, the laws of State A would preposterously take precedence over the laws of State B within the jurisdiction of State B!

It has been a stroke of luck that we have not experienced any serious embarrassments on this subject. According to the laws of several states, certain types of aliens who had committed certain reprehensible acts were kept from enjoying the full rights of citizenship in those states, as well as the privileges of being a resident. What would have happened if such a person, by residency or some other way, had become a citizen under the laws of another state, and then asserted their new rights (with regard to both their residency and citizenship) within the state that had initially punished them? No matter what the legal consequences may have been, there could have been other consequences which were too serious for the new Constitution to not protect against. The new Constitution has not only provided protections against these consequences, but has made up for all of the other defects of the Articles of Confederation on this subject by authorizing the Federal government to establish a uniform rule of naturalization throughout the United States.

The power of establishing uniform laws of bankruptcy is so closely connected with the regulation of commerce, and will also be incredibly useful in preventing frauds in cases where the property of the different parties involved is located in different states, that its usefulness will not likely be questioned.

The power to establish national laws that will lay out how the public acts, records, and judicial proceedings will be recorded, as well as the effect they shall have in other states is an obvious and valuable improvement over the corresponding clause in the Articles of Confederation, whose meaning is so ambiguous that it's ultimately of little importance to us, no matter how it is interpreted. This power could very well prove to be a very convenient and beneficial tool in the administration of justice, especially on the borders of adjacent states where the demands of justice on any person may suddenly, and without warning fall under some other jurisdiction.

The harmless power to establish post roads can never be objected to by anyone, especially since it could greatly increase the convenience with which the public communicates (so long as it is properly managed). Nothing that facilitates enhanced interaction between the states can ever be deemed unworthy of the public's interest.

—Publius

FEDERALIST NO. 43

The Message: Sometimes the business of government isn't idealistic but a matter of nuts and bolts, from copyrights and patents, to treason and debt. In this Paper Publius goes through a few of these issues and explains why the Convention arrived at the solutions it did.

Original Quote: "[A]s new-fangled and artificial treasons have been the great engines by which violent factions, the natural offspring of free government, have usually wreaked their alternate malignity on each other, the convention have, with great judgment, opposed a barrier to this peculiar danger, by inserting a constitutional definition of the crime . . ."

Relevance to Today: Throughout history, partisans from one group have called out their opponents as un-American, unpatriotic, and seditious. During the Bush presidency some Republicans made these kinds of accusations against anti-war Democrats, and Democrats, when in power, were suddenly less enamored with dissent when Republicans took aim at President Obama. But, as Publius pointed out, the charge of sedition is easily abused by government and therefore must be defined narrowly.

Original Quote: On the creation of a U.S. capital: "Without it . . . a dependence of the members of the general government on the State comprehending the seat of the government, for protection in the exercise of their duty, might bring on the national councils an imputation of awe or influence, equally dishonorable to the government and dissatisfactory to the other members of the Confederacy."

Relevance to Today: The idea of an independent capital makes perfect sense, but perhaps the Founders didn't envision how many politicians would embrace an independent capital city and make it home. Today, rather than worrying about Washington's being buffered from the states, we worry about buffering the states from Washington. Senators and congressmen regularly stay in Washington after their terms to take on jobs as lobbyists and influence the process in ways that can be harmful to a healthy republic.

NUMBER 43

A General Overview of the Powers to Be Vested in the Union by the Proposed Constitution (Continued)

JAMES MADISON

For the Independent Journal

The Constitutional Convention and the New Federalism

Constitutional References:
Article I: §3/1 | §8/8, 17 | §9/1, 4—Article III: §3/2—
Article IV: §3/1–2 | §4—Article V
Article VI: 1—Article VII

The fourth group comprises the following miscellaneous powers to be given to the new Federal government:

1. "[A power to] promote the progress of science and useful arts, by securing for a limited time, to authors and inventors, the exclusive right to their respective writings and discoveries."[1]

---

1. United States Constitution: Article I, Section 8, clause 8.

The usefulness of this power won't be questioned by anyone. The copyright of authors has been solemnly deemed in Great Britain as a right under Common Law. With equal reason, the right to useful inventions seems to belong to their inventors. The public good is completely compatible with the claims of these individuals. The states cannot provide adequate protection of these rights on their own, so in anticipation of this provision, most of them have already passed laws doing just that at the insistence of congress.

> 2. "To exercise exclusive legislation in all cases whatsoever, over such district (not exceeding ten miles square) as may by cession of particular states, and the acceptance of Congress, become the seat of the government of the United States; and to exercise like authority over all places purchased by the consent of the legislature of the state, in which the same shall be, for the erection of forts, magazines, arsenals, dockyards, and other needful buildings."[1]

The necessity of complete authority at the seat of government (the Capital) is indisputable. Because of its general supremacy, every legislature of the Union, I might even say the world, exercises this power. Without it, the public authority would be insulted and its proceedings interrupted with impunity. The dependence of the members of the Federal government on the state in which the seat of government was located for their protection would severely damage the majesty and influence of the Federal government, something that would be just as dishonorable to the Federal government as it would be to any other state.

---

1. United States Constitution: Article I, Section 8, clause 17.

This idea is even more significant if we consider that the gradual improvement of infrastructure at the stationary residence of the government will be a responsibility too big to give to any one state, and it would also place many obstacles in the way of the government's independence in case it ever decided to move to another location. Also, the size to which this government district will be limited is too small to arouse any jealousy on the part of any state.

All of the imaginable objections to a new capital using land ceded by the states should be answered by the following points. First, the state will ensure that the rights and the consent of the citizens involved will be respected. Second, the citizens of the land to be ceded will have many reasons to be a party both to the negotiations and to the actual execution of the cession of land, as they will have their voice heard by the state government that negotiates this agreement with the Federal government. Third, a municipal legislature (i.e.: city council) for this district, and one elected by the citizens of that district, will no doubt be set up for them. Lastly, by voting to ratify the Constitution, the authority of every one of the People of that state, including the inhabitants of the ceded piece of land, will be behind the agreement.

The necessity of having the same authority over forts, magazines, etc. established by the Federal government is obvious. The public money used to build such buildings, as well as the public property that will be placed within this district, requires that they all be exempt from the authority of any one state. Likewise, it would not be appropriate for the location on which the entire security of the Union may depend to be dependent on any member state. All other objections are nullified by the fact that the agreement of whichever state is involved in this transaction will be required.

3. "The Congress shall have power to declare the punishment
   of treason, but no attainder of treason shall work
   corruption of blood, or forfeiture, except during the life of
   the person attained."[1]

Since it is possible that treason will be committed against the
United States, then the United States ought to have the authority to punish it. But since the invention and creation of artificial
"treason" has long been a tool of violent factions that attempt to
harm one another, and since violent factions are the natural result
of a free government, the Convention has very wisely not included
in the Constitution a definition of the crime, but instead what is
required to prove it and obtain a conviction. The Constitution also
restricts Congress from extending punishment to anyone other
than the actual person who was tried and convicted of treason.

4. "New States may be admitted by the Congress into this
   Union; but no new state shall be formed or erected
   within the jurisdiction of any other state; nor any state
   formed by the junction of two or more states, or parts of
   states, without the consent of the legislatures of the states
   concerned, as well as of the Congress."[2]

The Articles of Confederation contain no provision to deal
with this important subject. Canada, by joining the actions of the
United States, was supposed to be admitted by right as a state,
while the other colonies (formerly British colonies) were to be admitted at the discretion of the nine states.[3] The eventual establish-

---

1. United States Constitution: Article III, Section 3, clause 2.
2. United States Constitution: Article IV, Section 3, clause 1.
3. The First Continental Congress sent three letters to the people of Quebec Province
(which was in British hands) in a failed attempt to get them to join the Revolutionary

ment of new states seems to have been overlooked by the framers of the Articles of Confederation. We have seen how inconvenient this has become, and how a lack of any provision forces Congress to overstep its powers. Therefore, with great wisdom, the new system has fixed the dilemma. It features a safeguard that no new states will be formed without the agreement of the Federal government or the states involved and is entirely appropriate for such transactions. The safeguard against creating new states by splitting up larger ones satisfies the concerns of the larger states, and the similar safeguard against joining two smaller states together satisfies concerns of the smaller states.

> 5. "The Congress shall have power to dispose of, and make
> all needful rules and regulations, respecting the territory
> or other property, belonging to the United States, with
> a proviso, that nothing in the Constitution shall be so
> construed, as to prejudice any claims of the United States,
> or of any particular state." [*sic*] [1]

This is a power of great importance, and one that is required for many of the same reasons as the previous power. It was probably necessary to include such a provision because of all the obvious jealousies and questions involved with the western territories.

> 6. "The United States shall guarantee to every state in the
> Union a republican form of government; to protect
> each of them against invasion; and on application of the

---

cause. In 1775, American troops invaded the province and engaged the British, but were defeated.

1. United States Constitution: Article IV, Section 3, clause 2.

legislature or of the executive (when the legislature cannot be convened), against domestic violence."[1]

In a Union based on republican principles and consisting of republican states, the Federal government should have the authority to defend such a system against changes that are aristocratic or monarchical in nature. The more intimate such a Union is, the more interest each state will have in each other's institutions, and thus the greater right they will have to insist that the form of government which existed when the compact (the Federal compact) was originally entered into should be *substantially* maintained.

In case a right is violated, where better to place a solution than the Constitution? Governments based on different forms and principles have been found to be less capable of entering into a Federal Union than governments that are based on similar forms and principles. As Montesquieu said: "As the confederate republic of Germany consists of free cities and petty states, subject to different princes, experience shows us that it is more imperfect than that of Holland and Switzerland . . . Greece was undone as soon as the king of Macedon obtained a seat among the Amphyctions."[2] In the case of Greece, no doubt the greater strength of the Macedonian King [Philip II], as well as the fact that he was a monarch, had a role to play.

Some may ask why there is a need for such a provision in the Constitution, and also whether or not it could be used by the Federal government as a pretext to alter a state's government without its consent. These questions deserve solid answers.

If the interference of the Federal government is never re-

---

1. United States Constitution: Article IV, Section 4.
2. *The Spirit of the Laws,* Book 9, Chapter 2. (Referenced in more detail in Federalist 9.)

quired, then this particular provision in the Constitution will be harmless and unnecessary. But who can say that none of the state governments, under the leadership of ambitious leaders who may possibly be under the influence of foreign powers, would never attempt to do away with the republican form of government? As to whether this provision could be used as a pretext to alter a state's government without its consent, I will simply state that if the Federal government acts based on the authority of this provision, then it will be bound by the requirements of this authority as well. This authority only *guarantees* a republican form of government, which requires that a republican government exist before any Federal action is taken in the first place. Therefore, as long as the republican governments that now exist in the states continue to exist, they are guaranteed by the Constitution. If any of the states choose to substitute another form of republican government, they will have the right to do so, a right that will be guaranteed by the Federal government. The one restriction states will have to abide by is that they cannot substitute for a republican government an anti-republican government, a restriction that I don't believe anyone would object to.

Society has the responsibility to protect every part of itself against invasion. This broad statement does not only include protecting each state against foreign hostility, but also from the hostility of any of its ambitious or vindictive neighbors. The history of both ancient and modern confederacies proves that the smaller states have every right to be concerned.

It is equally appropriate that protection from domestic violence is included. It is interesting that even the Swiss Cantons, who do not live, technically, under a single government, still require this protection from one another. Indeed, the history of their league shows that mutual aid such as this has been frequently claimed and given by both the most and the least democratic of the Cantons. A recent event[1] should be a warning about how we should prepare for similar emergencies.

On first thought, it may not seem to square with republican principles that a majority would not have the right to make such a decision, or that a minority would have the ability to subvert the government, and consequently that Federal interference would be inappropriate. But this is a case where theoretical thinking must give way to realities.

If, for some reason, a majority in a state (or a county or district of that state) united together for the purpose of engaging in violence, and it was appropriate for the authority of that state to be used to defend the local government, why should the Federal government not have a similar authority to protect the government of a state? Besides, there are certain parts of the state constitutions that are so interwoven with the Federal Constitution that it would be impossible to violate one without violating the other. Insurrections in a state will never require Federal interference unless the insurrectionists equaled or outnumbered those who were friendly to the state government. If the latter was the case, then it would be better for the Federal government to get involved rather than allow the insurrectionists to engage in their bloody and stubborn rebellion. The very fact that the Federal government will have a right to interfere will most likely prevent it from ever having to do so.

It is true that under a republican government, the use of force and the right to use force are necessarily on the same side. Isn't it possible that a minority could have more money, military talents, or experience, or possibly the help of a foreign power, all of which would make its appeal to violence all the more attractive?

---

1. Shays' Rebellion (1787). Explanation is given in Federalist 6.

Wouldn't a violent minority like this, which also happened to be highly organized, prove to be dangerous even against a force of superior numbers, but one which might be organized in such a way that it would be incapable of quickly exerting its full strength?

Nothing is more imaginary than the assumption that greater numbers will have the same effect in battle as they do in a census or an election. So is it not possible that a minority of *citizens* could, even with the support of alien residents and other non-citizens who do not have the right to vote under the Constitution, become a majority of *persons*? I am not even including the unhappy portion of the population that is common in some of the states, a group that during regular times of peace can be considered as being below the level of men, but who during stormy times of civic violence emerge as fully human and provide whatever side they wish to be on with superior strength.

In cases where two violent, destructive factions were ripping a state to shreds, what better umpire than the representatives of the states of the Union, who are not heated by the same local flame? Additionally, the objectivity of judges would unite them together as friends. Free governments everywhere would be happy if their weaknesses could be cured in this manner, and how wonderful it would be if such an effective project could be established for the universal peace of mankind.

Is there a better cure for addressing an insurrection that was spreading throughout the states and was perhaps the stronger force, than a constitutional right? If such an event occurred, one which was outside the limits of human cure, and so fortunately outside the limits of what is humanly probable, the best safeguard against it can be found in the new Federal Constitution, which diminishes the chances of this event ever occurring. At the end of the day, no constitution can ever completely cure or prevent such events.

As Montesquieu notes, one of the important advantages of a
Confederate Republic is "... that should a popular insurrection
happen in one of the states, the others are able to quell it. Should
abuses creep into one part, they are reformed by those that remain
sound." [1]

7. "All debts contracted, and engagements entered into,
   before the adoption of this Constitution, as being no less
   valid against the United States under this Constitution,
   than under the Confederation." [sic] [2]

This declaratory statement was probably inserted (among
other reasons) to alleviate the worries of the foreign creditors of
the United States. They are no doubt familiar with the doctrine
believed by some that a change in the political structures of a
society magically dissolves its moral obligations. Among the less
serious critiques of the Constitution has been the one that argues
that this provision should not have applied just to the debts of the
United States, but also to the debtors of the United States. But, as
happens all too often with small-minded critics, the lack of such a
provision has been blown up and magnified into some plot against
our very national rights. Those who make this criticism ought to
be told what hardly anyone else needs to be reminded of: Since
financial agreements are by nature reciprocal, asserting validity
on one side automatically asserts their validity on the other side.
As such, since this provision is merely declaratory, the establishment of this principle in one case establishes it in every case. They
should also be reminded that every constitution must limit whatever protections are included in it to dangers that are *real* and not

1. *The Spirit of the Laws,* Book 9, Chapter 1. (Referenced in more detail in Federalist 9.)
2. United States Constitution: Article VI, clause 1.

simply imagined. With this in mind, there is no chance whatsoever that the government would *dare*, with or without this provision, to not pay on the debts which are justly owed to the public.

    8. "The Congress, whenever two-thirds of both Houses
       shall deem it necessary, shall propose Amendments
       to this Constitution, or, on the application of the
       legislatures of two-thirds of the several States, shall call
       a Convention proposing Amendments, which, in either
       case, shall be valid to all intents and purposes, as part
       of this Constitution, when ratified by the legislatures of
       three-fourths of the several States, or by Conventions in
       three-fourths thereof, as the one or the other mode of
       ratification may be proposed by the Congress; provided
       [that no amendment that may be made prior to 1808
       shall in any manner affect the first and fourth clauses in
       the Ninth Section of the First Article; and] that no State,
       without its consent, shall be deprived of its equal suffrage
       in the Senate."[1]

It is beyond doubt that helpful changes based on new events
will be suggested for the Constitution. Therefore, it was necessary
to provide a way in which this could be done. The method that the
Convention preferred to put in the Constitution seems to be entirely appropriate. It protects the Constitution from being changed
too easily, while also preventing whatever faults or errors it may
have from going on forever. It allows the process of amending
the Constitution to be initiated by either the states or the Federal
government, depending on whose experiences seem to justify it.
The exception in favor of the equal representation in the Senate

---

1. United States Constitution: Article V.

was probably meant as recognition of the remaining sovereignty of the states. This sovereignty, as it is both implied and secured by equal representation in that House of Congress (the Senate)[1] was likely insisted upon by those states who are particularly concerned about their equality. The other exception was probably included based on the same reasoning which produced the privilege defended by it.[2]

> 9. "The ratification of the conventions of nine states, shall
> be sufficient for the establishment of this Constitution
> between the states ratifying the same."[3]

This provision speaks for itself. The explicit authority of the People alone can give this Constitution validity. To have required the unanimous ratification of all thirteen states would have been to put the interests of the whole at the mercy of the whims or corruption of a single state. Such a requirement would have proven to be an incredible lack of foresight on the part of the Convention, and one that our own experience would render inexcusable.

Two very delicate questions come to mind when discussing this issue. First, on what principles can the Union, which is based on a solemn compact between the states, be overruled without the unanimous consent of all the states to the new Constitution? Second, what type of relationship will exist between the nine or more states who decide to ratify the Constitution, and the remaining few who do not?

The first question can be answered by the absolute necessity of the Constitution, as well as by referring to the great principle of

---

1. United States Constitution: Article I, Section 3, clause 1.
2. Reference to the prohibition of any constitutional amendment against slavery before the year 1808, in accordance with Article I, Section 9, clauses 1 and 4.
3. Constitution of the United States, Article VII.

self-preservation and to the transcendent law of nature and of nature's God, both of which say that the safety and happiness of society are the goals of all political institutions. *Perhaps* we can also find an answer to this question within the principles of the Federal compact of the Union itself. It was previously mentioned that one of the defects of the current Confederation is that in many of the states, it received no higher approval than that of a mere ratification by the legislature. The principle of agreements being reciprocal seems to require that the same standard should have been used in all of the states. An agreement between independent sovereigns based on the authority of legislative acts can pretend to be nothing more than a treaty between the parties. It is an established principle of treaties that all of their stipulations are mutually binding on both parties, meaning that a breach of one is a breach of the whole treaty, and that if either party breaks the treaty, it absolves the others and allows them, if they please, to pronounce the treaty null and void. If we need to appeal to these delicate truths to justify allowing a few states to cause the dissolution of the Federal pact (the Union), won't these same states have a difficult time justifying the *numerous* and *significant* infractions of this pact which they themselves have committed? The time span required of all of us to not mention these ideas has passed. The times have changed, the scene is different, and the motives behind this question must be adjusted accordingly.

The second question is just as delicate (the relationship between the states who ratify, and those who don't ratify the Constitution), but fortunately, it is a hypothetical and unlikely scenario, which means that we don't have to overanalyze it. If it were to happen, however, it would be one of those situations that must be allowed to work itself out. Generally speaking, although a political relationship between those states that ratify and those that don't ratify the Constitution cannot exist, the moral relationship will remain unchanged. Rightful claims to justice will exist on both sides and will be enforced and fulfilled. Also, the rights of humanity must in all cases be appropriately and mutually respected.

Finally, our common interests, and above all, our memories of those past events which brought us all so close together, as well as our hope that all the obstacles to re-Union will be overcome, will, I hope, encourage *restraint* on one side, and *prudence* on the other.

—Publius

NUMBER 44

A General Overview of the Powers to Be Vested in the Union by the Proposed Constitution (Continued and Concluded)

JAMES MADISON

For the New York Packet: Friday, January 25, 1788

The Constitutional Convention and the New Federalism

Constitutional References:
Article I: §3/1 | §8/3, 18 | §10/1–3—
Article II: §1/2, 8—Article VI: 2–3

A fifth group of provisions in the new Constitution that restrict the authorities of the states in favor of the Federal government reads as follows:

1. "No state shall enter into any treaty, alliance, or confederation; grant letters of marquee and reprisal; coin money; emit bills of credit; make anything but gold and silver a legal tender in payment of debts; pass any

FEDERALIST NO. 44

The Message: With Anti-Federalists concerned over the powers being taken from the states in favor of the federal government, Publius took this opportunity to go through each power individually and explain why it was necessary for the central government to have it.

Original Quote: "Had they attempted to enumerate the particular powers or means not necessary or proper for carrying the general powers into execution, the task would have been no less chimerical; and would have been liable to this further objection, that every defect in the enumeration would have been equivalent to a positive grant of authority."

Relevance to Today: Proponents of a living and malleable Constitution will often point that the founding document doesn't specifically *prohibit* [*insert new right here*]. But, as the Founders clearly explained, the Constitution doesn't explicitly lay out everything the government *can't* do because they understood that covering all the bases was impossible. But nowhere does that imply that Americans have a Constitutional right to health care or solar panels.

Original Quote: "Bills of attainder, *ex post facto* laws, and laws impairing the obligation of contracts, are contrary to the first principles of the social compact, and to every principle of sound legislation."

Relevance to Today: In 2009, the Obama administration named the country's first pay czar, who quickly used the weight of the United States government to break private-sector contracts—not only for executives at companies that accepted taxpayer bailout funds, but also for CEOs tangentially involved with those corporations. This broke one of the fundamental rules laid out by the Founders.

bill of attainder, *ex post facto* laws, or laws impairing the obligation of contracts; or grant any title of nobility." [*sic*][1]

A provision that doesn't allow the states to form treaties, alliances, and confederations is also contained within the current Articles of Confederation, and was copied into the new Constitution for reasons that require no explanation. The prohibition of letters of marque[2] is another part of the old system that has been extended in parts to the new one. In the old system, letters of marque could be granted by the states after a declaration of war, but according to the new system, the states must obtain licenses for these from the government of the United States both before a declaration of war, and during a war itself. This change is justified because of the necessity of uniformity in everything that is related to, or connected with, our relationships with foreign nations, and also because it gives the nation that is immediately responsible for these relationships the ability to control all aspects of them.

The right to coin money was removed from the states in this provision, but it was actually left in their hands as a concurrent right with congress under the Confederation, with the exception that congress had the right to regulate the alloy (the makeup of the metal in the coins) and the value. The new provision is an improvement over the old one. While the alloy and value depended on the general authority of congress, the right of each state to coin the money resulted in many expensive mints, and also a great variety of designs and weights amongst the coins in circulation. The inconvenience of all of these different designs and weights defeated the purpose originally given to the federal government in the first place, and even though the existence of multiple mints

---

1. United States Constitution: Article I, Section 10, clause 1.
2. *letters of marque*: Referenced and defined in Federalist 41.

may have made it inconvenient to send gold and silver to the central mint for re-coinage, the same goal could be accomplished by simply establishing local mints under the authority of the Federal government.

Every citizen who loves justice and is aware of the sources of public prosperity must have been enormously relieved when they saw that bills of credit had been banned. The loss that America has suffered since the peace from the plague-like effects of paper money on the necessary confidence between one man and another and between citizens and their government, on the productivity and morals of the People, and on the character of republican government itself, has resulted in the states accumulating enormous debts that they will not be able to pay anytime soon. Rather than debt, it is more like an accumulation of guilt, atoned for in no other way than voluntarily sacrificing the power that caused these problems in the first place on the altar of justice.

In addition to these persuasive points, it should be pointed out that the same reasons it is necessary to deny the states the ability to regulate coin also prove that they should not have the ability to substitute paper money in place of coin. If every state has the right to regulate the value of its own coin, then there might be as many different currencies as there are states, which would have obstructed interstate commerce. The value of coin might have been retroactively changed, which would have resulted in the injury of the citizens of other states by the government(s) of another and aroused hostilities between the states themselves. Citizens of foreign countries might also suffer from the same fate, and thus the Union could be discredited and dragged into a conflict by the indiscretion of just a single state.

Any one of these problems could result from the states having the power to issue paper money, as well as gold or silver. Therefore, the power to use anything but gold and silver as legal tender to pay off debts has been taken away from the states, based on the same principle under which the power to issue paper money was also taken away.

Bills of Attainder,[1] *ex post facto*[2] laws, and laws that interfere with contractual obligations are contrary to the first principles of the social compact,[3] and to every principle of sound legislation. Both Bills of Attainder and *ex post facto* laws are explicitly prohibited in the introductions to some of the state constitutions, and all of them are prohibited by the spirit and scope of these fundamental charters. Nevertheless, our own experiences tell us that additional barriers against these dangers should be included. Therefore, the Convention very appropriately added this constitutional safeguard to protect both personal security and private rights.

The sober people of America have grown weary of the constant changes that have taken place throughout our governments. With regret and great anger, they have witnessed how the sudden changes and intrusions of the legislatures into cases affecting their personal rights ended up becoming jobs in the hands of enterprising and influential speculators, while at the same time becoming

---

1. *Bills of Attainder:* This is a legislative act that pronounces a person guilty of a crime (typically treason) without the benefit of a trial, and subjects that person to capital punishment or attainder (a judgment against treason or a felony that involves the loss of all civil rights). (Referenced in Federalist 84.)

2. *ex post facto:* Latin, meaning "after the fact"; this would be a law that would allow someone to be retroactively punished for "breaking" that law, despite the fact that the law did not exist at the time that the "crime" (as defined by the *ex post facto* law) was committed. (Referenced in Federalist 84.)

3. *social compact:* Commonly referred to today as the "social contract," which refers to the large group of political theories related to the forming of states and governments as a method of securing social order. It is described by the political philosopher Jean-Jacques Rousseau (1712–78) in his *Du Contrat Social* ("The Social Contract"), written in 1762: "Each of us puts his person and all his power in common under the supreme direction of the general will; and in a body we receive each member as an indivisible part of the whole."

traps to the harder working and less informed part of the community. They have also seen that one intrusion by the legislature is but the first link of a very long chain, with each successive intrusion being the natural and expected result of the one before it. Therefore, they have correctly concluded that some sort of reform is needed that will do away with uncertainty over government actions, and which will inspire a general sense of wisdom and productivity, in addition to providing a sense of regularity and predictability to the business of society.

The ban on titles of nobility is copied from the Articles of Confederation and needs no comment.

> 2. "No state shall, without the consent of the Congress, lay
> any imposts or duties on imports or exports, except what
> may be absolutely necessary for executing its inspection
> laws, and the net produce of all duties and imposts laid
> by any state on imports or exports, shall be for the use of
> the treasury of the United States; and all such laws shall
> be subject to the revision and control of the Congress. No
> state shall, without the consent of Congress, lay any duty
> on tonnage, keep troops or ships of war in time of peace;
> enter into any agreement or compact with another state,
> or with a foreign power, or engage in war, unless actually
> invaded, or in such imminent danger as will not admit of
> delay." [1]

All the arguments that prove the necessity of giving the Federal government the power to regulate trade [2] also support the idea of restricting the power of the states over imports and exports.

---

1. United States Constitution: Article I, Section 10, clauses 2–3.

2. United States Constitution: Article I, Section 8, clause 3.

Therefore, it would be useless to comment on this subject any further, except to say that the exclusion included in this provision seems appropriate in order to afford the states a reasonable amount of freedom with regard to the convenience of their own imports and exports, and to the United States a reasonable check against the abuse of this freedom. The rest of this particular provision is justified by reasoning that is either so obvious, or has been so fully developed in other papers that we need not comment on it any further.

The sixth and last group of powers to be given to the new Federal government consists of those powers and provisions that will make all of the other ones effective.

> 1. "[The Congress shall have power] to make all laws which shall be necessary and proper for carrying into execution the foregoing powers, and all other powers vested by this Constitution in the government of the United States or in any department or officer thereof." [1]

Few parts of the Constitution have been as excessively attacked as this one. Yet, upon a fair and closer examination of it, no part of the Constitution can be more completely invincible, as has been shown in another paper. Without the *substance* of this power, the whole Constitution would be a dead letter. Those who object to this provision can only mean that the *form* of the provision is inappropriate. But have they considered whether or not a better form could have been substituted for it?

The Convention could have used four other possible methods as far as this subject is concerned:

---

1. United States Constitution: Article I, Section 8, clause 18.

1. They could have copied Article II of the Articles of
   Confederation, which would have prohibited the
   exercise of any power that was not *explicitly* given in the
   Constitution;
2. They could have attempted to list every power that could
   possibly exist under the general terms "necessary and
   proper";
3. They could have attempted to list every power that
   could *not* be included under the "necessary and proper"
   category;
4. They could have remained silent on this subject, leaving
   the definition of "necessary and proper" powers up to
   speculation and deduction.

Had the Convention used the first method of adopting Article
II of the Articles of Confederation the new Congress would be exposed to the danger of either interpreting the term "explicitly," or
with so much freedom that the restriction would become worthless. If it interpreted the term explicitly, the government would be
disarmed of all real authority whatsoever.

It would be easy to show that not a single power that has been
delegated to congress by the Articles of Confederation (both those
that have been used, or could be used) could have been used without more or less falling back on the doctrine of *speculation* and
deduction. Since the powers that will exist under the new system
are more extensive, the new government would have to deal with
the troubling alternative of either betraying the public interest
by doing nothing, or of violating the Constitution by exercising
a power which was absolutely necessary and proper, but which
at the same time was not *explicitly* granted, had the Convention
established the first method.

Had the Convention attempted to list every power possible

under the general terms "necessary and proper," it would have necessitated a complete collection of all laws on every subject not affected by the Constitution, and not just for the present time and circumstances, but for all possible changes the future may bring. Under this scenario, this step would be necessary, because whenever a general power is applied to a specific purpose, the *specific powers* that are needed in order to accomplish the *purpose* of the general power would always have to change and adapt in order to meet that purpose, even while the purpose remained the same.

Had the Convention attempted to list every power that could *not* be included under the "necessary and proper" category of powers that were needed to carry out the general powers, the task would have been just as unrealistic and worthless. This would have also been liable to the criticism that every defect in the list would have been equivalent to a positive grant of authority, since anything not included on the list *could* be considered "necessary and proper." If they tried to avoid this by only including a partial list of the exceptions, and described whatever may have been left out by the general terms "not necessary or proper," then the list would naturally include only a few of the excluded powers. Since this partial list would only include the powers which were *least* necessary or proper, then all of the powers that were not specifically included on the list would be less actively guarded against than if no list had existed at all.

Had the Constitution been silent on the subject, then it would have unavoidably implied that every power required in order to carry out the general powers of the government would have indeed become the government's to use. There is no principle more clearly established in either law or reason than whenever a specific goal is required, the means to accomplish it are authorized, and wherever a general power to do something is given, then every specific power necessary for doing it is included. Therefore, had this last method been used by the Convention, every objection so far being made against their Plan would be plausible. If the Convention kept silent on this subject, then the states could very well fabricate some sort of pretext allowing them to question the essential powers of the Union, perhaps even during emergency situations.

If I were to be asked, "What would the consequences be if Congress did misinterpret this part of the Constitution, and did exercise powers that it was never meant to have?" I would answer that the consequences would be the same as if they had misinterpreted or enlarged any other power that had been delegated to them, or if they had violated any of the specific powers which were necessary in order to carry out a general power. In short, the same thing that happens if any state legislature should violate their respective constitutional authorities.

In the case of a violation by Congress, the success of such a violation would depend on the Executive and Judicial Branches, both of which are there to enforce and interpret all acts of Congress. If worse came to worst, a solution would have to come from the People, who would be able to repeal the acts of the usurpers by electing more faithful representatives. In all honesty, we would be able to place more trust in this method of ultimate redress (having the violation corrected) with regard to unconstitutional acts of Congress, as opposed to unconstitutional acts of the state legislatures. The reason for this is simple: Every unconstitutional act of Congress will be an invasion of the rights of the state legislatures, which will always be on the lookout for such things in order to sound the alarm to the People, and to exert local influence so that they can bring about a change in their state's Federal representation. Since there are no such intermediaries between the state legislatures and the People who can act as a watchdog on the legislature, violations of the state constitutions are more likely to remain unnoticed and un-redressed.

> 2. "This Constitution, and the laws of the United States which shall be made in pursuance thereof, and all treaties made, or which shall be made, under the authority of the United States, shall be the supreme law of the land, and the judges in every state shall be bound thereby, anything in the Constitution or laws of any state to the contrary notwithstanding."[1]

To attack this section of the Constitution—and it would be radically defective without it—has betrayed again the reckless zeal of its adversaries. To fully understand this absurdity, we must assume for the moment that there is a clause in the Constitution guaranteeing the supremacy of the *state* constitutions. To begin with, as these constitutions invest the state legislatures with absolute sovereignty in all cases (unless otherwise specified by the Articles of Confederation), all of the authorities that extend beyond those of the Confederation and that are listed in the new Constitution would have become null and void. And the new Congress would have been reduced to the same weak condition as the current one.

Second, as some of the state constitutions do not even explicitly recognize the existing powers of the Confederacy, any explicit guarantee of the supremacy of the state constitutions would bring into question every power that is contained within the proposed Constitution.

Third, since the state constitutions are unlike each other, it

---

1. United States Constitution: Article VI, clause 2.

might so happen that a treaty or national law of great and equal importance to every state would interfere with some of their constitutions and not with others, which would result in the treaty or law being valid in some states, and dead-on-arrival in others.

Finally, the world would have seen for the very first time a system of government founded upon the inversion of the fundamental principles of all government. It would have seen the authority of the whole society subordinated to the authority of the parts. It would have seen a monster in which the head was being controlled by the rest of the body.

3. "The Senators and Representatives, and the members of the several state legislatures; and all executive and judicial officers, both of the United States and the several states, shall be bound by oath or affirmation, to support this Constitution."[1]

It has been asked why it was necessary for the officials of the state governments to be bound by oath to support the Federal Constitution, while it's been deemed unnecessary that a similar oath should be required of the officers of the United States with respect to the state constitutions.

Several reasons could be given for this difference, but I will limit myself to one, which is both obvious and conclusive: The officials of the Federal government will have no part in enforcing the state constitutions. The members and officials of the state governments will play an essential role in enforcing the Federal Constitution. The election of both the President and the Senate will always depend on the state legislatures,[2] and the election of

---

1. United States Constitution: Article VI, clause 3; Article II, Section 1, clause 8.

2. United States Constitution: Article II, Section 1, clause 2; Article I, Section 3, clause 1.

the House of Representatives will depend just as much on the same authority. Additionally, the election of Representatives will likely forever be carried out by the officers and laws of each state.

Among the provisions that allow the Federal powers to be effective, we could also include those within the Executive and Judicial Branches. But since these will be examined in another place, I won't bother with them now.

We have now completed a detailed review of all of the provisions in the new Constitution that make up the sum or quantity of power that will be delegated to the Federal government, and we are brought to the undeniable conclusion that none of these powers is either unnecessary or improper for accomplishing the necessary purposes of the Union. Therefore, the question of whether or not these powers will be granted hinges on another question: whether or not a government equal to the demands of the Union shall be established, or, in other words, whether the Union itself shall be preserved.

—Publius

FEDERALIST NO. 51

The Message: The Constitution will create three separate branches of government. Because of the unique relationships each branch will have with the people, and with each other, this system will shield the nation from tyranny.

Original Quote: "In framing a government which is to be administered by men over men, the great difficulty lies in this: you must first enable the government to control the governed; and in the next place oblige it to control itself. A dependence on the people is, no doubt, the primary control on the government; but experience has taught mankind the necessity of auxiliary precautions."

Relevance to Today: Whenever Republicans or Democrats control the House, Senate, and presidency (as both George W. Bush and Barack Obama did at one point) they've faltered and abused their power. Ultimately the American people exerted their will by diluting the hold on power that the majority party had.

Original Quote: "We see it particularly displayed in all the subordinate distributions of power, where the constant aim is to divide and arrange the several offices in such a manner as that each may be a check on the other—that the private interest of every individual may be a sentinel over the public rights."

Relevance to Today: Few acts in Washington sparked more outrage around the country than the passing of the Patient Protection and Affordable Care Act. Americans took to the streets . . . and to the ballot box, and elected representatives who promised to overturn the legislation. A newly Republican House then immediately began finding ways to legally undermine the law. Lawyers and attorneys general from around the country challenged the constitutionality of the legislation and, in the end, took it to the Supreme Court. Politics can be ugly, but the Constitution guarantees that the people have the ultimate power as "sentinels" over public rights—it's just up to us to use that power.

The Structure of the Government Must Furnish the Proper Checks and Balances Between the Different Departments

JAMES MADISON

For the New York Packet: Tuesday, February 5, 1788
The Constitutional Convention and the New Federalism

How will we maintain, in practice, the necessary separation of power between the Branches of government as laid out in the Constitution?

Since all the provisions that describe each separate Branch are merely surface-level solutions, the defect must be corrected by arranging the interior structure of the government in such a way that the mutual relationships between each Branch will turn out to be the way in which each Branch is kept within its own appropriate limits. While I won't be presumptuous enough to attempt to fully develop such an important idea in this paper, I will hazard a few general points that will hopefully shed some light on the subject and enable us to correctly judge the principles and structure of the government proposed by the Convention.

In order to build a strong foundation and ensure that the powers of each Branch will be exercised freely and separately, powers that everyone, on some level, admits are essential to the preservation of liberty, it is clear that each Branch should have a will of its own. Therefore, they should be structured in a way that the members of each Branch will play as small a role as possible in the appointment of the members of the other Branches. However, if we strictly followed this principle, then it would require that all appointments to the supreme Executive, Legislative, and Judicial Branches should come from the same fountain of authority, and through channels that have absolutely no communication with each other; in other words, the authority of the People.

It may be the case that this could be accomplished more easily than it may appear. Since some additional difficulties and expenses will crop up in the actual execution of such a plan, we must accept that, from time to time, we will depart from the principle of separation of powers. For example, it might be inadvisable to insist on strictly adhering to the principle as far as the makeup of the Judicial Branch is concerned. The reasons for this are: First, since it is essential that each member of the Judicial Branch have unique qualifications, our primary interest is to find a method of appointment that will do the most to ensure we appoint judges with those qualifications; and second, because judges have lifelong terms in office, their sense of dependence on the authority that appointed them in the first place would be completely destroyed if the Judicial Branch were kept completely separate and distinct.

It is equally obvious that the officials of each Branch must depend as little as possible on the other Branches for their salaries. If the President or the judges absolutely depended on Congress to determine their salaries, then their independence to everything else would be mere mockery.

What will ultimately provide the greatest security against the gradual accumulation of the powers into a single Branch will be giving everyone who actually administers the different Branches the constitutional ability, as well as the personal motives, to resist the invasions of the others. The provisions in the Constitution that allow each Branch to defend itself must (as always) be equal to the risk of one Branch being attacked by, or attacking, another. Ambition must be made to work against ambition, and the interests of each man must be connected with the constitutional rights that his position will afford him. Perhaps it is a reflection on human nature that such devices should be necessary in the first place to control the abuses of government. But what is government itself, but the greatest of all reflections on human nature? If men were angels, no government would be necessary, and if angels were to govern men, then neither external nor internal controls on government would be necessary. In framing a government administered by men over men, the great difficulty lies in this: You must first enable the government to control the governed, and in the next place obligate it to control itself. Without a doubt, the primary control on the government will be its dependence on the People, but experience has taught mankind that other precautions will be necessary as well.

The idea of making up for man's lack of virtue by putting his interests in opposition to those that rival his own is not a new one. This notion can be seen throughout all of the private and public affairs of humanity. Specifically, we see this idea on display in every subordinate distribution of powers (such as in a bureaucracy), where the goal is always to divide and arrange each department in such a way that each acts as a check on the other. This way the private interests of every individual may serve as a lookout of sorts for the rights of the public. These wise inventions are as necessary in the distribution of the supreme powers of the state.

It isn't possible to give each Branch an equal power of self-defense, since in republican government the legislative authority is inevitably the strongest. The way to make up for this inconvenience is to divide the Legislature into different Houses and to disconnect them from each other. This can be accomplished by using different methods of election and assigning each House its own unique powers and procedures. It may even be necessary to provide more safeguards against dangerous invasions of power. Since the great importance and strength of the legislative authority requires that it be divided into separate Houses, then the natural weakness of the executive authority may actually require that *it* be strengthened.

At first glance, it may appear that giving the Executive an absolute veto power on any law the Legislature passes would be a smart and natural idea. But perhaps such a power would be neither completely safe nor, on its own, adequate. On ordinary occasions, such a power may not be used with enough firmness, while during extraordinary times it might be treacherously abused. Isn't there some way to fix the difficulties involved in giving the Executive such an absolute and final veto power? Could it be fixed by a spelled-out connection between the weaker Executive Branch, and the weaker House of the stronger Congress, and in such a way that Congress could be made to respect the constitutional rights of the President and, at the same time, remain confident enough in its own rights?

If these principles (which I am convinced are correct) were applied as a standard to the state constitutions and to the proposed Federal Constitution, I believe that, even if the Federal Constitution didn't perfectly comport with them, the state constitutions would be infinitely less capable of passing the same test.

Furthermore, there are two considerations that apply especially to the Federal system of America, and will allow us to look at our system from a very interesting point of view.

First, in a single republic, all the power that is surrendered by the People is submitted to the administration of a single government, and abuses of that power are protected by dividing that government into distinct and separate Branches. In the compound republic of America, the power that is surrendered by the People is first divided between two distinct governments (state and Federal), and then the portion that each has for itself is further subdivided into distinct and separate Branches. As a result, the rights of the People are provided with double security, since the two different governments control each other, and will at the same time control themselves.

Second, it is important in a republic to not only protect society against the oppression of its rulers, but to protect each part of society against the injustice of the others. Different classes of citizens have different interests, and if some common interest were to unite a majority of citizens, then the rights of the minority would be at risk. There are only two ways to protect against this evil: first, by creating within the community itself a will or authority that is independent of the majority, or in other words, society itself (i.e., such as a monarch); or second, by having so many different types of citizens within society it would be extremely unlikely, if not completely impractical, for a majority of citizens to ever combine together for the sake of oppressing their own fellow citizens.

The first method is common to all governments that have a hereditary or self-appointed authority (i.e., monarchies). This security is at best a precarious one, since a power that is independent of society supports the unjust views of the majority as much as the rightful interests of the minority, or better yet, may possibly turn against both of them. The second method, however, will be exemplified by the Federal Republic of the United States. While the authority of this government will be derived from and be dependent on society, the society itself will be broken into so many parties, interests, and classes, that individual and/or minority rights will be in very little danger against any sinister alliance on the part of the majority.

In a free government, the security for civil rights must be the same as that for religious rights; the security for the first will be provided for by society's great variety of interests, just as the security for the second will be provided for by society's many religions. The amount of security for each depends on the number of interests and religions, which is itself dependent on the size of the country, and the number of people who will live under the same government.[1]

From this point of view, it seems that any sincere friend of republican government has good reasons to support the idea of a well-constructed Federal system. It shows that, in this country, oppressive majorities will be easier to form in exact proportion to how much the territory of the Union decreases. The Union becoming more diverse and more divided into different confederacies or states is the best possible security that can be had under the republican form of government for the rights of every class of citizen. As a result, the stability and independence of some Branch of government (the only other security for such rights) would have to be proportionally increased.

Justice is the goal of government, it is the goal of civil society, and it has, and always will be, pursued until it is either obtained, or until liberty is lost in its pursuit. In a society in which the stronger faction can easily come together to oppress the weaker, it can be said that society anarchy is just as prevalent as it is in nature,

---

1. Refer to Federalist 10.

where the weaker species is always in danger from the stronger. And since, even in a state of anarchy, the stronger individuals may wish to submit to a government that protects the weak as well as themselves (because of the uncertainty of their own safety and well-being), in the same way, under a Federal government, the more powerful factions or parties will be gradually persuaded by the same motive to wish for a government that protects all parties, both the weak as well as the powerful.

It is almost certain that if the state of Rhode Island were to be separated from the Union and left on its own, individual rights under a government that was so confined would become so insecure (because of the oppressions of the majority) that a power completely independent of the People would be called on by the very same factions whose own misrule had required such a power in the first place. However, in the immense republic of the United States, with its numerous and diverse interests, parties, and religions, the formation of a majority coalition throughout all of society would probably only happen if it were based on the principles of justice and the general good. And since under the system established by the Constitution the minority will be in less danger of being oppressed by the majority, there will be even fewer reasons to further protect the security of the minority by introducing into the government a will that was not dependent on the majority, or in other words, a will that was independent of society itself (i.e., such as a monarch).

Also, contrary to the opinions of some, it is just as certain that the larger the society, the more capable it will be of self-government (so long as it exists within a practical amount of territory). Fortunately for the *republican cause*, the amount of territory that has been deemed "practical" can be greatly enlarged by a wise modification and application of the *Federal principle*.

—Publius

PART THREE

A REPUBLIC,
IF YOU CAN KEEP IT

L eaving the Constitutional Convention of 1787 on the last day of debate, Benjamin Franklin was stopped by someone outside Independence Hall and was asked what kind of government the Convention had decided on.

"A Republic," Franklin replied, "if you can keep it."

Benjamin Franklin was a brilliant man and he knew well that a true republic—tried in its purest form for perhaps the first time in the history of the world—was not something that would be easy to maintain. It would require constant vigilance over the delicate balance of power between the national and state governments, and it would put an almost-overwhelming demand on the citizens to recognize when that balance got out of whack.

Given all of that, some people wonder why the Founders didn't choose to structure the country as a simple democracy. The truth is that they weren't in love with democracy. Writing in Federalist 10, James Madison said that "a republic is more capable of controlling the effects of faction than a democracy . . ." That may surprise some Americans. After all, in grade school many of us were taught that America is a "democracy"—but we're not. America is a republic and the distinction isn't minor.

A *representative* democracy, which more accurately describes our model of government, means that we cede decision making to our elected officials but maintain ultimate authority through the right to vote. There are a lot of challenges, of course: How can a republic grow and still stay true to its principles without straying from them? How can it defend the rights of the individual while at the same time creating a strong union?

Throughout the Federalist Papers, Publius reminded readers that the Constitution would establish a republican government, *not* a democracy. Federalist 39 reemphasized that key point while also explaining how the Constitution would enable the country to maintain the characteristics of both a national and federal government. Like "democracy" and "republic," we often use the terms "national" and "federal" synonymously, but they have very different meanings. "National" refers to a union of all the people of a nation, along with the government duties and policies that promote the common welfare of all people. "Federal," on the other hand, refers to the structure of government that pertains to the union of individual states which combine in a federation.

This distinction was perhaps the defining issue of the debate over the Constitution. Anti-Federalists, like Patrick Henry, believed strongly that the states should be empowered to act on behalf of the people, not a central government. At the Virginia Ratifying Convention he spoke in opposition to the Constitution:

> "What right had they to say, We, the people? My political curiosity, exclusive of my anxious solicitude for the public welfare, leads me to ask, Who authorized them to speak the language of, We, the people, instead of, We, the states? States are the characteristics and the soul of a confederation. . . . The people gave them no power to use their name. That they exceeded their power is perfectly clear."

On the other hand, Federalists like James Wilson, who was a signer of the Declaration of Independence and strong ally of Madison, had the opposite point of view. At the Pennsylvania Ratifying Convention he argued:

"This, Mr. President, is not a government founded upon compact; it is founded upon the power of the people. . . . They wish
a principle established, by the operation of which the legislatures may feel the direct authority of the people."

As powerful as Washington has become, the truth is that it is
there to act as our agents in matters that would be impossible for
individual states to effectively execute on their own (i.e., national
defense, international treaties, commerce among states, etc.).

The authors of the Federalist Papers continually stressed
that states are essential parts of the Constitution and not merely
tangential offshoots of the federal government, as they are
often treated today. Publius reminded readers of a fact that modern citizens often forget: There are some powers that the states
retain that the federal government can do *nothing* to change or
affect. The Founders believed that the secret was to create a centralized power to maintain unity and order and to deal only with
problems that would affect the entire nation. They would leave the
rest up to local governments. As Madison stated in Federalist 14:

"In the first place it is to be remembered that the general government is not to be charged with the whole power of making
and administering laws. Its jurisdiction is limited to certain
enumerated objects, which concern all the members of the
republic, but which are not to be attained by the separate provisions of any. The subordinate governments, which can extend
their care to all those other subjects which can be separately
provided for, will retain their due authority and activity."

They knew it would be immensely difficult to pull off, so
Alexander Hamilton began Federalist 9 with a "tour of failure"
recounting past republics that had failed. His point was that, just

because others have tried and failed or perverted true republican government, the baby shouldn't be thrown out with the bathwater. Republicanism was the best chance that man had to enjoy true freedom—but no one had attempted a pure form of it. It was up to America to give it a try.

The article then introduced what French political theorist Montesquieu called the "enlargement of the scope" of a republic, which is just a fancy way of explaining how to grow in size and maintain the union.

Most important, "Publius" explained how the Constitution would create a government with the flexibility and freedom to grow while still providing continuity through a commitment to core principles. Federalist 9, therefore, set the perfect stage for James Madison's famous Federalist 10.

"Liberty Is to Faction What Air Is to Fire"

That quote, from Federalist 10, underscores James Madison's brilliance. Unlike some who would assume that government's role would be to create eternal peace and harmony among its citizens, Madison realized that was simply not possible. One of the consequences of liberty is faction (different groups of people with shared special interests who bind together to effect change that is not always in the best interest of the community as a whole), just as one of the consequences of air is fire.

Madison and our other Founders realized that faction is natural. "The very causes of faction," he wrote, "are thus part of the very nature of man . . ." Instead of trying to eliminate something that is a part of human nature, Madison instead sought to craft a government that could direct that spirit to the benefit of society.

A union organized as a republic, Madison argued, would be the most effective system at controlling the various groups who would no doubt eventually try to exert their influence. But the Anti-Federalists weren't convinced. It was considered common knowledge at the time that other so-called "republics" throughout history had failed—often in violent and spectacular fashion. Republics were thought to be politically unstable by their very nature. How, the Anti-Federalists asked, could a republic work on such a massive scale as was being proposed if it hadn't even worked in small countries, like Poland and the Netherlands? The Anti-Federalists maintained that a Republic could work only in a small, homogenous geographic area, where citizens all maintained shared backgrounds and interests.

Madison turned their logic around. The reason it *would* work in America was precisely because of the scope and scale of the experiment. With so many people involved, the factions would have a much harder time reaching the critical mass necessary to effect real change. (How prophetic. American history has shown that it has so far been impossible to maintain a permanent governing majority.) That, combined with the fact that this republic would likely be the first ever tried as a true representative democracy, eventually convinced enough people to support the proposed structure.

But political theory is one thing—putting a true republic into practice is quite another.

Making the Sausage

Publius knew that simply telling people "don't worry about it" when it came to the inner workings of the government wasn't going to fly. They needed to outline specifically why this government was different. Why the people should trust them. Why a tyrant wouldn't rise as one had in almost every other republic in history. Why people who had fought so hard for individual rights should willingly lend their power to a new government, the seat of which might be thousands of miles from them.

Beginning with Federalist 52, and continuing through No. 77, Publius goes through the various seats of power (in sometimes excruciating detail) and explains how they are formed, how they operate, the powers they have, and how those powers will be checked and balanced.

For example, No. 57, which focused on the House of Representatives, served to allay the fears that only the wealthy or well connected would be able to serve. Madison explained that the rich and poor, educated and uneducated, the heirs and the humble, would all have an equal chance to be elected. There was no standard of wealth, land ownership, religion, or occupation that would preclude anyone from running (except minimum age and citizenship requirements).

It was these characteristics, he argued, that would make the House of Representatives *exactly that:* a body of Congress that would represent the people who elected them. And since the makeup of the House would be based on the population of each state, the larger states would have a larger say—unlike in the Senate, where representation would be equal. Put another way, the House would infuse the new government with a more republican sensibility, because it would symbolize representation of the people, whereas the Senate would bring with it a spirit of federalism because it would provide equal representation of each state as a political entity.

But Madison's greatest evidence as to why the House would never become at odds with the people was simple: They would have to live under the laws they passed. Unlike the republics that operated in name only, our leaders would be subject to the very same rules that citizens were. No special treatment. No exemptions or carve-outs. No different sets of rules for those in office. Madison wrote:

> [The House of Representatives] can make no law which will not have its full operation on themselves and their friends, as well as on the great mass of the society. This has always been deemed one of the strongest bonds by which human policy can connect the rulers and the people together. It creates between them that communion of interests and sympathy of sentiments, of which few governments have furnished examples; but without which every government degenerates into tyranny.

Madison also had a stern warning about what would happen to our republic should that ever change: "If this spirit shall ever be so far debased as to tolerate a law not obligatory on the legislature, as well as on the people, the people will be prepared to tolerate any thing but liberty."

When it comes to spending the people's money, Madison reminded readers that the House of Representatives—the people's house—would solely hold the power of the purse. All fiscal appropriations would begin in the House, never the Senate. That would give citizens great comfort, Madison reasoned, because every operation of government, whether good or ill-conceived, requires money. That meant that every taxpayer would have a say through their congressperson as to how or if their dollars will be spent. The current process through which some in the House are attempting to "defund" the Obama health care plan is a good example of how this check on power works in practice.

In Federalist 62, Madison turned his attention to the Senate. It's been hailed as "the world's greatest deliberative body" but we often forget that, until the passage of the Seventeenth Amendment, the state legislatures appointed their state's senators. Why was it designed that way? Because the Founders believed that state legislatures could provide a check against some demagogue being able to stir up populist passions and win an election. The Senate was to be the representative body of the states themselves.

As to the more basic question of why the Senate was even necessary when the House represented the people directly, Madison offered a pretty convincing reply. "[The Senate]," he wrote, "doubles the security to the people, by requiring the concurrence of two distinct bodies in schemes of usurpation or perfidy, where the ambition or corruption of one would otherwise be sufficient."

And this corruption was not exactly a trivial concern. It had happened in other republics, and citizens were concerned that America was setting itself up for the same kind of failure. The Senate, therefore, was part of the answer, as it would provide a check against House members who, Madison wrote, "are prone to act on the basis of sudden and violent impulses, and can at times be easily seduced by factious or partisan leaders into passing hotheaded and harmful resolutions or legislation."

Unfit for a King

While no one would want another tyrant in charge, history had proven that, one way or another, that's what always seemed to happen. The Founders feared that citizens might one day be hypnotized by the seductive eloquence of an unqualified candidate with motives that ran counter to the Constitution. That's why they pressed so hard for a republican, not democratic, union that would use an Electoral College system to elect a president. This system was designed to act as a sort of "emotional backstop" that would prevent voters from making ill-informed decisions based purely on a "sudden breeze of passion."

The Electoral College allowed for a fresh set of electors to be chosen by each state every four years so that states' interests would be protected. Furthermore, electors could not be members of Congress and were to be virtuous citizens with access to facts and information necessary to "carry out such a complicated investigation."

The other big aim of the Electoral College was to find a president who was not so beholden to special interests, or even to his own supporters, that he could not make the right decisions for the country: a president who "would rely on everyone except the People for continuing in his office," as Hamilton put it in Federalist 68.

Sounds kind of radical, doesn't it? It is. And it's interesting to think about how different history might have turned out had we maintained the course that our Founders originally envisioned. But the historical context of the time is critical. With men like George Washington and John Adams alive and waiting in the wings, their assumption was that men of goodwill and virtue would emerge and serve the nation faithfully. "This process of election will afford a moral certainty that the Presidency will seldom be occupied by anyone who is not eminently qualified for it," Publius wrote. "I do not think it would be an exaggeration to say that this office will likely always be filled by men of superior ability and virtue."

Some might say that sentiment is beautiful in its optimism, tragic in its error—but the truth is that it's been the ultimate check against power, the *people*, who have allowed that vision to go so far off course. Remember, one of the overarching principles of the Constitution was that the people would always be engaged enough in the public debate to understand what was going on and to hold their leaders accountable for the consequences.

But is that really happening today? Are the majority of people

engaged? Have we successfully kept the "factions" at bay, or are
the factions basically running the show? And what about the bills
we pass? Publius worried that "[o]ur governments seem the most
susceptible to the disease of too easily writing and passing an excessive number of new laws." Isn't that exactly what's happening?
Bills are so large, so complex, and passed so quickly that some
representatives have confessed that they are not even able to read
them before voting to pass them.

We've come so far from the process described in this set of
papers that you have to wonder if that conversation outside Independence Hall on the day the Convention finished debate was a
lot more prescient than anyone ever realized.

We may still have a Republic, but Franklin's question remains
just as valid: Can we keep it?

NUMBER 9

How the Union Will Act as a Safeguard Against Domestic Divisions and Rebellion

ALEXANDER HAMILTON

For the Independent Journal

The Importance of a Strong Union to Our Safety and Prosperity

Constitutional References:
Article I: §3/1

Astrong Union will be the single greatest protector of the peace and liberty of the states, and will also act as a barrier against domestic rebellions.

When you read the history of the republics of Greece and Italy, you see all the petty troubles that constantly distracted and disturbed them, as well as all the revolutions that kept them alternating between anarchy and tyranny. If they ever appeared to enjoy periods of calm, those periods didn't last long and were quickly replaced by furious storms. If you read about periods of happiness now and then, you always feel a certain sense of regret, since you know that such a pleasant scene will soon be overwhelmed by horrible internal and party conflicts. The rays of light that temporarily break through the gloom also remind us of how

FEDERALIST NO. 9

The Message: History teaches us that republics have continually been overcome by insurrection, but this republic, with a strong union as its core, will be different.

Original Quote: "The chaos that characterizes the history of these republics [Greece Italy, etc.] has not only provided the advocates of despotism with arguments against the forms of republican government, but against the very principles of civil liberty. They have declared that all free government is inconsistent with the order of society . . ."

Relevance to Today: The Founders placed institutions like the Electoral College into the Constitution precisely because they wanted to match order with liberty. These kinds of mechanisms are in place to ensure that domestic insurrection, which has brought down many other republics, is not able to gain a foothold here. Those who favor eliminating these mechanisms (like those who desire to get rid of the Electoral College system) have not learned from history.

Original Quote: "The proposed Constitution, rather than suggesting the destruction of the state governments, makes them constituent parts of the national sovereignty by allowing them to have direct representation in the Senate, while leaving in their hands certain exclusive and very important portions of sovereign power. This fully lines up in every way with the idea of a federal government."

Relevance to Today: It's a recurring theme throughout the Papers: The Founders did not want to concentrate power at the federal level. In fact, they clearly stated that state governments were an integral part of a properly functioning federal government. But today the states are far more dependent on Washington than Washington is on the states.

sad it is to see that dysfunctional governments were the norm in the same ancient Greece that gave us so many great leaders and institutions.

The chaos that characterizes the history of these republics has not only provided the supporters of tyranny with arguments against the republican form of government, but also against the very principles of civil liberty. They have declared that all free government is inconsistent with an orderly society, and have been malicious toward its friends and participants. Fortunately for mankind, history has provided us with fantastic examples of governments based upon liberty that have flourished for many years—examples that have sometimes soundly refuted these enemies of freedom. I trust that America will also serve as an impressive example that will stand as monuments to their error.

It cannot be denied, however, that the picture of republican government that these enemies of freedom have used in their arguments is in fact a fair representation of the originals from which their examples were taken. Hypothetically, if it was impossible to come up with a more perfect model of government, then the friends of liberty would be forced to abandon the cause of republican government. However, like most other sciences, the science of politics has greatly improved. Principles that were either unknown, or known only imperfectly to the ancients, are now well understood. Among those principles that are either completely new or have made the most progress in modern times are the distribution of power into distinct departments or branches, legislative checks and balances, the institution of courts made up of judges who hold their office during good behavior, and the representation of the People in the legislature by representatives whom they elect. These principles form the basis of republican government, as well as a way in which its imperfections can be mitigated or avoided. I will dare to add one more principle to this list, however novel it may appear to some, since it is a principle that some have used in order to argue against the new Constitution: the *enlargement of the scope* of such a republican system, either with respect to the size of a single state, or the consolidation of several smaller states into a single great confederacy—which is exactly what we are currently focusing on. It will also be useful to examine this principle with respect to a single state, but this will be done at a later time.

The ability of a confederacy to control internal violence and maintain the internal tranquility of its states, as well as increase their external security and strength, is really not a new idea at all. This has not only been practiced in different countries and at different times, but has also been approved by the most reputable political theorists. With great effort, the opponents of the new Constitution have quoted and distributed the ideas of Montesquieu[1] in which he apparently argues that the republican form of government can only exist within a smaller territory. But they seem to have forgotten not only the opinions that the very same man expressed in another part of his work, but also the consequences of this principle that they so readily defend.

When Montesquieu recommends that republics remain territorially small, the idea he had in mind for their size was much smaller than almost every single one of our states. Neither Virginia, Massachusetts, Pennsylvania, New York, North Carolina, nor Georgia can be compared to the models he used or described in his reasoning. If we accept his ideas as fact, then we are forced to conclude that we should either take refuge in the arms of mon-

---

1. *Montesquieu:* Formally known as Charles-Louis de Secondat, Baron de La Brède et de Montesquieu. Montesquieu (1689–1755) was a French social commentator and political thinker who lived during the Enlightenment, and is most famous for articulating the theoretical foundations of the political principle of "separation of powers." He also popularized the terms "feudalism" and "Byzantine Empire." (Referenced in Federalist 43 and 47.)

archy, or divide ourselves into an infinite number of small, jealous, clashing, disorderly states, which are themselves the sources of endless conflict and viewed with universal pity or contempt.

Some of the opponents of the Constitution seem to have been aware of this problem, and have been bold enough to suggest that the division of the larger states into smaller pieces is actually a desirable thing. Such crazy ideas and desperate suggestions might satisfy those who are unable to see beyond their own personal interests, but they could never promote the greatness or happiness of the American People.

If you look at Montesquieu's theory with regard to just a single state, it would only require that some of the larger states of the Union be reduced in size, but would have nothing to say on whether or not the states should be joined together into a single confederate government, which is the question we are now discussing.

Rather than suggest anything that would be contrary to a general Union of the states, Montesquieu actually very specifically treats the idea of a *confederate republic* as the answer to the problem of extending the reach of popular government, while also reconciling the advantages of a monarchy with those of a republic.

It is very probable that mankind would have been obliged, at length, to live constantly under the government of a single person, had they not contrived a kind of constitution, that has all the internal advantages of a republican, together with the external force of a monarchical government. I mean a Confederate Republic. This form of government is a convention by which several smaller states agree to become members of a larger one, which they intend to form. It is a kind of assemblage of societies, that constitute a new one, capable of increasing by means of new associations, till they arrive to such a degree of power as to be able to provide for the security of the united body. A republic of this kind, able to withstand an external force, may support itself without any internal corruption. The form of this society prevents all manner of inconveniences. If a single member should attempt to usurp the supreme authority, he could not be supposed to have an equal authority and credit in all the confederate states. Were he to have too great influence over one, this would alarm the rest. Were he to subdue a part, that which would still remain free might oppose him with forces, independent of those which he had usurped, and overpower him before he could be settled in his usurpation. Should a popular insurrection happen in one of the confederate states, the others are able to quell it. Should abuses creep into one part, they are reformed by those that remain sound. The state may be destroyed on one side, and not on the other; confederacy may be dissolved, and the confederates preserve their sovereignty. As this government is composed of small republics, it enjoys the internal happiness of each, and with respect to its external situation, it is possessed, by means of the association, of all the advantages of large monarchies.[1]

I felt it was necessary to quote these interesting passages at length because they not only brilliantly summarize the main arguments in favor of the Union, but they should also remove any false ideas that may have been created by the Constitution's critics when they misapplied other parts of this great man's work. This passage is also directly connected with the purpose of this paper, which is to show that the Union would help suppress domestic faction and rebellion.

Some have tried to bring up the slight difference between

---

1. Montesquieu, *The Spirit of the Laws,* Book 9, Chapter 1.

a *confederacy* and a *consolidation* of the states, a difference that tends to be more subtle than accurate. Some have said that the primary characteristic of a *confederacy* is the placing of authority in the hands of the member states collectively, which wouldn't affect the individual states themselves. It is argued that in a confederacy, the national council should not concern itself with matters of internal administration, and that each member state should have exactly the same amount of power in terms of voting. However, such opinions are mostly arbitrary, and aren't supported by either principle or history. While these types of government have generally operated in this way (which is why it has been assumed that it is in their nature to do so), there are many exceptions to these rules that show that there's not a single, completely correct example of a confederacy. It will also become increasingly obvious throughout this discussion that, as far as these supposed principles of a confederacy are concerned, they have actually been the cause of incurable disorders and weaknesses in the government.

The definition of a *confederate republic* seems to simply be "... an assemblage of societies ..." or an association of two or more states into one state. As far as the federal authority is concerned, its extent, the modifications made to it, and the things to which its authority applies are mere matters of opinion. So long as each member state remains independently organized and exists for the purposes of local governance, while still remaining subordinate to the general authority of the Union, it would be, both in theory and in fact, an association of states, or a confederacy. The proposed Constitution, rather than suggesting the destruction of the state governments, makes them essential parts of the national government by allowing them to have direct representation in the Senate,[1] while leaving certain exclusive and very important pow-

---

1. United States Constitution: Article I, Section 3, clause 1.

ers in their hands. This fully lines up in every way with the idea of a federal government.

In the Lycian confederacy, which was made up of twenty-three cities or republics, the largest were entitled to *three* votes in their common council, the next largest to *two*, and the smallest to just *one*.[1] Their common council had the power to appoint all the judges and magistrates of each city. Of all the powers that it had to interfere within the cities themselves, this was certainly the most controversial one, simply because of the fact that, if there is any power that seems most appropriate for local government, it is the power to appoint its own officers. Yet Montesquieu, speaking of this confederacy, said, "Were I to give a model of an excellent confederate republic, it would be that of Lycia."[2]

Therefore it's obvious that those who oppose the Constitution are not basing their arguments on the ideas of this enlightened writer, but rather on an attempt to peddle their own theory, and a wrong one at that.

—Publius

---

1. *Lycian confederacy:* A confederacy made up of many small communities that was established on the southwestern coast of Asia Minor in 200 BC. It managed to survive repeated invasions until the Romans conquered it in 43 AD.

2. Montesquieu, *Spirit of the Laws,* Book 9, Chapter 3. Hamilton uses this to refer to the idea of inequality between the members of a confederacy. Opponents of Hamilton's position typically utilized the "celebrated Montesquieu" to challenge the idea of unequally strong members existing within the same confederacy, as a way to warn that large states would swallow up smaller ones.

NUMBER 10

How the Union Will Act as a Safeguard Against Domestic Divisions and Rebellion (Continued)

JAMES MADISON

For the Independent Journal: Friday, November 23, 1787
The Importance of a Strong Union to Our Safety and Prosperity

None of the benefits that a well-constructed Union brings deserves to be considered more than its tendency to decrease and control the violence that typically comes with opposing political factions.

The friends of popular government are understandably alarmed by the tendency of the factions within any government to engage in violence. Violence always puts both the character and the fate of the government at risk. If this is the case, then these friends of popular government would be wise to carefully consider a Plan that, far from violating their principles, actually provides a cure for this problem. The instability, injustice, and confusion that often occur within the institutions of popular government have also caused them to fail everywhere. In fact, the enemies of liberty have used these very problems to most aggressively attack the idea

FEDERALIST NO. 10

The Message: Faction, the idea that a group can unite with a common impulse or purpose that either violates individual rights or the common good, has brought down many other republics—but ours has been able to control its effects.

———————

Original Quote: "Enlightened statesmen will not always be at the helm."

Relevance to Today: This one is pretty obvious—our Founders knew that if our system required that all politicians be "enlightened statesmen" then it was doomed to fail. This has clearly been proven true, as even the worst, most corrupt politicians have failed to bring down our republic. While it's easy to get frustrated when we look at some of those elected to serve us, it should inspire some confidence that our Founders planned for the occasion.

———————

Original Quote: "Theoretic politicians, who have patronized this species of government, have erroneously supposed that by reducing mankind to a perfect equality in their political rights, they would, at the same time, be perfectly equalized and assimilated in their possessions, their opinions, and their passions."

Relevance to Today: The Founders believed that people have different abilities and ambitions and there is no guarantee of equality of outcome. But these days various programs, regulations, and tax policies attempt to redistribute wealth and ability in a failing effort to make everyone equal in their possessions.

of popular government, though their arguments tend to be very shallow, and only superficially appealing.

While the American Constitution makes many valuable and admirable improvements on both the ancient and modern models of popular government, it would be untrue and unfair to claim that, if ratified, it would completely prevent these dangers as well as might be hoped or expected. Everywhere you go, you hear our most thoughtful and honorable citizens (both public and private), who are themselves friends of both public and personal liberty, say that our government is too unstable because of party conflict. Such party conflict too often leads to actions that do not reflect either justice or the rights of the minority, but rather the interests of a superior and tyrannical majority. However much we might wish that these complaints were baseless, there is simply too much evidence that proves they are true. If we step back and examine our situation objectively, we will find that while *some* of the problems we face are not related to the operation of our governments, our biggest and most urgent ones can have no other explanation than the growing distrust that the People have of government, and the concern they have for their own individual rights, a concern that stretches from one end of the continent to the other. These problems are primarily, if not entirely, caused by the instability and injustice in government brought about by the spirit of faction.

By "faction," I mean a group of citizens (either a majority or a minority) who are united and have a common interest that is dangerous to either the rights of other citizens, or the permanent and cumulative interests of the community.

There are two methods of solving the problems associated with faction: either remove its causes, or control its effects. There are two methods of removing the *causes* of faction: either destroy the liberty that is required for it to exist, or somehow ensure that every citizen has the same opinions, the same feelings, and the same interests.

The first cure is worse than the disease. Liberty is to faction what air is to fire—a requirement without which it would instantly disappear. But it would be just as dangerous and foolish to abolish liberty (which is essential to political life) simply because it nourishes the spirit of party, as it would be to wish that air (which is essential to animal life) did not exist because it allows fire, which can be destructive.

To ensure that every citizen had the same opinions, feelings, and interests would be as unrealistic as abolishing liberty would be unwise, for as long as man's reason remains imperfect and he is free to use it, there will always be different opinions. As long as his reason is continuously connected with his own love of himself, his passions will always cling to his opinions, since they will have a shared and reciprocal influence on one another. The many different skills and abilities that people have, which are the source of property rights, also represent an insurmountable obstacle to uniform interests. The protection of these unequal skills and abilities is the first duty of government. By protecting those abilities that are used to acquire property, different types of property are the obvious result. The effect that these types of property have on the feelings and opinions of their owners ensures that different interests and parties will always exist in society.

The very causes of faction are thus part of the very nature of man that we, to one degree or another, see everywhere (depending on the circumstances of civil society). The fact that people have dramatically different opinions about religion, government, or different types of people, and that they also have different opinions about different leaders (who themselves ambitiously fight for power and prestige), has resulted in the division of mankind into parties that mutually dislike each other and make it more likely that they will provoke and oppress each other rather than cooperate for their common good. This tendency of mankind is so strong that even without some sort of unique occasion or event, the smallest and most unimportant differences have not only provoked unfriendly feelings, but have also brought about the most violent conflicts.

The most common and tangible source of faction has been the various types and unequal distribution of property, since those who have property and those who do not have it always form different interests in society, just as creditors and debtors do as well. A land interest, a manufacturing interest, a commercial interest, a financial interest, as well as many others, necessarily exist in a civilized society, and divide that society into different classes that have different outlooks and views. Therefore, the primary purpose of legislation is to regulate these various and conflicting interests, and this requires the spirit of party and faction in the ordinary operations of government.

No man is allowed to be a judge in his own case, since his own interests would make him biased and most likely corrupt his integrity. With equal, if not greater reason, a group of men is unfit to be both the judges and a party in a legal case at the same time. Yet aren't the most important pieces of legislation simply decisions that affect the rights of many citizens, and not just single individuals? Also, aren't legislators, under the guise of a political party, advocates of the causes that they legislate? Are laws that affect only private debts ever passed? No, they aren't. Instead, creditors are the party on one side and debtors on the other, and it is the role of justice to mediate between the two. Yet political parties are, and are required to be, the judges, with the expectation being that the most numerous and powerful party will prevail. Those of the land-owning and manufacturing classes would most likely answer the following question differently, and probably not with justice or the public good as their primary goal: "Should we encourage domestic manufacturers by placing restrictions on foreign ones, and if so, to what degree?"

The apportionment[1] of different taxes for different types of property is a decision that seems to require the greatest objectivity, and yet no legislative act provides as much opportunity or temptation for the party in power to act unjustly as this one. Every dollar they overtax the minority is a dollar that goes into their own pockets.

To say that some enlightened statesman would be able to mediate between these different and opposing interests so that they all work together for the public good is naïve. Enlightened statesmen will not always be in power, and even if such mediation could happen, it would rarely take place with long-term interests in mind, since the immediate "here and now" interests of the party in power would most likely win the day at the expense of the rights of the other party, or the good of the whole.

Therefore, the conclusion we must make is that the *causes* of faction cannot be removed, so we must seek instead to find a way to control its *effects*.

If a faction is less than a majority, then the republican principle provides safety because it allows the majority to defeat the evil plans of the faction through a regular vote. While it may be able to obstruct the administration or shake up society, a faction such as this would be unable to put its plan into action, or use the Constitution to defend its use of violence. If, on the other hand, a faction is in the majority, the system of popular government would enable

---

1. According to *The New Dictionary of Cultural Literacy,* The rule of apportionment: "The allocation of seats in a legislature or of taxes according to a plan. In the United States Congress, for example, the apportionment of seats in the House of Representatives is based on the relative population of each state, whereas the apportionment in the Senate is based on equal representation for every state." (Referred to in Federalist Nos. 15 and 54.)

it to endanger not just the public good, but the rights of other citizens for the sake of its own interests. Thus, the ultimate goal is to secure both the public good and the private rights of citizens against the danger of such a majority faction, while at the same time preserving the spirit and system of popular government. The achievement of this great goal, I might add, would save this form of government (popular government) from the disgrace it has maintained for so long, and would finally make it respectable and worthy of adoption.

So, how then are we to reach this goal? There are only two ways: We must either prevent any majority that holds the same views and opinions from existing at any given time, or, if such a majority exists, it must be rendered incapable of organizing and executing any plan to oppress other citizens. If the desire to oppress others and the opportunity to do so coincide, we know very well that neither moral nor religious motives would be capable of stopping such a plan. Such motives aren't even powerful enough to control the injustice and violence of individuals, and are even less effective as more and more people combine together. In other words, moral and religious motives are used in proportion to how useful they are.

With this in mind, we can conclude that a pure democracy, where a society of a small number of citizens assembles and administers the government in person, would be incapable of avoiding the troubles of faction. In almost every case, a common passion or interest will be held by a majority of the whole, while at the same time there would be nothing to act as a check on any troublesome individual, or the desire to harm the weaker party. Such things are made possible by the form of government itself! It comes as no surprise then that such democracies have proven to be as short in their lives as they were violent in their deaths, having been examples of turbulence and conflict, and thus incompatible with personal security or property rights. Political scholars who have advocated this type of government have mistakenly assumed that by making all people perfectly equal in their political rights, they would also at the same time become perfectly equal in their possessions, opinions, and interests.

A republic, a form of government in which the People elect representatives, allows for different possibilities, and in fact promises the cure that we are seeking. By examining where it differs from democracy, it's easier to understand how it both cures the problems of that form of government and also how it would become even more effective under the Union.

A democracy and a republic differ in two major ways: First, in a republic, the power of governing is delegated to a small number of citizens who are elected by the rest; and second, a republic can handle a much larger population, and can be extended over a much larger territory than a democracy.

The advantage of representation (the first difference) is that it refines the views of the public by passing them through a small body of select citizens whose wisdom will be more capable of identifying the true interests of the country. The patriotism and love of justice of these citizens will also make it unlikely that they will sacrifice the interests of their country to those that are only temporary or biased. Under such a system, it may prove to be the case that the voice of the public, as expressed by the representatives of the People, will be more in the interests of the public good than if they were expressed by the People through a popular vote. On the other hand, the effect may be the opposite. Men of party spirit, local prejudice, or those who have their own shameful and selfish plans may, by dishonesty, corruption, or some other way, receive the votes of the People and then betray their interests. So the question then becomes, "Which is more favorable to the election of true guardians of the public's well-being, small or large republics?" Large republics are clearly the answer, and for two obvious reasons.

First, no matter how small the republic may be, there must be enough representatives to guard against the plots of a few, and no matter how large the republic may be, the number of representatives must be limited to a certain number in order to avoid the confusion of a mob. Since the number of representatives in both cases will not be proportional to the number of constituents (which would be proportionally the greatest in the small republic), and since the proportion of worthy candidates is probably equal in the large as much as it is in the small republic, the larger republic will be the better option.

Second, since in the large republic each representative will be chosen by a greater number of citizens than the small one, it will be more difficult for unworthy candidates to engage in the nasty political tactics that too often win elections. Lastly, since the People will be able to vote freely, they will more often focus on those who have the most merit, and who are also the most widely known and established citizens.

However, it must be admitted that, even with this advantage, as with most other things, there exists the possibility of difficulties on both sides. If there are too many constituents per each representative, the representatives would not be familiar enough with all the local circumstances and interests of their constituents. On the other hand, if there are too few constituents per representative, the representative would attach too little importance to those local interests, and would be incapable of comprehending and dealing with important national issues. As far as this is concerned, the proposed Federal Constitution takes the middle road, since all the great interests of the whole country will be referred to the

National Legislature (Congress), and the more specific and unique interests of each community will be referred to the state legislatures.

The other difference between a republic and a democracy is the greater number of citizens and larger amount of territory that can be brought under a republican government, as compared with a democratic one. This makes the possibility of some sort of large, dangerous faction ever coming to power less of a threat in a republic than in a democracy. The smaller the society, the fewer the people and interests in any one party; the fewer the parties and interests, the more frequent a majority of the same party will exist; and the smaller the number of people in a majority, the more concentrated power they will have, making it possible for them to organize and execute their plans to oppress their fellow citizens. If you increase the number of people involved, you naturally increase the number of parties and interests involved, making it less likely that a majority of the People will have a common motive to invade the rights of their fellow citizens. Even if such a motive existed, it would be more difficult to find like-minded citizens, which would make acting in unison more difficult as well. In addition to other obstacles, it is also true that whenever people are aware of any unjust or dishonorable motives on the part of others, their communication is always hindered by distrust, which takes place in proportion to the number of people whose agreement is required for any plan of action to move forward.

It therefore appears that a republic is more capable of controlling the effects of faction than a democracy, just as a large republic is more capable than a smaller one of doing the same thing, and just as the Union would be more than the states. But is this because of the People's elected representatives, whose enlightened opinions and virtuous conduct make them less likely to be affected by local prejudices and unjust schemes? It's undeniable that the representatives of the Union will most likely have these characteristics. Is it because of the greater security provided by the greater number and variety of interested parties, making it unlikely that a single interest or party could outnumber and oppress the others? Indeed, more security would be provided by the Union for this reason. Finally, is it because of the greater number of obstacles which the Constitution and the Union put in the way of an oppressive majority ever being able to oppress the rest of the People? Here, again, the Union provides the greatest and clearest advantage.

The influence of rebellious leaders may, from time to time, ignite unrest in particular states, but that unrest will be unable to spread throughout a large portion of the other states; a religious sect may degenerate into some sort of a political faction in a part of the confederacy, but the great variety of faiths and sects throughout the Union would protect the National government from any sort of violence from that source; any craze for paper money, the elimination of debts, an equal division of property, or any other unacceptable or wicked plot would be less capable of spreading throughout the entire Union than within a particular state, in the same way that such a problem would most likely affect a single county or district rather than an entire state.

Therefore, we find within both the size and the structure of the Union a republican solution to the problems most common to a republican government. In the same way that we feel pleasure and pride in being republicans, we ought to be just as enthusiastic to have both the spirit and character of federalists.

—Publius

FEDERALIST NO. 39

The Message: The government created by the Constitution is a Republic, not a democracy, and the government derives its power directly from the people, not merely the elite.

———————

Original Quote: "We may define a republic to be, or at least may bestow that name on, a government which derives all its powers directly or indirectly from the great body of the people, and is administered by persons holding their offices during pleasure, for a limited period, or during good behavior. It is *essential* to such a government that it be derived from the great body of the society, not from an inconsiderable proportion, or a favored class of it. . . ."

Relevance to Today: Policy in Washington is increasingly directed and guided by elites for the benefit of elites. The massive bailout of Wall Street is a billion-dollar example. As one writer put it in *Forbes* magazine, "The wealthy speculators who are behind the Average Joe's current pain are going to be allowed to stay on top—not because of diligent work or creative genius, but because a group of friendly bureaucrats have decided to use Joe's hard-earned money to finance the preeminence of those who lost it."

———————

Original Quote: "Could any further proof be required of the republican complexion of this system, the most decisive one might be found in its absolute prohibition of titles of nobility, both under the federal and the State governments . . ."

Relevance to Today: We don't have titles like "King" or "Princess" in America today, but we do increasingly have unelected elites making decisions for us. From "Czars" to advisory boards, like the Independent Payment Advisory Board (which will control the health-care decisions of individual Americans) power has been shifted from direct representatives of the people to unelected surrogates.

NUMBER 39

How the Constitution Conforms to Republican Principles: An Examination of the Objection to the Powers of the Convention

JAMES MADISON

For the Independent Journal

The Constitutional Convention and the New Federalism

Constitutional References:
Article I: §2/1, 3 | §3/1 | §9/8—Article II: §1/1–4—
Article III: §1 | §2/1–2—Article IV: §4
Article V—Article VII

S ince the previous paper concluded my honest thoughts on the general structure of the government proposed by the Convention, we are now free to move forward.

The first question that comes to mind is whether the general form and nature of this government can be truly labeled "republican." It is obvious that no other form of government would be compatible with the genius of the American People, the fundamental principles of the Revolution, or the honorable convictions of every supporter of freedom. Therefore, no other form of government is worthy of us entrusting to it the results of any, and perhaps all, experiments on mankind's capacity for self-government. If the Constitution abandons the republican character in any way, its supporters must abandon it as an indefensible document.

What are the unique characteristics of the republican form of government? If I was to answer this question by referring to how the term "republican" is used by different political writers when they refer to the state constitutions, as opposed to what the term means in principle, then it would be impossible to provide a satisfactory answer.

Holland has almost universally been referred to as a republic, and yet not one bit of the supreme authority of its government is derived from the People. The same has happened to Venice, even though absolute power is exercised in the most tyrannical way by a small group of hereditary nobles over the majority of the People. Poland, whose government is a mixture of the worst forms of aristocracy and monarchy, has been dignified by the same term. The government of England, which has just one republican branch (the House of Commons), combined with a hereditary aristocracy (the House of Lords)[1] and monarchy (the King), has just as frequently and inappropriately been placed on the list of "republics."

These examples, which are nearly as different from each other as they are to a true republic, show how this term has been inaccurately used throughout the works of political scholars.

If we defined this term by referring to the different principles which form the basis of other forms of government, then we could

---

1. *House of Lords:* The upper house of the British Parliament. The House of Lords is made up of the Lords Spiritual (bishops in the Church of England) and the Lords Temporal, which are hereditary aristocratic positions (lords, dukes, etc.). The current House of Lords has only a small number of hereditary lords (after several reforms). (Referenced in Federalist 47–48, 63, 65, and 81.)

define a republic as being a government which derives all of its powers directly or indirectly from the majority of the People, administered by representatives who hold their offices/positions at the pleasure of the People, for a limited time period, or during good behavior. It is essential to this form of government that its power and authority be derived from the majority of society, not from a minority or some favored class. Otherwise, a handful of tyrannical nobles could simply delegate their powers to whomever they chose, and then claim for their government the honorable title of "Republic."

It is sufficient in the republican form of government that those who administer it are appointed either directly or indirectly by the People, and that they are able to maintain their positions only during good behavior, or at the pleasure of the People. If this was not the case, then every government in the United States, as well as every other popular government that has ever existed, or which can be well organized or well administered, would be unworthy of the name "republican."

According to the constitutions of every state in the Union, at least some government officials are appointed indirectly by the People. According to most of the constitutions, the executive is appointed in the same way, and in one of them, the same method is used to appoint the members of one of the branches of the legislature. Also, according to all of the state constitutions, the terms for the highest offices are set at a specific period of time, and in many others, the terms of both the legislative and executive branches are limited to a certain number of years. Again, according to the provisions of most of the state constitutions, as well as the most respectable and widely acknowledged opinions on the subject, the members of the judicial branch can only hold their offices during good behavior.

If you compare the Constitution drawn up by the Convention

with the standards of republican government which we have just laid out, you will immediately see that it is completely compatible with them. The House of Representatives is elected directly by the majority of the People, just as at least one branch of each of the state legislatures is.[1] The Senate, like the current congress and the senate of Maryland, is appointed indirectly by the People via the state legislatures.[2] The President (the Executive), like in many of the states, is indirectly chosen by representatives of the People.[3] Even the judges, along with all of the officials of the Federal government, will be indirectly chosen by the People themselves, just like in many of the states.

Even the term length of each Federal office is compatible with the republican standard, and with the state constitutions as well. Like all of the states, the House of Representatives is periodically elected and their term of two years mirrors the term in South Carolina. Senators are elected for a term of six years,[4] which is just one more than the senate of Maryland, and just two more than those of New York and Virginia. The President is elected for a four-year term,[5] while the executives of New York and Delaware are elected for three years, and two years in South Carolina. In the other states, the executive is elected annually.

In some of the states there is no explicit provision in their constitutions on impeaching the executive, and in Delaware and Virginia, he can't even be impeached until he is out of office. The President of the United States, on the other hand, can be impeached at any time during his term.[6] As they no doubt should,

---

1. United States Constitution: Article I, Section 2, clause 1.
2. United States Constitution: Article I, Section 3, clause 1.
3. United States Constitution: Article II, Section 1, clauses 1–4.
4. United States Constitution: Article I, Section 3, clause 1.
5. United States Constitution: Article II, Section 1, clause 1.
6. United States Constitution: Article II, Section 4.

judges will hold their offices so long as they show good behavior.[1] The tenure of officials throughout the different government departments will generally be regulated by the law, which is in line with the examples of the state constitution, and is entirely appropriate.

If I could provide any more proof of the republican nature of this new system, the most decisive one might be the fact that all titles of nobility under both the Federal and state governments are absolutely forbidden,[2] as well as the Constitution's explicit guarantee of the republican form of government to each of the states.[3]

"But," say the adversaries of the Constitution, "it isn't enough that the Convention adhered to the republican form of government." They say that the Convention should have preserved the *Federal* form of government (which regards the Union as a *Confederacy* of sovereign states), rather than framing a *National* government (which regards the Union as a *consolidation* of states).[4] Additionally, they ask by whose authority this bold and radical change was made in the first place. The significance of these arguments to the ratification of the Constitution requires that I address it precisely.

Without going into whether or not the distinction (Federal vs. National) upon which this objection is based is accurate, three things will be required to determine whether the objection is valid:

---

1. United States Constitution: Article III, Section 1.

2. United States Constitution: Article I, Section 9, clause 8.

3. United States Constitution: Article IV, Section 4.

4. The term that is typically used today to refer to what is called in this paper a "National" government is "unitary" government, in which the central government has complete legislative, executive, and judicial authority, which is superior in every way to the authorities that its subordinate/state/provincial governments have (if they have any). A modern example of a unitary government would be China.

1. We must determine the true nature of the proposed government;
2. We must find out by what authority the Convention proposed such a government in the first place;
3. And lastly, how much the duty which the Convention owed to their country could make up for a lack of regular authority.

First, in order to determine the true nature of the new government, we should consider the following:

a. The foundation on which it will be established;
b. The source of its ordinary powers;
c. The function of those powers;
d. How far those powers will extend;
e. The authority by which future changes in the government will be made (amendments).

In regard to the foundation of the new government, on one hand it appears to be founded on the agreement and ratification of the American People via representatives who were elected to the Convention for that special purpose.[1] On the other hand, this agreement and ratification will be given by the People not as individuals of one nation, but as the citizens of each of their respective separate and independent states. Thus, this agreement and ratification of the new Constitution will ultimately be based on the agreement and ratification of the states, derived from the supreme authority in each state, which is the authority of the People themselves. Therefore, the act that will establish the Constitution will not be a *National* act, but a *Federal* act.

---

1. United States Constitution: Article VII.

Since this will be a Federal and not a National act (as far as these terms are understood by the Constitution's opponents), as well as an act of the People as citizens of independent states and not one unified nation, it is obvious that it will not be the result of the decision of a *majority* of the People of the Union, nor that of a *majority* of the states. Rather, for those states who wish to live under it, their agreement must be *unanimous*, the only difference being that this agreement will not be expressed by the state legislatures, but by the People themselves.

If the People's decision on this subject was whether or not to form one nation, then the will of the majority of all the People of the United States would overrule the minority, just as would be the case in each state. Either way, the will of the majority of the People of the United States must be determined by either individual votes, or the will of a majority of the People in each state. However, neither of these methods has been adopted. Each state, in ratifying the Constitution, is considered a sovereign power, independent of all others, and bound only by its own voluntary choice. Because of this, if the new Constitution is established, it will be a *Federal* and not a *National* Constitution.

The next thing we must consider is the source of the new government's ordinary powers. The House of Representatives will derive its power from the American People, and the People will be represented to the same degree and according to the same principles as they are represented in their own state legislatures. So far, the government is *National*, not *Federal*. The Senate will derive its powers from the states in their capacity as co-equal sovereignties that will each be represented equally in the Senate, just as they are in the current congress. So far, the government is *Federal*, not *National*. The source of the Executive power (the President) will be mixed.

The election of the President will be conducted by the states in their political capacity (via the Electors, and according to the total number of Representatives and Senators each state has in Congress). The votes allotted to each state will be allotted according to a compound ratio, one that considers them both as distinct and co-equal sovereignties (derived from their representation in the Senate), and also as unequal members of the same society (derived from their representation in the House of Representatives). The election itself will be carried out by Electors from each of the states, whose number shall be equal to the number of Representatives and Senators of that state in Congress (but will not include any *current* Representatives or Senators). This way, each state will have its own delegation. From this point of view, it appears that the government will have as many *Federal* characteristics as *National* ones.

Those who oppose the Constitution have said that the difference between a Federal and a National government, as far as how the government actually functions, is that the powers of a Federal government will operate on the states in their capacity as independent governments, whereas the powers of a National government would operate on each of the individual citizens of the entire nation in their capacity as individuals. If we examine the Constitution from this point of view, it is in fact *National* rather than *Federal*—though perhaps not as much as some have said. Sometimes, the states must be treated by the Federal government as distinct and partially independent governments, particularly in court cases in which states are one of the parties (which is why these cases fall within the original jurisdiction of the Supreme Court).[1] However, given the fact that the Federal government's normal and essential powers will function and act on each citizen

---

1. United States Constitution: Article III, Section 2, clause 2.

as an individual, this would make it, according to its opponents, a *National* government. But if the proposed government is a National one in relation to the *function* of its powers, then it changes once we view it in light of the *extent* of those powers. For a government to be National, it must have authority over not just individual citizens, but also over every person and every thing, so long as it is lawful to do so. For a people who are consolidated into one nation, this supremacy would be entirely vested in the National Legislature. For communities (states) who are united for specific purposes, this supremacy is partially vested in the National Legislature (Congress), and partially in the state legislatures. In the first example, all local authorities are subordinate to the supreme authority, and may be controlled, directed, or abolished at its pleasure. In the second example, however, the state authorities have their own distinct and independent legal supremacy, which is no more subject to the National authority than the National authority is subject to them within its own sphere of authority. Therefore, from this point of view, the proposed government cannot be called a *National* one, since its jurisdiction extends only to certain specified things, and leaves to the states sovereignty and power over everything else, which cannot be violated by the National government.

It is true that whenever there is a controversy over the boundary separating these two jurisdictions, the dispute will ultimately be decided by the Supreme Court,[1] which will be a part of the Federal government. But that does not mean that the principle in question is changed or violated. The decision will be made objectively according to the rules of the Constitution, and every effort has been made to ensure such objectivity. It is clear that such a

---

1. United States Constitution: Article III, Section 2, clause 1.

court will be essential if we are to avoid any appeal to, or use of, violence to resolve such conflicts—which would dissolve the Federal compact between the states. Therefore, this court ought to be established under the Federal, rather than the state governments; or, to say it more appropriately, the fact that it could be safely placed only under the Federal government is a position that is not likely to be challenged.

If we examine the Constitution in light of the authority by which future changes in the government will be made (amendments), we see that the process of amending the document is neither completely *National* nor completely *Federal*. If this process were completely National, then supreme and ultimate authority would reside in the majority of the People of the Union, and this authority would at all times be capable of altering or abolishing the established government, just as every other majority in a National society is. Yet, if it were completely Federal, the agreement of every single state in the Union would be required for every change that is proposed for the Constitution to go into effect.

In reality, the method devised by the Convention for amending the Constitution isn't based on either of those principles. By requiring more than a majority to pass an amendment, and by not calculating the vote of each state according to the number of *citizens* it has, the amendment process is less *National* and more *Federal*. But by not requiring the unanimous agreement of all of the states in order to pass an amendment, it is less *Federal* and more *National*.[1]

Therefore, the proposed Constitution, even according to the standards set by its opponents, is neither a completely National nor a completely Federal Constitution, but is a mixture of both. Its foundation is Federal; the sources of its ordinary powers are

---

1. The amendment process is referenced in Article V of the United States Constitution.

partly Federal and partly National; the function of those powers is National; the extent of those powers is again Federal; and, finally, the method of introducing and passing amendments is neither completely Federal nor completely National.

—Publius

FEDERALIST NO. 56

The Message: Federal government must focus on three main areas: commerce, the militia, and taxation. Also, while it is vital that representatives understand their constituents on these issues, there is no reason for them to be experts on topics outside their legislative authority.

Original Quote: "An ignorance of a variety of minute and particular objects, which do not lie within the compass of legislation, is consistent with every attribute necessary to a due performance of the legislative trust. In determining the extent of information required in the exercise of a particular authority, recourse then must be had to the objects within the purview of that authority."

Relevance to Today: There are countless examples of representatives who take unpopular positions. Take ethanol subsidizes, for example. Though disliked by most Republicans, GOP House members in corn-belt states regularly vote for the continuation of this policy because their local constituents support it.

Original Quote: "A proper regulation of commerce requires much information, as has been elsewhere remarked; but as far as this information relates to the laws and local situation of each individual State, a very few representatives would be very sufficient vehicles of it to the federal councils."

Relevance to Today: The House, with its diverse and large population of elected officials, controls the budget of the United States. This large population is also why representative are far more likely to be blamed when unpopular legislation gets passed. After the health-care reform bill became law, the House saw a historic turnover, while members from across the country were forced to explain their votes to smaller population centers.

NUMBER 56

The Total Number of the House of Representatives (Continued)

JAMES MADISON

For the New York Packet: Tuesday, February 19, 1788

The House of Representatives and Federal Election System

Constitutional References:
Article I: §2/3 | §8/1, 3, 14–16

The second accusation made against the House of Representatives asserts that the body has too few Representatives to possess an appropriate amount of knowledge concerning the interests of all constituents. While this objection was made by someone who compares the proposed number of Representatives[1] with the great size of the United States, it does not take into account the unique qualities that distinguish Congress from other legislative bodies. In order to provide the best answer to this objection, I will be brief in explaining those unique qualities.

---

1. United States Constitution: Article I, Section 2, clause 3.

While it is true and vital that Representatives should be familiar with the interests and circumstances of their constituents, this principle can go no further than the actual interests and circumstances that will fall under the authority and care of the Representative. In fact, it would be consistent with the duties and characteristics of a legislator if a Representative was ignorant of a variety of minute details that didn't happen to fall within the scope of what that Representative would legislate. Therefore, in order to determine how much information is required in order to exercise authority, we must examine those things that fall within the scope of that authority.

So, to what things will Federal legislation be applied? Those things that are the most important, and also seem to require the most amount of local knowledge, are commerce,[1] taxation,[2] and the militia.[3]

As noted in previous papers, in order to regulate commerce appropriately you need a great deal of information. However, a very small number of Representatives would be more than capable of relaying the information regarding the laws and local circumstances of each state to the Federal government.

For the most part, taxation will fall under the duties involved in the regulation of commerce, which would in turn be included under the category of those local laws and situations we discussed in previous comments. As far as the internal collection of taxes is concerned, it may be necessary to have more widespread and general knowledge of the circumstances of each state. But it is really hard to imagine that intelligent men elected throughout the state will be without an adequate level of such knowledge. If

---

1. United States Constitution: Article I, Section 8, clause 3.

2. United States Constitution: Article I, Section 8, clause 1.

3. United States Constitution: Article I, Section, clauses 14–16.

you divided the largest state into ten or twelve districts, you would find there would be no unique district interests in any of them that a Representative would not know about. Other than this source of information, the laws of each state can be a sufficient guide, since they are framed by the representatives from each part of the state who are in that state's legislature. In many cases, every state has created, and must continue to create, tax and commercial regulations that will frequently leave very little for Congress to do, outside of reviewing them and condensing them into one general (Federal) law.

Even a skilled person, with access to all of the local laws of each state, would be capable of writing tax laws for the entire Union, and all without ever having heard anything about them from anyone else. Whenever internal taxes may be necessary, particularly when uniformity throughout the states would be required, it is likely that those things that are easier to tax will be preferred. However, in order for us to fully realize just how much states help with this type of Federal legislation, all we need to do is imagine that the state were divided into several different parts, and that each part had its own power of legislation. Isn't it obvious that the amount of information and preparation found in the laws of each of these parts would not only cut down on the amount of work that the state legislature would have to do, but would also make it so that a much smaller number of representatives would be required in order to carry out such work?

Congress will reap the benefits of another great advantage as well: Not only will the Representatives bring information about their state's laws, along with local knowledge about each of their respective districts, but all of them will probably have been, at one time or another (or even just before they were elected), a member of their state's legislature, where all local information and interests had been assembled, and from that it would be easy for only a few people to convey the same information to the Congress of the United States.

As far as regulating the militia is concerned, there are hardly any reasons to believe that local knowledge would be needed. The required knowledge needed would concern the general terrain of the country (such as whether it was mountainous or flat) in order to determine which areas would be the best territory for infantry or cavalry military operations. The art of war, though, teaches general principles of organization, movement, and discipline, principles that apply universally.

Readers who have been paying close attention to my argument understand that this reasoning does not conflict with the logic previously used to detail what information each Representative ought to be familiar with, or the time necessary for him to acquire it. Insofar as this type of information is related to local matters, it is necessary. Taking each state on its own, its laws are the same and its interests are not very diverse, so only a few knowledgeable men will be required to represent the interests of the state. If the issues of each individual state were uniform throughout, then deep knowledge in one part would mean knowledge in every other part. This would make it possible for the entire state to be represented in Congress by a single competent representative from only one part of it. However, when comparing the different states with each other, we find that there are great differences between their laws, and many of these circumstances may fall under the jurisdiction of Federal legislation.

Because of this, all of the Federal Representatives should be familiar with them. So while a few Representatives from each state may bring an appropriate level of knowledge about their home state with them, every Representative will have to familiarize themselves with the concerns of other states. The comparative situation of each of the states, the effects and changes of time will tend to integrate and bring them closer, while on the other hand, the effects of time and change on the internal affairs of each state will have the opposite effect. Currently, some of the states are predominately farming societies, and only a few of them have advanced industrially, which is the type of advancement that ultimately complicates and varies the affairs of a nation. Then again, each state will inevitably advance in this way as population grows, which will mean that each state will require more representation. With this in mind, the Convention made sure that the People's representation in the representative Branch of the government will also grow.[1]

Throughout these papers, I have frequently used the historical experience of Great Britain as an example, since it teaches us many excellent political lessons and offers us numerous warnings. That historical experience confirms that the conclusions we have just reached are accurate. The population of the two kingdoms of England and Scotland is no less than eight million, and they are represented in the House of Commons[2] by 558 representatives. Of these 558 representatives, one-ninth are elected by 364 people, and one-half by 5,723 people.[3] It cannot be argued that those 279 representatives (the half), elected by only 5,723 people, and who do not even live among the People themselves, contribute anything to either the security of the People against the government, or to any knowledge of their circumstances and interests in Parliament. On the contrary, they are notorious for being the instruments and pawns of the King rather than the guardians and advocates of the popular rights of the People. Because of this, it would be appropriate not to consider them the true representatives of the People.

---

1. United States Constitution: Article I, Section 2, clause 3.

2. *House of Commons:* Referenced in detail in Federalist 6.

3. James Burgh (1714–75), *Political Disquisitions.*

However, we will leave it at that, and not bother with those who do not live among their own constituents, hardly feel any connection with them whatsoever, and have very little specific knowledge about their interests.

Only 279 people would be acting on the safety, interests, and happiness of eight million people. In other words, there will only be one representative who will maintain the rights and explain the situation of *28,670 constituents* to Parliament. Not only this, but Parliament is an institution that is exposed to monarchical influence, and its authority extends to every possible object of legislation within a nation whose affairs are extremely diverse and complicated. And yet, we can be quite certain that under these circumstances, not only has a valuable portion of freedom been preserved for the British people, but many of the defects in British law cannot in any significant way be blamed on Parliament's ignorance of the People's circumstances. So, if we fully allow this fact to sink in as much as it should, and also compare it with the House of Representatives as I previously explained it, we can be quite certain that a single Representative for every *thirty thousand inhabitants*[1] will render the House of Representatives a safe and capable guardian of the interests which shall be entrusted to its care.

—Publius

---

1. United States Constitution: Article I, Section 2, clause 3

NUMBER 57

The Supposed Tendency of the Constitution to Elevate the Privileged Above the Common (Continued)

JAMES MADISON

For the New York Packet: Tuesday, February 19, 1788

The House of Representatives and Federal Election System

> Constitutional References:
>
> Article I: §2/1

The third accusation made against the House of Representatives is that its members will come from a class of citizens who will have very little sympathy for the majority of the People, and will therefore be likely to sacrifice the interests of the many in order to serve the interests of the few. Of all the objections against the new Federal Constitution, this is perhaps the most extraordinary. While the objection itself is made against an imagined oligarchy, the principle behind it strikes at the very foundations of republican government.

First, the goal of every political constitution is (or ought to be) to find rulers of men who will not have just the wisdom to discern,

FEDERALIST NO. 57

The Message: Frequent elections in the House of Representative will ensure the honest character of politicians whose performances will be based on meritocracy and not their class or position in society.

———————————

Original Quote: "Who are to be the electors of the federal representatives? Not the rich, more than the poor; not the learned, more than the ignorant; not the haughty heirs of distinguished names, more than the humble sons of obscurity and unpropitious fortune."

Relevance to Today: One thing that can be definitively said about Americans of all political persuasions is that they have little concern about the class status of their candidates. Many of our presidents have risen from meager beginnings. In fact, the failure of so many rich, famous, and powerful candidates in the past few decades makes it clear that Americans have little interest in class or "distinguished names" and are far more interested in the merits and accomplishments of the person. That said, we must continually be on guard. Trying to "buy your way" into office is one thing—succeeding is another.

———————————

Original Quote: "All these securities, however, would be found very insufficient without the restraint of frequent elections. Hence, in the fourth place, the House of Representatives is so constituted as to support in the members an habitual recollection of their dependence on the people."

Relevance to Today: As we've seen over the course of American history, unlike the Senate, the House will often experience dramatic turnovers. With elections every two years, representatives are far more sensitive to the immediate needs of the local electorate and far more likely to feel the unhappiness of their voters.

but the virtue to pursue the common good of society. Second, it is to take all the necessary precautions and keep those rulers virtuous, so long as they continue to hold the public trust. The defining characteristic of republican government is the utilization of elections in order to obtain rulers. There are a whole host of methods that this form of government relies on to prevent the corruption of elections. The most effective one is limiting term lengths to a period of time that forces the Representatives of the People to maintain an appropriate level of responsibility to the People.

Let me ask: How exactly does the House of Representatives violate the principles of republican government? Or, which part of it favors the elevation of the few over the ruins of the many? Isn't it true that, on the contrary, every aspect of this type of government strictly relies on republican principles, and is in fact very carefully non-biased toward the rights of every class and type of citizen?

Who will elect the Federal Representatives? Indeed, not the rich any more than the poor, or the educated any more than the ignorant, or the arrogant heirs of fortune any more than the humble sons of obscure and modest backgrounds. In other words, the electors shall be the great body of the People of the United States.[1] They will be the very same people who exercise the exact same right to vote and elect members of the corresponding house of each state's legislature in every state. Who will be elected by the choice of the People? Every citizen whose own merit will make them worthy of the respect and confidence of his country. There is no qualification of wealth, birth, religious faith, or occupation/profession that will stand in the way of the People's choice.

Those who are elected by the freely given votes of their fellow citizens will find that the Constitution has taken every imaginable precaution to ensure their loyalty to their constituents. Since they

---

1. United States Constitution: Article I, Section 2, clause 1.

will be honored by the votes of their fellow citizens, we assume that, in general, they will be at least somewhat distinguished by the qualities that earned them the support in the first place. This will help guarantee that any Representative of the People will behave carefully and sincerely.

Yet, the approval and goodwill bestowed on them by their constituents will most likely be temporary. Inside every person, there is a desire to be honored, favored, and respected. Other interests aside, such things are typically given in the hope that there will be some sort of reward in return. Ingratitude is a well-known and frequently discussed defect in human nature, and it must be confessed that there are far too many blatant examples of it in both public and private life. But the fact that it arouses such extreme resentment only proves how much its opposite, gratitude, is appreciated.

The ties that bind a Representative to his constituents will be strengthened by motives that are more selfish in nature. The pride and vanity of each Representative will help connect them with a form of government that allows them to rise to such a position, and also be awarded and take part in the distinction of being a part of it. No matter what the hopes and plans of a few ambitious Representatives may be, generally, the great majority of them will tend to want to preserve their influence with the People rather than become involved in government actions that undermine the authority of the People, since it is that influence that allowed them to have their position in the first place.

However, even these precautions would be wholly inadequate without the additional protection provided by frequent elections.[1] That's why the House of Representatives is structured to encourage members to constantly remember their dependence on the

---

1. United States Constitution: Article I, Section 2, clause 1.

People. Before their sense of gratefulness to the People is erased, before they receive and use their powers, they will be forced to anticipate a time when those powers will no longer be theirs. Once they descend to the level from which they were raised by the voters, they will remain there forever, unless, having faithfully carried out their duties, they earn the right to have those powers renewed by the People.

There is an additional restraint that will prevent the Representatives from becoming oppressive: Any law they make will be just as applicable to themselves and their friends as it is to the rest of society. This has always been considered one of the strongest ties by which men can bind the People and their rulers together. It creates a common interest and feeling between the two. Few governments have provided this example, but all governments degenerate into tyranny without it. If someone asked: "What will keep the House of Representatives from engaging in any sort of legal discrimination in favor of themselves and a particular class of society?" I would answer: the genius of the whole system, the nature of just and constitutional laws, and above all, the vigilant and courageous spirit that stirs the American People, a spirit that nourishes freedom, and is in return nourished by it.

If this spirit is ever corrupted to the point that it will tolerate a law that does not apply to both the legislature and the People, then the People will be prepared to tolerate anything but liberty.

This is how the relationship between the House of Representatives and their constituents will be. Duty, gratitude, interest, and ambition itself will be those things that will bind each Representative to the idea of loyalty and sympathy for the great mass of the People. Ultimately, these may not be enough to control the impulses and wickedness of men, but in the end, do they not represent everything that we can expect from government and the best that human wisdom can come up with? Are these not the genuine

and characteristic means by which republican government provides liberty and happiness of the People? Are they not identical
to the methods every state in the Union relies on to attain the
same goals? What then are we to make of the objection that I have
been confronting in this paper? What should we say to men who
profess the most fervent passion for republican government, and
yet boldly call into question its fundamental principles? Men who
claim to be champions of the People's right and ability to choose
their own rulers, yet also claim that they will choose rulers who
will immediately and fully betray their trust?

If a person had not actually read the method devised by the
Constitution for choosing Representatives, and then heard these
objections, they would think that the right to vote had some out-
rageous property requirement attached to it, or that only those
from particular families or fortunes could run for election. Or, at
the very least, that the method of election laid out in the state constitutions in some way grossly departed from the method found
in the Constitution. We have already seen how wrong such an
assumption would be with regard to the first two points and the
same is true for this one. The only possible difference between the
two examples is that each Representative of the United States will
be elected by five or six thousand citizens, while in the individual
states, the election of a representative is left to about five or six
hundred citizens. Are people really claiming that this difference is
enough for citizens to be attached to their own state governments,
but to hate the Federal government? If that is the basis of the objection, then it deserves our attention.

Is this objection supported by *reason*? This cannot be said
without also saying that five or six thousand citizens are less capable of choosing an appropriate Representative, or are more likely
to be corrupted by an inappropriate one, than five or six hundred
citizens. To the contrary, it's common sense that with such a great

number of citizens, an appropriate and qualified Representative would most likely be found, and the People's decision would not be affected by the schemes of the ambitious or the bribes of the rich.

Is the premise of this unreasonable argument even acceptable? If we say that five or six hundred citizens is the maximum number of people that can safely and jointly exercise their right to vote, wouldn't we have to deprive the People of their right to choose their own public servants whenever the administration of the government did not require even one representative for that amount of people?

Is this argument warranted by *facts*? I showed in the last paper how the representation in the British House of Commons amounts to little more than thirty thousand inhabitants for every one representative. In addition to other significant reasons that do not play as much of a role in this country, but which benefit those of high rank and wealth in Great Britain, no person there is eligible to be a representative of a county unless he has real estate of a net value of six hundred pounds sterling per year, nor of a city or borough unless he has an estate of half that annual value.

In addition to this qualification for county representatives, the right to vote is limited to persons who have a freehold estate [1] with an annual value of more than twenty pounds sterling, according to the present currency rate. Putting aside for the moment such unfavorable circumstances, as well as some very unequal laws in Great Britain, it cannot be said that the representatives of that nation have elevated the few upon the ruins of the many.

But we don't need to resort to foreign examples on this sub-

---

1. *freehold estate:* "Exclusive right to enjoy the possession and use of a parcel of land or other asset for an indefinite period. In contrast, a leasehold estate is for a fixed, definite period." (Owning versus renting.)

ject, since our own experiences clearly speak for themselves. The districts in New Hampshire where citizens choose their own state senators are nearly as large as the ones that will be required for their Representatives in Congress. Those in Massachusetts are in fact larger than what will be required for that purpose, and those of New York are still larger.

It makes no difference whether citizens vote for several representatives at the same time in each of these senatorial districts and counties. If these citizens are capable of choosing four or five representatives at the same time, then they are certainly capable of choosing one. Pennsylvania is an additional example, as some of the counties that elect state representatives are almost as large as the districts which will be required for her to elect her Federal Representatives. Supposedly the city of Philadelphia has a population of somewhere between fifty and sixty thousand people, which would form nearly two districts for the sake of electing Federal Representatives. However, it forms only one county from which every voter inside it will select its representatives for the state legislature. The whole city actually elects a *single member* for the state's executive council. This is the case in all of the other counties of that state as well.

Don't these facts provide satisfactory proof that the argument that has been used to criticize the Federal House of Representatives is simply wrong? When put to the test, does it appear as if the senators of New Hampshire, Massachusetts, and New York, or the executive council of Pennsylvania, or the members of the assembly in the last two states, have shown any particular tendency to sacrifice the many to the few, or are in any way less worthy of their offices than the representatives and magistrates appointed in other states, who are sometimes elected by very small portions of the People?

There are even stronger examples than the ones I have already provided. One branch of the Connecticut legislature is structured in such a way that each member of it is elected by the whole state. The same is true of the governor of that state, of Massachusetts, and of New York, as well as the president of New Hampshire. I leave it up to every person to decide whether the result of any of these examples will make it at all likely that such widespread methods of choosing the Representatives of the People will in any way elevate traitors above the People, or undermine public liberty.

—Publius

FEDERALIST NO. 58

The Message: Despite our republican inclinations, citizens must also have direct representation so that their voices can be heard. This is why the House of Representatives, one that grows with the population, is vital to the republic.

Original Quote: "Within every successive term of ten years a census of inhabitants is to be repeated. The unequivocal objects of these regulations are, first, to readjust, from time to time, the apportionment of representatives to the number of inhabitants, under the single exception that each State shall have one representative at least . . ."

Relevance to Today: The census is taken every ten years to determine the population of the United States. But the census is also used to define the number of congressional seats apportioned to each state—and as a blueprint for congressional districts within states. Every ten years, parties battle over this important process, but we must ensure that the process itself remains pure.

Original Quote: "In the ancient republics, where the whole body of the people assembled in person, a single orator, or an artful statesman, was generally seen to rule with as complete a sway as if a sceptre had been placed in his single hand."

Relevance to Today: In the 2010 midterm elections, the Republicans won a historic victory by winning back the House and creating a more balanced and divided government. Though, not always as impressive, midterm elections during the first term of a new president often see the opposing party winning large numbers of seats. Having so many direct representatives of the people, as Publius argued, has often been a safety net against concentrated power.

NUMBER 58

Future Augmentations in the Number of Representatives (Continued)

JAMES MADISON

The House of Representatives and Federal Election System

Constitutional References:
Article I: §2/3 | §7/1

Let's examine the final accusation most often made against the House of Representatives. This charge claims that the number of Representatives will not be augmented fairly from time to time as the population grows. I have already admitted that if this accusation were well founded, it would certainly prove to be a good argument. The following points will show that, like most other objections against the Constitution, such a claim could only be made by someone biased against the document, or from someone who was so distrustful that they needed to distort the truth.

First, those who have made this objection seem to have forgotten that the Federal Constitution does not provide any less security than the state constitutions do for a gradual augmentation in the number of Representatives.[1] It has already been declared that the initial number of Representatives (sixty-five) will, for the short period of three years, only be temporary.

Every ten years, a census of all of the inhabitants of the United States will be taken.[2] The unambiguous purpose of this provision is to readjust the apportionment of the number of Representatives to the inhabitants, with the only exception being that each state shall have at least one Representative. Secondly, the census will allow the number of Representatives from each state to be augmented at the same time, with the sole limitation being that the overall number of Representatives shall not exceed one for every 30,000 inhabitants. If we carefully examine the state constitutions, we will find that while some of them have not spelled out regulations on this subject, others are much the same as the Federal Constitution.

In all of them, however, the most effective security put in place with regard to this subject is merely a provision in their constitutions that requires that they occasionally augment the number of representatives.

Second, experience has taught us that under the state constitutions, a gradual increase in the number of state representatives has at the very least kept up with the growing number of constituents in each state. It also appears that the constituents have gone along with such changes as often as their representatives have actually called for them.

Third, there is a unique feature of the Federal Constitution that will ensure that a majority of the People and their Representatives will carefully pay attention to the constitutional augmentation of the number of Representatives. It says that the House of

---

1. United States Constitution: Article I, Section 2, clause 3.
2. Ibid.

Congress is a representation of citizens (the House of Representatives), and the other of the states (the Senate), and consequently, the larger states will have the advantage in the House of Representatives, and the smaller states in the Senate. Because of this, it is almost certain that the larger states will vigorously advocate for increasing the number and importance of the House of Representatives, in which they are more powerful. And as it so happens, only four of the largest states will have a majority over all of the votes in the House of Representatives. Therefore, if the Representatives from the smaller states were ever opposed to a reasonable augmentation of the number of members in the House of Representatives, then a coalition of only a very small number of states would be able to overrule them. Putting aside for the moment the rivalries and local prejudices that may prevent them from coming together, this kind of coalition would certainly come together if the questions at stake were no merely ordinary matter, but questions involving basic fairness and the principles of the Constitution itself.

Some may allege that the Senate would have the same motives to engage a similar alliance, one that may be capable of defeating the fair and constitutional views of the House of Representatives (since the Senate's agreement would also be required). This may have aroused the most fear among those supporting a larger House of Representatives. Fortunately, it is a difficulty that only *appears* difficult because it quickly evaporates once it is carefully and accurately examined. I could be wrong, but I believe that the following points will prove to be both correct and conclusive on the subject.

Forgetting for the moment the equal authority between both Houses of Congress (except on money bills)[1]—since the House of

---

1. United States Constitution: Article I, Section 7, clause 1.

Representatives will not only have a greater number of members but will also be supported by the more powerful states—it will no doubt have an advantage over the Senate in any endurance contest between the two, especially when it is speaking and acting upon the known opinion of the majority of the People. The House of Representatives will be aware of these advantages, as well as the fact that they would be supported by right, by reason, and by the Constitution, just as the Senate would be aware of the fact that it would be contending with all of these powerful forces.

We must not forget that in the continuum between the smallest and largest states there are several states that, though likely to take the side of the larger states most of the time, are actually much closer in population and in size to the smallest states. Thus, it is by no means certain that a majority of votes, even in the Senate, would be capable of standing in the way of the number of Representatives in the House of Representatives being appropriately enhanced.

Additionally, it will not require us to look too far into the future to remember that Senators from new states could be won over to the legitimate views of the House of Representatives by a process that is too obvious to be overlooked. Since the population of these new states will increase rapidly for over many years, they will have an interest in there being frequent reapportionments of the number of Representatives per the number of inhabitants. Therefore, the larger states that will be dominant in the House of Representatives will have nothing to do except to make apportionments and augmentations mutually dependent on one another, just as the Senators from the most rapidly growing states will be required to argue for reapportionments because of the interest their states will have in an augmentation of their representation in the House of Representatives.

These thoughts suggest that there are plenty of checks and

balances, and that doubts we have on the topic should be appeased. However, even if for the sake of argument we admitted that all of these safeguards were incapable of protecting against the unjust demands of the smaller states (including their dominance in the Senate), the large states would still have a perfect, and at the same time constitutional, resource that would allow them to carry out their purposes at all times. The House of Representatives are also the only ones that can provide the necessary financial resources for the operations of the government. In a word, they hold the purse,[1] the very same power by which, in the history of the British constitution, an infantile and humble representation of the People (early Parliament) was able to gradually enlarge the sphere of its activity and importance, allowing it to eventually reduce the overgrown powers and privileges of all of the other branches of the government. In fact, this power over the purse may be regarded as the most effective weapon that the People's Representatives themselves can ever be given by a Constitution in order to obtain a redress of any grievance, and for carrying out every good and beneficial plan.

But won't the House of Representatives be just as interested as the Senate in maintaining the proper functions of the government, and wouldn't they be unwilling to stake an existence or reputation on the flexibility of the Senate? Or, if there were a contest between the two, wouldn't one be just as likely to yield as the other?

Such questions aren't difficult. In all cases, the smaller the number, the more permanent and visible the position of the men in power, the stronger the personal interest in whatever concerns the government. Those who represent the dignity of their country in the eyes of other nations (the Senate, because of their role in ratifying treaties) will be particularly sensitive to every possibil-

---

1. United States Constitution: Article I, Section 7, clause 1.

ity of public danger, or any dishonorable stagnation in public affairs. Because of things such as this, the British House of Commons was, and is to this day able to constantly triumph over the other branches of government whenever they use a money bill as a means to an end. Whenever the House of Commons used this tactic, they have neither feared nor ever experienced an absolute inflexibility on the part of the other branches of government, since this would cause general confusion throughout the entire government. Even the greatest amount of firmness imaginable on the part of the Senate or the President will not be able to resist the power of the House of Representatives when it is engaged in actions that will be supported by constitutional and patriotic principles.

Until now, I have not commented on the constraints that our current economic situation puts on us. These constraints might have played a role in decreasing the temporary number of Representatives prescribed by the Constitution. Of course, I'm sure that such an omission on my part will probably be taken advantage of, and will give the Constitution's critics just as much of an opportunity to criticize the argument as they have the initial number of Representatives. I will also refrain from commenting on the possible difficulties, given our present situation, of financially supporting the number of Representatives as the People will likely elect.

I must add one thought on the topic, because it requires serious attention: The greater the number in a legislative assembly, the fewer men there will be who will be directing its actions. In the first place, the more numerous any such assembly may be, no matter what type of people, the more likely it is that passion will take the place of reason. In the second place, the larger the number, the more Representatives there will be who lack information and ability, and it is *these* types of Representatives who can be most swayed by the eloquence and abilities of the few.

In the ancient republics, where the whole body of the People assembled in person to conduct public business, a single orator or a clever statesman could generally rule the assembly completely, as if a scepter had been placed into his hands alone. Based on this same principle, the more numerous a representative assembly is, the more it will experience the weaknesses that are a normal feature in any collective meeting of the People. Ignorance will fall prey to cunning, and passion will become the slave of sophistry and clever speaking and speeches. The People couldn't be more wrong if they believed that they can protect themselves better against a government of the few (an oligarchy) by multiplying their Representatives beyond a certain limit. On the contrary, experience will forever rebuke them that after securing the number of Representatives that are adequate for the purposes of safety, transmitting local information, and an overall sympathy with all of society, they will only act against their own interests if they continue to add more Representatives to this number. The government may appear more democratic, but its spirit will be more oligarchic. The machine will be enlarged, but the sources of its power and its movements will become fewer, and often more secret.

I will acknowledge another objection made against the Constitution as it relates to the number of Representatives that is apparently capable of, or necessary for carrying out legislative business. It has been said that more than a majority should be required to pass legislation (a quorum), and that in particular cases, if not all cases, more than a majority should have been required for a decision. It cannot be denied that some advantages could have resulted from such a precaution. It might have provided an additional shield to certain interests, and perhaps another obstacle to hasty and sloppy legislation. However, these advantages are far outweighed by the inconveniences that lie at the other end of the scale.

In every case where justice or the general good might require new laws to be passed or active steps to be taken, such a precaution would reverse the fundamental principle of free government. No longer would the majority rule, but the minority would. If such a privilege was limited to particular cases, then an interested minority might take advantage of them in order to keep themselves from having to make reasonable sacrifices to the general will, or they may force the majority to make unreasonable concessions during some particular emergency. Lastly, such a precaution makes it easier to engage in the destructive practice of secession, an action that has shown itself (even in states where only a majority is required) to be subversive of the principles of order and regular government, and has proven to be a practice that, more than any other yet used among us, can lead directly to public disturbances and the ruin of popular government.

—Publius

NUMBER 62

A General Overview of the Senate

JAMES MADISON
For the Independent Journal
The Senate

Constitutional References:
Article I: §3/1, 3 | §7/2

Since we have examined the makeup of the House of Representatives, as well as answered any objections to it, I will now begin to examine the Senate. The categories that this analysis will fall under are:

1. The qualifications of Senators;
2. The appointment of Senators by the state legislatures;
3. The equality of representation in the Senate;
4. The number of Senators and the length of their terms;
5. The powers vested in the Senate.

The qualifications of Senators differ from those of Representatives in two obvious but important ways: a more advanced age requirement, and a longer period of citizenship.[1]

---

1. United States Constitution: Article I, Section 3, clause 3.

FEDERALIST NO. 62

The Message: The House represents the people directly, but the union needs additional checks and balances, and buffers against corruption. The Senate, with its longer terms and direct election by state legislatures, won't be as sensitive to the vacillating emotions of the electorate and will be a more deliberative and reasonable legislative body.

Original Quote: "It is equally unnecessary to dilate on the appointment of senators by the State legislatures. Among the various modes which might have been devised for constituting this branch of the government, that which has been proposed by the convention is probably the most congenial with the public opinion."

Relevance to Today: There has been a renewed interest among Tea Party activists in rescinding the Seventeenth Amendment and, once again, allowing senators to be voted for by state legislatures rather than directly by voters. The Founders were obsessive about creating competitive interests and buffers to democracy—the Electoral College, for instance. Since Senators seem less responsive to state rights than ever, it is not surprising that Madison's arguments are being reexamined.

Original Quote: "It will be of little avail to the people, that the laws are made by men of their own choice, if the laws be so voluminous that they cannot be read, or so incoherent that they cannot be understood . . ."

Relevance to Today: The number of voluminous and incoherent laws Americans deal with today is amazing. Some of these laws are so large, in fact, that on the eve of passing the stimulus bill in 2008, New Jersey senator Frank Lautenberg explained to the press that though his colleagues would vote on the bill, they probably did not "have the chance" to read it. Similar situations emerged with the health-care reform and energy bills the next year. If politicians can't read or understand legislation, how can citizens be expected to? It's the ultimate display of arrogance.

A Senator must be at least thirty years old and have been a citizen for at least nine years, while a Representative must only be at least twenty-five and have been a citizen at least seven years. The nature of the Senatorial trust makes the reasons behind these differences obvious. A Senator requires a greater amount of information and stability of character, so an age requirement makes sense so that both of these characteristics can be adequately developed. Since Senators will be participating in our dealings with foreign nations,[1] the office should be held by those who have been thoroughly weaned of the biases and habits that sometimes result from foreign birth and education. A period of citizenship of at least nine years strikes a happy balance between completely excluding adopted citizens, whose merit and talents may make them worthy of the public trust, and indiscriminately and hastily welcoming them into a body as important as the Senate—which might provide a channel through which foreign influence could be exerted upon the Federal government.

It is equally unnecessary to expand on the appointment of Senators by the state legislatures.[2] Among the many ways that have been suggested for assembling the Senate, the method that has been proposed by the Convention is probably the most in line with public opinion. This method of appointment is doubly advantageous as it maintains the selective nature of the Senate while also giving state governments a role in forming the Federal government. This not only helps to secure their authority, but also forms a convenient link between the two systems.

The equality of representation in the Senate is another point that does not require much discussion. It was obviously the result

---

1. United States Constitution: Article II, Section 2, clause 2.
2. United States Constitution: Article I, Section 3, clause 1.

of a compromise between the larger and smaller states.[1] It is correct that among people forming one nation, every state ought to have a *proportional* representation in government, but it is also correct that, among independent and sovereign states, the members should have *equal* representation in a common government (as under the Articles of Confederation), however unequal they are in size. Therefore, it seems to make sense that in a compound Republic, which has both National and Federal characteristics, the government should be founded on a mixture of the principles of both proportional and equal representation. It would be useless to analyze this principle of the Constitution theoretically, however, when all have admitted that it was not the result of some theory, but "of a spirit of amity, and that mutual deference and concession which the peculiarity of our political situation rendered indispensable."[2]

A common government with a power equal to its stated goals is called for not just by voices, but more loudly by the political situation of America. A government that is founded on principles in line with the opinions of the larger states would not be acceptable to the smaller ones. Therefore, the only option left open to the larger states is adopting the proposed government, or one that is even more problematic. In a scenario like this, the wise thing to do would be to embrace the lesser of two evils, and instead of pointlessly worrying about the possible problems that might ensue, focus instead on the many possible advantages that make the sacrifice worthwhile.

In this same spirit, I will point out that the equal votes of all the states in the Senate is a way to constitutional recognition of

---

1. United States Constitution: same reference as previous footnote.
2. From a 1787 letter George Washington sent to the President of Congress along with the Constitution which the Convention had devised.

the sovereignty of individual states and a means of preserving that sovereignty. This equal vote should be just as acceptable to the large states as it is to the small ones, since both are just as eager to avoid, in every way possible, an improper consolidation of the states into one simple republic.[1]

Another advantage of the equal vote in the Senate is the additional security it will provide against inappropriate acts of legislation.

According to the Constitution, no law or resolution can be passed by Congress without the agreement, first, of a majority of the People (via the House of Representatives), and then, of a majority of the states (via the Senate).[2] It must be acknowledged that this complicated check on legislation may at times be more harmful than beneficial, and that the defense it specifically provides to the small states would make more sense if there was some common interest between them that was in danger. But since the large states will always be able to defeat unreasonable use of this right by the small states—since they control most resources, and since governments seem susceptible to the disease of writing and passing an excessive number of new laws—it seems quite possible that this part of the Constitution may perhaps be more convenient in practice than in theory.

We will now consider the *number of Senators and the length*

---

1. *simple republic:* By "simple republic," Madison is referring to a unitary government (it is called "National" in the Federalist Papers), a central government completely superior to the state/provincial governments of a nation. In other words, it is not a Federal government, since a Federal government by nature shares authority with the smaller governments that exist under it (i.e., the state governments). Madison was attempting to show how the Constitution not only forms a republican government, but would also avoid the subjugation of the state governments by the central government, which therefore made it a Federal, and not a unitary/National Constitution (i.e., "simple republic"), although it has the characteristics of both (which is a concept discussed in Federalist 39).

2. United States Constitution: Article I, Section 7, clause 2.

of their terms. In order to come to the right conclusion on both of these points, it would be appropriate to think about the objectives that need to be fulfilled by a Senate. To determine that, we must first review the problems that a republic would suffer if it happened to lack such an institution.

First, there is a problem peculiar to republican governments, and to a lesser degree other forms of government: Those who administer it can forget about their obligations to their constituents, and thus prove themselves unfaithful to their important public duties.

With this in mind, the Senate, as the second House of the Legislature that is distinct from and shares power with another, would always provide a beneficial check on the government. It provides extra security to the People, since any treacherous power-grabbing scheme would require the agreement of two distinct Houses of Congress, whereas before, the ambition or corruption of one would have been sufficient. This is a security based on principles understood so fully in the United States that it would be a waste of time to expand on them further. I will simply add that since the probability of there ever being any sinister plots to grab power will be proportional to how different the two Houses of Congress are, it would be wise to make them as different as possible while still allowing them to act together in harmony and in accordance with the genuine principles of republican government as far as appropriate and constitutional actions are concerned.

Second, a Senate is even more necessary given the fact that any single House and numerous assemblies are prone to act on the basis of sudden and violent impulses, and can at times be easily seduced by factious or partisan leaders into passing hotheaded and harmful resolutions or legislation. An infinite number of examples could be cited on this subject, both from within the United States, as well as from the history of other nations. But a position that won't be argued doesn't need to be proved. All that needs to be said is that any assembly meant to correct the defect of a numerous, single legislature, should not have as many members. It should also be a very durable body, and consequently its authority should be extended over a longer period of time, hence the six-year term for Senators.[1]

Third, the Senate can remedy another defect by featuring men who have an appropriate level of knowledge regarding the purposes and principles of legislation. [The following refers to the House of Representatives.] It is not possible for an assembly of men who, for the most part, have been called away from their own private pursuits, whose terms of office are short, and who have no deep-seated motives to study the laws, public affairs, or the overall interests of their country, to avoid a host of harmful errors in the process of carrying out legislative duties—especially if they were left completely to themselves. It can be strongly asserted that no small share of America's current embarrassments are the result of the blunders of governments, and that these came from the heads, rather than the hearts, of the authors. What can we possibly make of all the laws that repeal, explain, or amend past laws? Or those that fill and disgrace our massive codes of law? Can we see these as anything other than clear and simple evidence of a lack of wisdom? What about the many impeachments issued by each succeeding session of our legislatures against each preceding session? What are we to make of all of the warnings which have been given to the People by the critics concerning the benefits we could expect to receive from a well-structured Senate?

A good government implies two things: first, a loyalty to the purpose of government, which is the happiness of the People; and second, knowledge of how best to obtain that goal. While

---

1. United States Constitution: Article I, Section 3, clause 1.

some governments lack both these qualities, most governments lack in the first. I feel compelled to assert that in the American government, too little attention has been paid to the second. The new Federal Constitution avoids this error, and it deserves to be pointed out that it provides for the second in such a way that the security of the first is increased.

Fourth, the constantly changing nature of the government, resulting from the rapid succession of new members and public officials, however qualified they may be, strongly indicates the necessity for some sort of stable institution. Every election in the states ends up switching out fully half of the Representatives. This constant change of people means a change of opinions, and from a change of opinion, a change of policy. But a constant change in the policies of the government, even if they are productive, is inconsistent with every idea of prudence, as well as the possibility that such a government could be successful. This observation is just as true in private life, and thus becomes all the more fair, as well as important, when applied to national and government decisions.

It would take an entire book to write a history to catalog the negative effects resulting in a constantly changing government. I will simply mention a few here, but I'm sure they will bring to mind quite a few more. The first area sacrificed by a constantly changing government is the respect and confidence of other nations, and all the other advantages that stem from national character. Any individual who is constantly inconsistent in his plans, or perhaps goes through life without any plan whatsoever, is seen by wise people (both friend and foe) as the speedy victim of his own instability and foolishness. His more friendly neighbors may pity him, but they will decline connecting their own wealth and reputation with his, and some may even seize the opportunity of taking advantage of him. One nation is to another what one individual is to another, with the sad difference being that nations have fewer restraints which prevent them from taking advantage of the mistakes of other nations. Thus, every nation whose affairs seem to be lacking in wisdom and stability can count on being negatively affected by the more systematic policies of its neighbors.

The best source of instruction for America on this subject, sadly, is her very own situation. She has found that her friends do not respect her, she is ridiculed by her enemies, and she is the prey of every nation which has an interest in taking advantage of her frequently fluctuating government and the humiliated state of her public affairs.

The internal effects of constantly changing policies are even more disastrous, since it poisons the blessings of liberty itself. It won't matter much to the People that laws are made by men who chose themselves if there are so many that they cannot be read, or they are so incoherent that they cannot be understood. Additionally, it won't matter if the laws are repealed or revised before they are enforced, or undergo so many changes that no one who knows what the law is today can guess what it will be tomorrow. Law is defined as a rule of action, but how can something that is not very well known and not permanent be considered a rule?

Another effect of such public instability is the unreasonable advantage it gives to the shrewd, enterprising, and wealthy over the industrious and common mass of the People. Every new regulation concerning commerce or revenue, or which in any way affects the value of various types of property, presents an opportunity that can be taken advantage of by those who pay attention to the change and can determine its consequences. Ultimately, these opportunities are not of their own doing, but are the result of the troubles and hard work of the vast majority of their fellow citizens. This is really an example of a situation in which it can be said with some truth that laws are made for the *few*, not for the *many*.

An unstable government is harmful from another point of view as well: A lack of confidence in the government prevents every useful, beneficial, or entrepreneurial undertaking from ever taking place, since a certain level of permanence in the government, as well as pre-existing institutions and ways of going about things would be necessary for it to succeed. What practical merchant would risk his fortunes on a new commercial venture when he knows that any plans he may have may be pronounced unlawful before they can even be executed? What farmer or manufacturer would risk his livelihood on a particular crop or establishment without assurances that his preparation and progress will not become the victim of instability? In other words, any advances or praiseworthy enterprises requiring the protection of steady national policies cannot go forward.

But unstable government's most disastrous effect is its negative effect on the attachment and reverence the People have for their political system, a system that not only exhibits signs of weakness, but also disappoints their deeply held hopes. Just like an individual, no government can be respected for very long without being respectable, nor respectable without possessing a certain amount of order and stability.

—Publius

NUMBER 68

The Appointment of the President (Continued)

ALEXANDER HAMILTON

For the New York Packet: Friday, March 14, 1788

The Executive Branch

Constitutional References:
Article II: §1/2–4, 6

The method of appointing the President of the United States is seemingly the only important part of the Constitution that has not been severely criticized by opponents of the document. In fact, it received the slightest amount of approval from critics who have begrudgingly admitted that the election of the President is fairly well protected.[1] I would go even

---

1. This is a reference to the admission on the part of "Federal Farmer," which was the pen name of an Anti-Federalist writer who wrote an important and methodical examination of the proposed constitution. The assessment consisted of two pamphlets, the first of which was published in November 1787, and the second in May 1788. They were addressed to "The Republican" (which was most likely New York governor George Clinton), and some scholars have suggested that the "Federal Farmer" was possibly either Richard Henry Lee (1732–94), Virginian statesman who was most famous for calling for a resolution of independence during the Second Continental Congress, which resolution ultimately became the Declaration

FEDERALIST NO. 68

The Message: The Electoral College system of electing a president is one of the most effective ways to preserve the American republic. The presence of an independent group of electors will protect the presidency from special interests and insure that all citizens—even those who live in small or isolated areas, are proportionally represented.

Original Quote: "They have not made the appointment of the President to depend on any preexisting bodies of men who might be tampered with beforehand to prostitute their voices . . ."

Relevance to Today: A few years ago, George Soros' son Jonathan wrote an op-ed in the Wall Street Journal titled "It's Time to Junk the Electoral College." This idea, popular in progressive circles, is ostensibly meant to bring more "fair" and direct democracy to America. State legislatures across the country have joined in the crusade by either passing or proposing laws that would eliminate the Electoral College and throw all the states' votes to the candidate who won the nationwide popular vote. That would weaken the influence of smaller states and strengthen the control of big ones, like New York and California—which, big surprise, usually happen to vote for the Democratic Party. We all must remember why the Electoral College system exists in the first place, and the Federalist Papers are a great place to start.

Original Quote: "Talents for low intrigue, and the little arts of popularity, may alone suffice to elevate a man to the first honors in a single State . . ."

Relevance to Today: Scaremongering, deceit, and propaganda can all, in the short term, play on the emotions of the electorate. We regularly see these kinds of manipulations—"they're going to kill your grandmother!"—in political campaigns. The Electoral College's purpose was to weaken these kinds of emotional current in elections and allow citizens, through their state electors, to choose the best, most qualified person, not the one who was simply saying what they wanted to hear.

further and note that if the method is not perfect, it is at the very least excellent as it, in a rather noteworthy fashion, combines all the advantages we could possibly desire in the process.[1]

Obviously, it was desirable that the People have a large role in choosing the person who will be delegated a public trust as important as the Presidency. This has been accomplished by giving the right to make such a decision not to any preexisting body, but to men chosen by the People at the right time for this specific and unique purpose. It was equally desirable that the election of the President be made by men who are capable of analyzing the qualities needed for such an office, and who are able to cast their votes under circumstances favoring both a discussion and thoughtful consideration of the reasons and motives affecting their choice. It would be likely that a small number of people who had been selected by their fellow citizens to carry out such a complicated investigation will possess the information and wisdom required to do so.

It was also desirable to protect the process (as much as possible) against turmoil or disorder, considering it is the process that picks an Executive who plays a vital role in the administration of government. Fortunately, the new Constitution combines many precautions to protect this process against potential problems: The election of *several* people, who make up an intermediate body of Electors will elect the President, and this group will be less likely to arouse violent or tumultuous reactions in the community than the direct election of a single person. And since these Electors

---

of Independence; or Melancton Smith (1744–98), a New York delegate to the Continental Congress who made many of the same arguments as the Federal Farmer to the New York state ratification convention at Poughkeepsie in 1788. (Ultimately, Smith voted in favor of the Constitution with amendments.)

1. A reference to the Electoral College system; United States Constitution: Article II, Section 1, clauses 2–4.

will be chosen in each state, and will cast their votes in the state in which they are chosen, the election of the President will be detached and sprawled out to help protect the Electors against the reactions or the violence of the People more effectively than if they were all in the same place at one time.

Nothing, however, is more desirable than placing every practical obstacle possible in the way of secret plotting, intrigue, or corruption. While it might be expected that the dangerous adversaries of republican government would reveal themselves from more than one place, the primary danger would come from the desire of foreign powers to gain an inappropriate level of influence in our government. How could they achieve this goal any better than by raising one of their own citizens to the Presidency of the United States? But the Convention guarded against such dangers with the wisest and most appropriate foresight and attention. Instead of referring the appointment of the President to preexisting bodies of men, whose votes could have been tampered with beforehand, they have referred the choice to the People of America first, who will decide for themselves specific people whose temporary and sole purpose is to appoint the President.

Thus, without corrupting the People, those elected to carry out the appointment of the President will begin their task without any corrupt bias. They will only exist for a short time, and they will be spread out throughout each of the states, both of which give us satisfactory reasons to believe that the Electors will complete their task without falling under the influence of any bias. The task of corrupting large numbers of men would require both time and means, and it would be difficult (with all of them dispersed over thirteen states) to convince them to take one side or another. This may not technically be "corruption," but nonetheless it distracts them from carrying out their duty. Just as important, the

President will be in a position to rely on everyone except the People for continuing in his office. Otherwise, he might be tempted to sacrifice his duty for the sake of pleasing those who elected him into office in the first place. This will be avoided by making his reelection dependent on the same special body of representatives (the Electors) who will be chosen by society for the sole purpose of making this important choice.

The Plan devised by the Convention combines all of these advantages together by requiring that each state choose a particular number of people as Electors, equal to the number of Senators and Representatives of that state in the Federal government. They will then assemble within that state and vote for the person they believe is most qualified to be President.[1] Once their votes are cast, the votes will be sent to the seat of the Federal government (the Capital), and whoever happens to have a majority of the votes will become President. Since one man might not always receive the majority of votes, and since it might be unsafe to allow less than a majority to make the final decision, the House of Representatives, in such a contingency, would be required to choose from among the candidates with the five highest numbers of votes the man who, in their opinion, would be best qualified for the office of President.[2]

This process of election will provide us with a moral certainty that the Presidency will seldom be occupied by anyone not eminently qualified for it. It may be possible, and even sufficient, for someone who has a gift for political maneuvering and intrigue, as well as the petty desire to be popular, to rise to the highest office of a single state (i.e., governor); but it will require completely dif-

---

1. United States Constitution: Article II, Section 1, clause 3.
2. Ibid.

ferent talents and different kinds of qualities in order to earn the necessary respect and confidence of the whole Union (or of a large enough portion of it) in order to become a viable candidate for the distinguished office of President of the United States.

I do not think it would be an exaggeration to say that this office is likely to be filled by men of superior ability and virtue, and this should be considered no small accomplishment on the part of the Constitution, which recognizes how important a role the Executive has in the administration of every government, either for good or bad.

While we cannot accept the political heresy of the poet who declares:

> For forms of government, let fools contest . . .
> That which is best administered, is best[1]

we can at least safely conclude that the true test of a good government is its ability and tendency to produce a good administration.

The Vice President will be chosen in the same way as the President, with the only difference being that the Senate will do the same thing with respect to the Vice President as the House of Representatives does with the President (should that ever happen).[2] One of the useless and mischievous objections to this proposition is that an unusual person will be chosen as Vice President. It has also been alleged that it would have been preferable for the Senate to elect one of its own to fill the position of Vice President. However, two points seem to justify the ideas that the Convention used in this respect. The first is that in order to secure a conclusive

---

1. Alexander Pope (1688–1744), *An Essay on Man*. The original reads: "For forms of government let fools contest / whate'er is best administer'd is best" (Epistle 3, lines 303–4).
2. United States Constitution: Article II, Section 1, clause 3.

decision by the Senate, it would be necessary for the president of the Senate to cast a vote, not a tie-breaking vote.[1] And making the Senator of one state the president of the Senate would be the same as that state exchanging a constant ability to vote with only the occasional and contingent ability to vote. The second point is that as the Vice President may occasionally act as a substitute for the President, all of the reasons that support the method of election used for the President should apply with great, if not equal, force to the election of the Vice President.[2]

Again, it is simply remarkable that in this example, as well as in most of the others, the objections made against the proposed Constitution could just as easily have been made against the constitution of New York. For example, we have a lieutenant-governor who is chosen by the People at large, who presides over the state's senate, and acts as the constitutional substitute for the governor in situations which are similar to the ones which, under the new Constitution, would authorize the Vice President to exercise the authorities and carry out the duties of the President.

—Publius

---

1. United States Constitution: Article I, Section 3, clause 5.
2. United States Constitution: Article II, Section 1, clause 6.

FEDERALIST NO. 71

The Message: No more kings. Though a nation needs an executive who can act independently of the other branches, the president must also be, at the same time, both accountable to the people and a leader of men. The best way to create this balance is with a four-year term.

———————————

Original Quote: "The republican principle demands that the deliberate sense of the community should govern the conduct of those to whom they intrust the management of their affairs; but it does not require an unqualified complaisance to every sudden breeze of passion, or to every transient impulse which the people may receive from the arts of men, who flatter their prejudices to betray their interests."

Relevance to Today: Our Founders believed that our presidents should champion the public's views that have been thought out and developed over time, but they should not acquiesce to every whim. But is that really how it still works? Presidents these days seem to interpret overnight opinion polls as gospel. From gas prices to the stock market, chief executives now seem to react to the news of the day rather than drive forward an agenda based on the long-held views of society as a whole.

———————————

Original Quote: "A feeble executive implies feeble execution of the government. A feeble execution is but another phrase for a bad execution; and a government ill executed, what it may be in theory, must be, in practice a bad government."

Relevance to Today: We've seen it countless times—a president who is unsure how to proceed acts meekly in public and a bad situation gets worse. One of the most jarring examples of this were the actions of President George W. Bush during the early days of what turned into the "Great Recession." Weakness—or even the perception of it—in the nation's top executive can induce an entire nation to lose confidence.

NUMBER 71

The Length of the President's Term
in Office (Continued)

ALEXANDER HAMILTON
For the New York Packet: Tuesday, March 18, 1788
The Executive Branch

Constitutional References:
Article II: §1/1–2 | §2–§3

An adequately long term in office is the second component of an energetic Executive authority. This element
is directly related to two points: first, enabling the President to use his constitutional powers in a robust way, and second,
creating stability under his leadership.

As far as the firmness of the presidency is concerned, it must
be obvious that the longer he remains in office, the more likely he
will obtain such an important advantage. It is a general principle
of human nature that a man is interested in whatever he possesses
in proportion to how firmly (or how precariously) he possesses it.
So if he holds a certain title for only a brief time, then he will be
less attached to it. Therefore, he will risk more for the sake of one
than the other. This observation applies to any political privilege,

honor, or trust, as it does to any other ordinary piece of property. The conclusion to draw from this truth is that anyone serving as President, even those who know that in a very short time he *must* lay down his office, will likely find that he isn't interested in it enough to risk any of the serious criticism or uncertainty that may result from him exercising his powers independently. He may even want to avoid the bad feelings, however temporary, that may be felt by a large portion of the People or by the party in control of Congress. Even if he only *might* have to lay down his powers (in case he was reelected), both his personal desires and fears would have a powerful tendency to corrupt his integrity, or diminish his resilience, if he was in office for a short time. In either case, feebleness and indecisiveness would be the characteristics of his office.

There are some who might prefer, as the best solution, that the Executive power always be at the mercy of the prevailing mood or climate of the nation or Congress. But those who recommend such a thing have a crude notion about the purpose of government, as well as the true means by which public happiness can be promoted. While the republican principle demands that a deliberate sense of the People should govern the conduct of those to whom they have entrusted the management of public affairs, it does not require unconditional surrender to every sudden breeze of passion, or to every momentary impulse that may be aroused among the People by the cleverness of those who seek to appease their prejudices.

I believe it is fair to say that the People often *intend* the PUBLIC GOOD, but that this intention applies just as much to their mistakes as it does to their successes. Their common sense tells them that they should despise those who pretend to always know the *correct way* to promote the public good. They know from their life experiences that humans make mistakes. Yet, despite being at the mercy of self-serving politicians and greedy individuals, the ambitious, the desperate, and those who seek to possess power rather than earn and deserve it, the People rarely make mistakes. That is the true miracle.

When the feelings of the People are contrary to their real interests, then it is the duty of those they have appointed to act as the guardians and to persevere whenever the People may be swayed by some temporary passion, in order to give them both the time and opportunity for more calm and careful reflection. There are several examples of this kind of conduct on the part of the People's representatives, and it has saved them from the very fatal consequences of their own mistakes. Such conduct will forever stand as an enduring monument of the People's gratitude to those men who had enough courage and nobility to serve them, even at the risk of making them angry.

But no matter how inclined we may be to insist that the President should always be willing to bend to the inclinations of the People, it would be absolutely inappropriate for us to insist that he do the same with regard to every temporary whim of Congress. The People may sometimes be opposed to Congress, and at other times they may be entirely neutral. However, in both cases, it is certainly desirable that the President should be in a situation where he can dare to act decisively and with conviction on his own opinions.

The same reasoning that makes dividing power between the different Branches of government appropriate, also teaches us that that division should be done in such a way that it renders each Branch independent of the other. What would be the point of separating the Executive or Judicial Branch from the Legislative Branch if they were both structured in such a way that they had to be absolutely devoted to and dependent on the Legislative Branch?

A "separation" such as this one would be in-name-only, and

therefore incapable of achieving the goals that it establishes. It is one thing to obey the laws, but a completely different thing to be entirely dependent on Congress. The first is in line with the fundamental principles of good government; the second violates them. No matter what form the Constitution takes, placing all power into the same hands is tyrannical. The tendency of the legislative authority to absorb every other authority has already been fully discussed and illustrated in previous papers, and in purely republican government, this tendency is almost irresistible. In a popularly elected assembly, the representatives of the People sometimes seem to think of themselves as the People themselves, and as such they sometimes exhibit impatience or disgust at the smallest sign of opposition from any other quarter, almost as if by exercising their own rightful powers the Executive and Judicial Branches are infringing on the privileges of Congress, and committing an outrage against their dignity. Such assemblies often have a tendency to exert a domineering control over the other Branches, and since they often have the People on their side, they always act with a degree of momentum that makes it very difficult for the other Branches of government to maintain the balance of the Constitution.

Without the power to appoint or remove the other from office, some may ask how a short term in office for the President affects the Executive's independence as it relates to Congress. The principle that I alluded to at the beginning of this paper can provide at least one answer to this question: A man will only have a little bit of interest in any advantage that he has for only a short time. This would make it unlikely that he would expose himself to any significant inconvenience or danger for the sake of such an advantage. An even more obvious issue is the greater influence which Congress will have over the People. They might use this influence to prevent the reelection of a man to the Presidency who, because he may have resisted some of their sinister plans, they may resent.

It may also be asked whether a four-year term[1] in office for the President would actually achieve all of these goals. If not, wouldn't a shorter term in office be preferable, even though the longer period being discussed is still too short to endow the President with the desired level of firmness and independence?

I cannot say with absolute certainty that a four-year term in office for the President (or any other limited amount of time) would achieve all of the goals mentioned above. But I can say that such a term in office would contribute significantly to the spirit and character of the government. Between the beginning and the end of such a term in office, there would always be a large amount of time that the President would feel very little danger of being removed from office. Therefore, this longer period of time would not affect the conduct of anyone who had the necessary endurance, and would also give the President enough time in office to convince the People of the appropriateness or necessity of his actions.

Although it is likely that the President's firmness will decline as he approaches a new election, the People's opinion of both his conduct, as well as their confidence in him, will be strengthened by the previous opportunities he had while he was in office to defend his actions to the People, and thereby earn respect and goodwill. At that point, he will probably be wise enough to risk being criticized, depending on how much evidence he would be able to provide the People of his wisdom and integrity while he occupied an office that was gained through their respect and affection.[2] Therefore, while a four-year term will allow the President to retain

---

1. United States Constitution: Article II, Section 1, clause 1.
2. United States Constitution: Article II, Section 1, clause 2.

an adequate level of firmness (which will be a very valuable part of the government), it won't be long enough to justify any fears that it will be dangerous to the liberties of the public.

If, from the most humble beginnings, a British House of Commons, *merely with the power to agree or disagree to the imposition of a new tax*, was able to rapidly reduce the powers of the Crown and the privileges of the nobility within the limits which they thought appropriate to the principles of free government; if they could at the same time raise their own status to that of a co-equal house of the legislature (Parliament); if they could at one time abolish both the royalty and the aristocracy, while overturning the ancient institutions within both the church and the state; if they were capable of eventually making the king tremble at the prospect of them making their own changes and applying their own ideas to the government,[1] then what do we have to fear from an Executive elected every four years whose powers will be confined to the authorities that are given to the President of the United States by the new Constitution?[2]

Wouldn't all we have to fear be that he might not be equal to the task that the Constitution assigns to him? If anyone doubts that during a four-year term the President will not be firm enough, then they cannot at the same time also fear that he will infringe upon or violate his powers.

—Publius

---

1. "This happened recently regarding Mr. Fox's [Charles Fox, 1749–1806; MP from Midhurst, West Sussex] India Bill (1784), which was passed in the House of Commons (apparently with the complete satisfaction of the people), but rejected in the House of Lords."
2. United States Constitution: Article II, Sections 2–3.

PART FOUR

THE DELICATE BALANCE
OF POWER

But when a long train of abuses and usurpations, pursuing invariably the same Object evinces a design to reduce them under absolute Despotism, it is their right, it is their duty, to throw off such Government, and to provide new Guards for their future security.

—Declaration of Independence

This section isn't about a radical militia group or some wild conspiracy theory. This section is about a series of very real, very specific directives left to us by a group of people who had just thrown off tyrannical rule and were experiencing true freedom for the first time. Like all great wisdom, this set of instructions was meant to be passed down through the ages, understood, talked about, and, if necessary, acted upon.

Instead, it's been largely ignored.

First, some context: The Articles of Confederation lacked a specific means through which its laws could be enforced. As a result, the laws were more like "suggestions" that could be followed or ignored at will by the states. You can imagine how that turned out.

Not wanting to experience the same kind of near-anarchy

again, the Convention worked hard to come up with a solution that would allow for the central government to have enforceable power over the states and people, even though it was those very same states and people who gave the government its power in the first place. It was a complicated, controversial issue and, in this set of papers, Publius explained and defended the Convention's answer.

Emergencies could occur, as Alexander Hamilton explained in Federalist 28, or insurrections might arise that could pose a danger to the republic as a whole. If that were the case then the federal government would have "no remedy but force." Yes, *force*.

That, of course, is an extraordinarily dangerous power to give to a government. A government's use of force against its own citizens is often the hallmark of tyrannical regimes. So, of course, Hamilton explained, that power needed to be balanced—and he further explained that the Constitution offered two specific ways to do that.

First, the system was set up so that the states would always have the opportunity to stand up to the federal government—and vice versa. "Power being almost always the rival of power," Hamilton wrote, "the general [federal] government will at all times stand ready to check the usurpations of the state governments, and these will have the same disposition towards the general government."

In case there was still any doubt, he revisited the topic again later in the paper and was even more clear as to the role of the states: "It may safely be received as an axiom in our political system, that the State governments will, in all possible contingencies, afford complete security against invasions of the public liberty by the national authority."

We've already covered a few of the basic principles that I think our Founders were mistaken on, and now we can add another one to the list. In theory and on paper, yes, the federal government and the state governments were essentially equals. But in reality we all understand that that's no longer the way it works. The federal government is able to pass legislation having nothing to do with the powers enumerated to it and, all too often, the states sit back and take it. (Why? Money. But more on that later.)

The second way to balance the power given to the federal government was the cornerstone principle of the entire constitution: power to the people. If the states failed in their responsibility, then it would be up to the people to respond. "If the representatives of the people betray their constituents," Hamilton wrote, "there is then no resource left but in the exertion of that original right of self-defense which is paramount to all positive forms of government."

We don't often think of it in these terms, but what better way to refer to the process of standing up to a group that is trying to take something away from you than *self-defense*? If someone told you they were actively taking your life, you'd respond in self-defense. If someone told you they were actively trying to take your liberty, you'd respond in self-defense. If someone told you they were actively trying to stop you from pursuing happiness, you'd respond in self-defense. After all, self-defense in the face of an aggressor is a basic right. If the federal government abuses its authority and betrays its constituents, then citizens possess the right—in fact, they have the *responsibility*—to defend themselves.

All of this, of course, assumes that the people understand their rights and are willing to defend them. That wasn't a very big assumption at the time—people took a keen interest in their rights—but things are much different today. Convincing people that they should read and understand the Constitution, the Federalist Papers, and the rest of our important founding documents is like pulling teeth. But without that knowledge people cannot understand their rights, let alone the instructions that were left on how to defend them.

"The obstacles to usurpation," Hamilton wrote, "and the facilities of resistance increase with the increased extent of the state, *provided the citizens understand their rights and are disposed to defend them*." I added the emphasis to make it clear that this important little caveat wasn't forgotten by the Founders. Perhaps they underestimated how likely it might be to occur, but they certainly acknowledged that it was one of the keys to the system working as planned.

In Federalist 46, James Madison took over and expanded on many of the points that Hamilton had made earlier. Regarding the states standing up to the central government, he wrote, "Should an unwarrantable measure of the federal government be unpopular in particular States, which would seldom fail to be the case, or even a warrantable measure be so, which may sometimes be the case, the means of opposition to it are powerful and at hand."

States would fight for their rights, and so would individuals. Madison asked readers not to insult the nation's citizens by assuming that if they were once again violated they wouldn't defend the rights they had earned through blood. The expectation that Americans would defend themselves against tyranny—external or internal—was a given at the time.

As Madison wrote, "The ultimate authority, no matter where any of its derivatives may be found, resides in the People alone." When people have the power, they have no need to revolt against themselves. That is a core premise of the Constitution and it was a core promise made to the people being asked to ratify it at the time.

As I've noted before, the authors of the Federalist Papers could not foresee modern events, or they misjudged the incentives of government and those of politicians. Madison, for example, assured readers that while state governments might attempt to increase their power through appropriations from the federal government, they would be thwarted by the lack of support among members of the federal government who would not want to fund them. If Madison were alive today he would likely be shocked at just how often the national government desires to fund state projects as a means of controlling those states. The entire equation has been flipped upside down.

In Federalist 45, titled "Alleged Danger From the Powers of the Union to the State Governments Considered," Madison turned to focus on whether the federal government might be able to use its new powers to overrun the states. After running through a brief history of confederacies around the world, Madison presented an answer that turned the whole criticism on its head:

> The State governments will have the advantage of the Federal government, whether we compare them in respect to the immediate dependence of the one on the other; to the weight of personal influence which each side will possess; to the powers respectively vested in them; to the predilection and probable support of the people; to the disposition and faculty of resisting and frustrating the measures of each other.

Let's go through the reasons he listed one by one:

Dependence on each other: The states would play a huge role in determining who serves in the federal government (at that point through direct election of Senators and via their power of redistricting) and therefore the federal government would be dependent on the states. The federal government would play no role in determining who serves in the states. Advantage: The states.

Weight of personal influence: All politics are local. Given that the states would have much more direct influence on the happiness of their population, the people in each state would likely be more loyal to their state governments than to some distant central one. Advantage: The states.

The powers vested: The powers given to the federal government were enumerated specifically in the Constitution. The states and people retained everything else. While this principle was later solidified in the Tenth Amendment ("The powers not delegated to the United States by the Constitution, nor prohibited by it to the States, are reserved to the States respectively, or to the people"), it's clear that the Amendment was simply repeating what was already an accepted part of the Constitution itself. Advantage: The states.

Support of the people: Back then, a person's state may have well been their country, as transportation and communication options weren't exactly what they are today. That meant that state governments were far more important in the everyday lives of people than the federal government was. Assuming that those state governments were operating honestly and efficiently, they would enjoy more support from the people than politicians operating perhaps hundreds or thousands of miles away. Advantage: The states.

Resisting the measures of the other: Remember, at the time the Constitution was ratified, the states had direct authority over the Senate (via elections by each state legislature). That power, along with their ability to elect presidential electors and appoint others to federal offices, gave Madison and the other Founders great comfort in the states' ability to resist the federal government if necessary. Advantage: The states.

So, according to Madison it was a blowout: The states were far more powerful than the federal government. But has he been proven right? I guess everyone can make up their own mind, but here's something to think about: In the first quarter of 2009, the federal government, for the first time ever, became the largest source of revenue for state and local governments. Above property taxes, sales taxes, and every other tax and fee you can think of.

How large has that federal and state aid become? Since 1960, and accounting for inflation, it's up nearly 1,200 percent—from approximately $50 billion a year to over $650 billion a year now.

Without that money, which funds everything from state health programs to education, from transportation to agriculture, the states would not be able to function as they currently do. Consider that fact the next time someone tells you that federalism is alive and well. And consider what James Madison would say about that relationship, considering the core principle of the Constitution that he wrote about in No. 45: "The State governments may be regarded as constituent and essential parts of the federal government; whilst the latter is nowise essential to the operation or organization of the former."

Try telling your governor how nonessential the federal government is to your state the next time he's filling out his state budget.

FEDERALIST NO. 28

The Message: The people are to hold the power of the federal government in check to help prevent it from usurping power.

Original Quote: "In a confederacy the people, without exaggeration, may be said to be entirely the masters of their own fate. Power being almost always the rival of power, the general government will at all times stand ready to check the usurpations of the state governments, and these will have the same disposition towards the general government. The people, by throwing themselves into either scale, will infallibly make it preponderate."

Relevance to Today: Those who are fighting for smaller government are not simply expressing opinions; they are exercising the ultimate constitutional check on federal power. If the people stand by and accept the federal government's ever-expanding role, then there is no barrier left to eventual tyranny.

Original Quote: "It may safely be received as an axiom in our political system, that the State governments will, in all possible contingencies, afford complete security against invasions of the public liberty by the national authority."

Relevance to Today: The Founders believed that the union of states would have more power than the central government. And, in theory, they still do (don't forget, if two-thirds of state legislatures call for a national Constitutional Convention, the Congress must act). While the federal government has successfully used carrots and sticks to control the states, it's the states that have the ultimate power—they just have to use it. The lawsuits filed by 28 states against the federal health-care reform law is one example of how they can push back against an overreaching government.

NUMBER 28

The Necessity of an Energetic Government

ALEXANDER HAMILTON

For the Independent Journal

The New Powers of the Union Explained and Justified:

Constitutional References:
Article I: §8/12, 15

I t's undeniable that the Federal government may at some point have to resort to force. Our own experience with England has taught us that these types of emergencies sometimes occur in all societies, no matter how they are structured. Unfortunately, sedition and insurrection are just as inseparable from the people of a nation as tumors and disease are from the body. In fact, the idea that it is always possible to govern through the simple force of law, which some have said is the only acceptable principle of a republican government, is simply a dream of political scholars whose shrewd words ignore the lessons of experience.

Should such emergencies ever occur under the Federal government, there would be no acceptable remedy other than force. The amount of force used should be proportional to the seriousness of the emergency. An insurrection eventually endangers all government. Concern for the public peace would cause all citizens who had not been swept up by the insurrectionist spirit to oppose the insurgents. And, assuming that the Federal government had proven to be beneficial to the happiness and prosperity of the People, it would be irrational to believe that citizens would not come to its support.

If, on the contrary, the insurrection swept through an entire state, or even a big chunk of it, the use of a different kind of force would become unavoidable. For example, Massachusetts found it necessary to raise troops in order to suppress the commotions that occurred during Shays' Rebellion in 1787,[1] and Pennsylvania raised troops simply because they feared the same thing might happen among their citizens. But suppose the state of New York had desired to re-establish some of the jurisdiction it lost to New Hampshire in what became present-day Vermont?[2] Could New York have ever hoped to do so successfully if she simply used the militia or would New York have been forced to raise and maintain a group of regular soldiers in order to carry out her plans?

Such extreme situations at a state level would have to be dealt with by a force greater than a simple militia, and it is possible that the Federal government may one day have to do the same thing. So it's surprising that the men who declare their love for the Union in the abstract are the same ones who object to the new

---

1. *Shays' Rebellion:* Explanation found in Federalist 6.
2. This is a reference to the land dispute between New Hampshire and New York (New York refused to recognize land titles by which New Hampshire had created towns in present-day Vermont), a dispute that ultimately led to the creation of independent Vermont on January 18, 1777. On July 20, 1764, King George III established the boundary between New Hampshire and New York as being along the west bank of the Connecticut River. New York (Albany County, specifically), gained this land, which is present-day Vermont. (Referenced in Federalist 7.)

Constitution on the grounds that it may one day require the use of force to maintain its existence.[1] And isn't this possible use of force one of the means by which a civil society is maintained, just on a larger scale? Would anyone rather experience the perpetual conflicts and frequent revolutions that have characterized so many of the petty republics of the past and present, rather than leaving open the possibility of using force?

Let's examine this in another way. Suppose that instead of one National system, we formed two, three, or even four confederacies. Wouldn't each of them have to deal with the very same difficulties? Wouldn't each of them face the possibility of sedition or insurrection, and be obliged to take the same forceful actions in order to maintain their authority that are now being used to object to a single Union government for all of the states? Would the militia be any more ready and able to support those multiple governments than they would be for a single Union government? Anyone who's honest and intelligent must acknowledge that this objection is applicable to both options equally. Whether we have a single Union government for all the states, different governments for different parts of them, or as many separate governments as there are states, there is always the possibility that a force of armed regular soldiers (non-militia) will have to be used in order to preserve the peace of the community and maintain the authority of the laws against violent invasions that amount to insurrection and rebellion.

Those who desire a more immediate constitutional provision against regular military establishments in time of peace would be better off replying that the complete power of the proposed gov-

---

1. United States Constitution: Article I, Section 8, clause 15.

ernment will be in the hands of the representatives of the People.[1] This is the essential and, after all, the only effective means to secure the rights and privileges of the People in a civil society.

If the representatives of the People betray their constituents, then those constituents can exercise their original right of self-defense. This right is paramount to all positive forms of government, and would be infinitely more successful if it were employed against any usurpation of rights by the Federal government rather than against any individual state government. But if the government of an individual state began to seize power, the different counties of the state would be unable to organize any defense. The citizens of the state might enthusiastically take up arms but without any organization or system or resources, they would be united only by their courage and despair. The usurpers of power, having the illusion of the legal authority of the state, could easily nip the opposition in the bud. The smaller the territory, the more difficult it would be for the People to organize a regular, systematic plan of opposition to the government, and the easier it would be to defeat them. Since intelligence about the movements and preparations of the opposition can be more easily obtained by those in power, they would be able to direct whatever military force they had more quickly against the opposition. Thus, in this type of situation, a very unlikely set of circumstances would be required for the popular opposition to actually succeed.

Fortunately for us, the obstacles to usurpation, and the ease with which it can be resisted, are both enhanced when the territory grows larger, provided two things: first, that the People understand their rights, and, second, that they are willing to stand up and defend them. The natural strength of the People in a large community is much greater in proportion to the artificial strength

---

1. United States Constitution: Article I, Section 8, clauses 12 and 15.

---

of government than in a small community, and certainly much more capable of struggling with the government in order to prevent it from becoming tyrannical. But in a confederacy, it's not an exaggeration to say that the People are entirely the masters of their own fate. Power is automatically a rival of any other power, so the power of the Federal government will at all times be ready to prevent the usurpations of the state governments, just as the state governments will do the same for the Federal government. Whatever side has the support of the People will have a decisive advantage. If either of those powers invades their rights, then the People can make use of the other to rectify the injury. It would be wise of the People who cherish their Union to preserve for themselves this advantage—an advantage that can never be overestimated.

It is a fact of our political system that the state governments will always be able to provide complete security against invasions of the public liberty by the Federal government. Any attempts to usurp power by the Federal government would never escape the attention of the state legislatures or the People themselves. The state legislatures will be able to detect the coming danger from a distance, since they will have all the tools of civil power at their disposal, as well as the confidence of the People, and they will be able to immediately come up with an effective plan of opposition and combine all the resources of the community to carry it out. They could also communicate with the other states and unite their forces for the protection of their common liberty.

The enormous size of our country is also an excellent source of security. In fact, we have already experienced its usefulness in repelling the attacks of a foreign enemy, and the exact same thing would be true in defending against the schemes of overly ambitious politicians in the National government. If the Federal army were able to quell resistance in one of the states, the more distant states would have the ability to provide fresh new forces. The success of the Federal forces in one place would have to be abandoned in order to quell resistance in other places, and the moment they left the state which they first subdued, the efforts of the opposition would be renewed and their resistance would be revived.

We must remember that the size of the military force will always be dependent on the resources of the country. For many years to come it will not be possible to maintain a large army, but as our ability to do so increases, so will our population, and thus the natural strength of the community will increase as well. Will it ever be possible for the Federal government to raise and maintain an army capable of establishing a tyranny over the majority of the People of an immense empire? Not if the People themselves are capable, through the medium of their state governments, of providing for their own defense with all the quickness, training, and organization of independent nations. But fear concerning something that unlikely can only be considered a disease that is beyond the ability to cure with simple arguments and reasoning.

—Publius

NUMBER 45

***

The Supposed Danger
to the State Governments from
the Proposed Powers of the Union

JAMES MADISON
For the Independent Journal
The Constitutional Convention and the New Federalism

Constitutional References:
Article I: §2/1 | §3/1 | §8/1—Article II: §1/2

Having already shown that none of the powers to be transferred to the new Federal government are unnecessary or improper, the next question to be considered is whether *all* of the powers as a whole could pose a threat to the authority being left to the states.

Instead of trying to figure out the amount of power that is absolutely necessary for the new Federal government to have, the adversaries of the Constitution have instead spent their time questioning the possible consequences of leaving the states with the amount of power that has been proposed.

But if the Union, as has been shown, is essential to the secu-

FEDERALIST NO. 45

The Message: The federal government will not be able to infringe on the rights maintained by the states because the central government has only very specific powers. Local governments should be most directly involved in the lives of the people than should the federal government.

———————

The Original Text: "The number of individuals employed under the Constitution of the United States will be much smaller than the number employed under the particular States. There will consequently be less of personal influence on the side of the former than of the latter."

Relevance to Today: While total State government employees (3.8 million) still outnumber total federal government employees (2.8 million), the gap is nowhere near as large as the Founders intended—and both levels of government are far larger. Because the federal government exerts so much power but is so distant from the people and the consequences of its laws, the government is far less responsive to the people, far less efficient, and far less capable of real change.

———————

The Original Text: "The State governments may be regarded as constituent and essential parts of the federal government; whilst the latter is nowise essential to the operation or organization of the former."

Relevance to Today: This equation seems to have been stood on its head. Our Republic was structured so that the federal government would be unable to function without the states, but the states would function just fine without the feds. But now? From federal subsidies for Medicaid to federal funding for education and transportation, the states are completely reliant on Washington. We can never push back toward the vision of our Founders unless we first push for financial independence of the states.

rity of the People of America against foreign danger; if it is essential to their security against disputes and wars between the states; if it is essential to guard them against the violent and oppressive factions that poison the blessings of liberty, and against the military establishments that gradually poison liberty's fountain; if, in a word, the Union is essential to the *happiness* of the People of America, then isn't it ridiculous to object to the government which will accomplish all of those things on the grounds that it might belittle the importance of the individual state governments?

Was the American Revolution carried out, was the Confederacy formed, was the precious blood of thousands spilled, and the hard-earned livelihoods of millions generously sacrificed, not so that the People of America could enjoy peace, liberty, and safety, but so that the individual state and city governments might enjoy a certain amount of power and be arrayed with certain dignities and attributes of sovereignty?

We have heard the ungodly doctrine of the Old World that the People were made for kings, not kings for the People. Will this same doctrine be revived in a new shape in the New World? Will the happiness of the People once again be sacrificed to the views of political institutions—just institutions of a different form? It is too early for politicians to already be forgetting that the public good, the real welfare of the great body of the People, is the supreme goal of government, and that no form of government has any value whatsoever if it is not capable of accomplishing this goal.

If the Plan of the Constitutional Convention was detrimental to public happiness, then I would raise my voice and advocate that it be rejected. If the Union itself was inconsistent with the public happiness, then my same voice would call for it to be abolished. In the same way, since the sovereignty of the states can't be reconciled with the happiness of the People, the voice of every good citizen must be. Let state sovereignty be sacrificed for happiness. Exactly how much sovereignty needs to be sacrificed has already been shown—the question now is whether or not the residue of sovereignty that we've not yet relinquished has been put in danger.

Several important points have already been touched on in these papers that refute the theory that the Federal government will gradually prove fatal to the state governments. In fact, the more I think about it, the more convinced I am that it's increasingly likely that the balance will be disturbed more often by the state governments than by the Federal government.

Past confederacies demonstrate that the members of those governments typically exhibited the strongest tendency to hijack authority from the central government, while the central governments were typically unable to effectively defend themselves against the power-grabs of their members. Although the systems of governments which were used in most of these examples were so different than the one we are considering that it makes them difficult to compare, they should not be entirely discounted since a large portion of active sovereignty will be retained by the states under the Constitution.

It is likely that the federal head of the Achaean League had a level and type of power that made it rather similar to the government framed by our Constitutional Convention. The Lycian Confederacy must have been even more similar to ours based on its principles and form. Yet history proves that neither of them formed into one consolidated government. On the contrary, we know that one of them was ruined by the inability of the federal authority to prevent the local quarrels, and finally the disbanding of the members. These examples are made even more relevant because the external causes that brought the individual parts together were much greater and more powerful than in our case.

That made it possible for the internal ties that bound each member to the central authority and to each other to not have to be as strong.

We have seen similar examples with a feudal system. Notwithstanding the lack of appropriate sympathy between local leaders and the People, and sometimes between the king and the People, it was usually the case that the local leaders were able to prevail in their rivalry with the king. If external dangers had not brought about and enforced some level of internal harmony and submission on the part of the local leaders toward the king, and particularly if the local leaders had ever won the love of the People, then the great kingdoms of Europe would instead be just a collection of independent princes.

The state governments will most likely have the advantage over the Federal government in most cases, whether we compare the immediate dependence each of them will have on the other, the amount of personal influence they will each have, the powers respectively vested in either of them, the preference and probable support of the People, or finally the tendency and ability which each will have to resist and obstruct the actions of the other.

The state governments may be regarded as integral and essential parts of the Federal government, while, on the other hand, the Federal government is not essential to the operation and organization of the state governments. Without the intervention of the state legislatures, the President of the United States will not even be able to be elected.[1] States will always have a great role to play in his appointment, and will perhaps actually determine who the President is in most cases. The Senate will be elected exclusively by the state legislatures.[2] Even the House of Representatives, though

---

1. United States Constitution: Article II, Section 1, clause 2.
2. United States Constitution: Article I, Section 3, clause 1.

directly elected by the People,[1] will be elected under the influence of the same types of men whose influence over the People had been integral in getting them elected into the state legislatures as well. Therefore, each of the principal Branches of the Federal government will more or less owe its existence to the support of the state governments, and will therefore feel a dependence on them which is more likely to be characterized by compliance than any sort of domineering attitude. Also, the component parts of the state governments will in no way be appointed through the direct actions of the Federal government, and will be subject very little, if at all, to the local influence of their members.

The number of individuals who will be employed under the Constitution of the United States will be far smaller than the number of people employed by the states. Consequently, there will be less personal influence on the side of the Federal government when compared with the state governments. Consider those to be hired by the thirteen (and eventually more) states: the members of the legislative, executive, and judicial branches, the justices of the People, officers of the militia, other justice officials, along with all of the county, corporation, and town officers—and all for three million or more citizens who are so familiar with every class and circle of people. This must dramatically exceed, both in number and influence, every possible type of person who will be employed in the administration of the Federal government.

Upon comparing the members of the three branches of power in each of the thirteen states (not including justices of the peace under the judicial branches) with the members of the corresponding Branches of the single government of the Union; or the number of militia officers of three million people with the probable, or even the possible number of military and naval officers of the

---

1. United States Constitution: Article I, Section 2, clause 1.

Union (from any establishment), it's obvious that the states have a decisive advantage. If the Federal government has officers in charge of collecting revenue, then the state governments will have theirs as well. But since there will only be a few Federal revenue collectors and they will be primarily concentrated on the seacoast, while there will be many state revenue collectors who will be spread throughout the whole country, then, again, it's obvious that the advantage still belongs to the states.

It is true that the Union will possess, and may exercise, the power of collecting both internal and external taxes throughout the states.[1] But it is likely that this power will not be used except to provide a supplemental source of revenue, after which the states will be given the option to collect the remaining tax revenues they need via the same types of taxes, and that the actual collection of taxes under the immediate authority of the Union will generally be carried out by state officers who must act according to the laws of each state. It is extremely likely that in other instances, particularly in organizing the Judiciary, state officers will be invested with the corresponding authority of the Union. However, should the Federal government appoint its own revenue collectors, the influence of that group as a whole would not be able to compare with the far greater number of state officers on the opposite side of the scale. Within every district that a Federal revenue collector may be assigned, there would be at least 30–40 state officers of all types, many of whom would be important, reputable people with great influence on the states.

The powers delegated by the proposed Constitution to the Federal government are few and defined. Those which are to remain with the state governments are numerous and undefined. The powers of the Federal government will be primarily concen-

---

1. United States Constitution: Article I, Section 8, clause 1.

trated on external matters, such as war, peace, diplomatic negotiation, and foreign commerce, which the power of taxation will,
for the most part, be connected with. The powers reserved to the
states will extend to all the objects normally concerning the lives,
liberties, and properties of the People, as well as the internal order,
improvement, and prosperity of the states themselves.

The operations of the Federal government will be at their
most extensive and important in times of war and danger, while
those of the state governments will be the most important in times
of peace and security. Since periods of war and danger will probably occur much less than times of peace and security, the state
governments will enjoy yet another advantage over the Federal
government. In fact, the more the Federal government's powers
are adequate for the national defense, the less frequently we'll be
in the periods of danger that require the Federal government to
use its maximum amount of power.

If the new Constitution is accurately and honestly examined
then it's obvious that the biggest change that it proposes is not so
much the addition of NEW POWERS to the Union, but rather the
revitalization of its ORIGINAL POWERS. It is true that the regulation of commerce is a new power, but it seems to be one that is
opposed by few and feared by no one. The powers related to war
and peace, armies and fleets, treaties and finance, along with the
other important powers, already exist within the existing congress
under the Articles of Confederation. The proposed changes do
not enlarge these powers, but merely substitute a more effective
method of administering them. The changes related to taxation
are probably the most important. While the current congress
has had the complete authority to REQUIRE unlimited amounts
of money from the states for the common defense and general
welfare (the quota and requisition system), the future Congress
will have just as much authority to require money from indi-

vidual citizens. But citizens will be no more bound than the states themselves have been to pay any of the quotas that are imposed on them. Had the states promptly complied with the Articles of Confederation, or if their compliance could have been peacefully enforced in a way that would also be successful on individual citizens, then they would have eventually lost their constitutional powers and would have gradually been consolidated under the federal government—a conclusion that is not supported by our experiences. To insist that such an event would have happened under the old system would be the same as saying that the state governments can never exist under any system of government that accomplishes the essential purposes of the Union.

—Publius

FEDERALIST NO. 46

The Message: The power of the state governments is greater than that of the federal government, which is supposed to be a distant and largely insignificant force in our daily lives.

Original Quote: "[It's] beyond doubt that the first and most natural attachment of the people will be to the governments of their respective States. . . . With the affairs of these, the people will be more familiarly and minutely conversant."

Relevance to Today: Instead of having a "natural attachment" to our local government, many Americans often turn to the federal government for assistance. From disaster relief to food stamps to Medicare, individual reliance on Washington has convinced many that the federal government is an indispensable part of their lives.

Original Quote: "But ambitious encroachments of the federal government, on the authority of the State governments, would not excite the opposition of a single State, or of a few States only. They would be signals of general alarm. Every government would espouse the common cause. A correspondence would be opened. Plans of resistance would be concerted. One spirit would animate and conduct the whole. . . . But what degree of madness could ever drive the federal government to such an extremity."

Relevance to Today: In answering critics who believed that the federal government could become too powerful, Publius reasoned that this could not happen because the States would undoubtedly resist the challenge to their authority. But he was wrong. By making States (and individuals) financially dependent on them, they've been able to usurp their rights without so much as whimper.

How can the balance of power be restored? First, by each state's becoming financially independent and saying "no" to blackmail disguised as support; and second, by states' using lawsuits and other constitutional powers to stand up to Washington. The lawsuits against the health care bill are an example of how this can work in practice.

The Relative Influence
of the Federal and State Governments
(Continued)

JAMES MADISON

For the New York Packet: Tuesday, January 29, 1788
The Constitutional Convention and the New Federalism

Constitutional References:
Article I: §8/16

Continuing with the subject of Federal and state power, I now want to examine which group has the advantage when it comes to obtaining the support of the People.

Putting aside for the moment the different ways in which both of these governments are appointed, we must consider that both are substantially dependent on the majority of the citizens of the United States. For now I will assume this is true with respect to the Federal government and I will provide proof of that later.

The Federal and state governments are in fact simply different agents and trustees of the People, and, as such, are instituted with different powers and designated for different purposes. The adversaries of the Constitution seem to have completely lost sight of the People in their arguments, and seem to view the different Federal and state establishments as not only mutual rivals and enemies, but also as being able to undermine each other without answering to any superior force. Those who have made these arguments are wrong. They must understand that the ultimate authority, no matter where any of its derivatives may be found, resides in the People alone, and that it does not come from nor depend upon the different governments, or whether either of them is able to grow their power at the expense of the other. Truth and decency require that their actions should depend on the support and the approval of their common constituents.

Many considerations, not including those which have been suggested in previous papers, seem to prove beyond any doubt that the first and most natural attachment of the People will be to their respective state governments. A greater number of citizens will be expected to serve in state administrations than in the Federal one and, as a gift of these state governments, a greater amount of offices and compensation will follow. All of the domestic and personal interests of the People will be regulated and provided for via oversight of the state governments. The People will be much more familiar with the details of their state's affairs, and a greater proportion of them will either be connected by family or party ties, or personally acquainted with, or have as friends members of their state's government. Therefore, the popular bias of the People will more likely bend toward their state.

Experience teaches us the same lesson. While it has been defective in comparison with what we hope for under a better system, the federal administration (under the Articles of Confederation), both during the war, and particularly when paper money was being independently issued as credit, carried out actions and had an importance as great as it will ever have, no matter what the future may hold. It was also engaged in a series of actions that were entirely meant to protect everything we hold dear, as well as acquire everything that could be desirable to the People at large. However, after the short-lived enthusiasm for the first Congresses came to an end, it was nearly always the case that the attention and attachment of the People again turned toward their own state governments. The Congress was never exactly the idol of public popularity, and those who wished to build up their own political importance on the prejudices of their fellow citizens were typically the ones who were also against the proposed enlargements of Congress's powers and importance.

If, in the future, the People begin to prefer the Federal government to their own state governments, it is very likely the Federal government is being run better. If that is the case, the People should not be prevented from giving their support to those whom they feel are most worthy of it. But, even if this were the case, the state governments would have little to fear because the powers of the Federal government could only be advantageously used within a certain jurisdiction.

The remaining points I want to cover on this topic concern the tendencies and abilities that the Federal and state governments would have to resist and thwart the actions of the other.

It has already been proven that the members of the Federal government will be more dependent on the members of the state governments, not vice versa. It also seems as if the support of the People, on whom both governments will depend, will be more on the side of the state governments than the Federal government. Insofar as the tendencies of each government toward the other may be influenced by this support, the state governments obviously have the advantage.

There is also another distinct and very important viewpoint that leaves the advantage with the states. The biases of everyone who will serve in the Federal government will generally be favorable toward the states, while those who serve in the state governments will rarely have a bias in favor of the Federal government. A local bias will always be much more prevalent in the members of Congress than a National bias will be prevalent in the legislatures of the states.

It's common knowledge that many of the errors committed by the state legislatures resulted from the tendencies of their members to sacrifice the overall and permanent interests of the state to the particular and separate interests of the counties or districts which they represented. And if they cannot even take into account the overall welfare of their own state, then how can we think they'll take into account the overall prosperity of the Union, as well as the dignity and respectability of the Federal government, in their actions and discussions? For the same reason that it is unlikely that the members of the state legislatures will adequately consider the interests of the Union, the members of Congress will also likely be too attached to their own local concerns. The states will be to Congress what the counties and towns are to the states. Government actions will too often be taken with the prejudices, interests, and pursuits of the governments and people of the individual states in mind instead of National prosperity and happiness.

What has been the spirit which has generally characterized the proceedings of the current congress? A brief glance through their journals, as well as the candid acknowledgments of those who have served in the current congress, reveal that its members have more often acted like partisans of their respective states rather than as objective guardians of a common interest. While there have been occasional examples of local interests being improperly sacrificed for the sake of aggrandizing the federal government, it's clear that, overall, the interests of the nation have suffered a hundred times more because of an inappropriate and excessive amount of attention being focused on the local prejudices, interests, and views of the individual states.

I don't mean to imply that the new Federal government will not embrace a larger and more comprehensive policy than the current federal government, or even that its views will be as biased as those of the state legislatures. I am simply trying to point out that the new Federal government will do both things to a degree that is unlikely to invade the rights of the individual states, or the powers of their governments. Any attempt on the part of the state governments to increase their power via appropriations of money from the Federal government will be thwarted by the lack of support for this among members of the Federal government.

If we were, however, to assume that the Federal government may feel the same tendency to extend its power beyond their proper limits as the state governments, then the state governments would still have the advantage. If any particular state acted in an unfriendly way toward the Federal government, and if that action was popular and did not violate the oaths of the state officials too much, then that action would be executed immediately on the spot, and its success would depend on the state alone. If the Federal government was opposed to this action, or if Federal officials attempted to interfere, that would just inflame the passions of all of those who were on the side of the state, and the evil could not be prevented or corrected without employing methods that must always be used as a last resort. Then again, if the Federal government engaged in unwarranted actions that were unpopular in particular states (which would happen often), or even in warranted actions that were still unpopular (which might sometimes be the case), then the states would have powerful means at their disposal to oppose such actions. The uneasiness of the People, along with their hatred of, and perhaps refusal to cooperate with, officers of the Union, the disapproval of the state's executives, and the embarrassments that might result from any legislative actions of Congress meant to help smooth over such a situation, would all come together in a large state to create very serious obstacles to the Federal government. If the views of several neighboring states happened to be in unison, then yet another obstacle would be created that the Federal government would likely be very unwilling to take on.

If the Federal government ever ambitiously intrudes on the authority of the state governments, then not only would the opposition of a single state or a few states rally, but a general alarm would sound for all states. Every government would espouse a common cause, communication between them would open up, resistance plans would be organized together, and all states would come together with a single purpose. In short, the same rallying together which would occur if there was danger of foreign oppression would also result from a fear of Federal oppression. Unless the intrusions of the Federal government were voluntarily abandoned, then the appeal to force that would occur in response to foreign oppression would also occur in response to oppression from the Federal government.

But what degree of madness could ever drive the Federal government to such extremes? In the war against Great Britain, one part of the empire was fighting against the other, and the more populated part had invaded the rights of the less populated part. And while the attempt on the part of the British could certainly be labeled as unjust and unwise, it was also never considered absolutely unrealistic either. In our own example, what would be the source of conflict? Who would the different sides be? A few representatives of the People would be opposed to the People themselves, or rather one set of representatives would be fighting against thirteen sets of representatives, with the whole body of the People being on the side of the thirteen.

The only option left for those who prophesy the downfall of the state governments is the imaginary claim that the Federal government may have previously built up a military force for the purposes of its own ambition. The arguments in these papers must have been pretty useless if it is now necessary to disprove such an imaginary danger. In order for such a plan to succeed, it would require that the People and the states should, for an adequate period of time, elect an uninterrupted series of representatives who would be ready to betray them both. It would require that throughout this whole time the traitors would have had to uniformly and systematically pursue some agreed-upon plan to enlarge and strengthen the military establishment. And it would require that the governments and the People of the states would silently and patiently observe the gathering storm, all the while continuing to supply it with the materials it needed until it's finally ready to burst on their own heads. This theory must appear to everyone to be the incoherent dreams of a delirious jealousy, or the mistaken exaggerations of some fake passion or enthusiasm, rather than the fears of a genuine patriotism.

As outlandish as this hypothesis is, let's assume for the moment that it is true. Let's say that a regular army, fully equal to the resources of the country, was formed, and let's even say that it was fully devoted to the Federal government. Even then, it would not be going too far to say that the state governments, with the People on their side, would be able to repel the danger. According to the best calculations, the greatest number of men who could be a part of such an army would not exceed one-hundredth of the entire population, or one-twenty-fifth of those who are able to bear arms. In the United States, this proportion would yield an army not greater than 25,000 or 30,000 men. Matched against this army would be a militia of nearly half a million citizens with arms in their hands, whose officers would be men chosen from amongst themselves, who would be fighting for their common liberties, and who would be united under and directed by the state governments, which would have both their love and their confidence. It should be doubted whether a militia like that could ever be conquered by regular troops.

Those who are most familiar with this country's successful resistance against the arms of Great Britain will be inclined to say that it would be impossible to defeat such a militia. In addition to the advantage of being armed (an advantage Americans have over the people of almost every other nation in the world), the existence of subordinate governments that have the support of the People, and by which militia officers will be appointed,[1] will together form a barrier against the ambitious plans of the Federal government, a barrier which will be more insurmountable than any that a simple government of any form would be capable of.

Not including the actual military establishments in some of the kingdoms of Europe (which are maintained as much as public resources will allow), the governments of Europe are quite simply afraid to trust the People with arms. Even then, it is not certain that if they were able to bear arms they would be able to defeat their oppressors. But, if the European people had the additional advantage of local governments that they had chosen, as well as militia officers who were appointed by those governments and loyal to them and to the militia, it could be confidently claimed that every tyrannical throne in Europe would be quickly overthrown in spite of the legions of regular troops which surround them.

---

1. United States Constitution: Article I, Section 8, clause 16.

Let's not insult the free and thoughtful citizens of America by suspecting that they would be less capable of defending the rights they have already earned for themselves than the violated and oppressed subjects of arbitrary power in Europe would be able to rescue theirs from the hands of their oppressors. Also, let's not insult the people of America by assuming that they would blindly submit to the many insidious actions that would have to occur before they ever took up arms in the first place.

My arguments on this subject can be stated very briefly and conclusively: Either the Federal government will be constructed in such a way that will render it sufficiently dependent on the People, or it will not. If it is made sufficiently dependent on the People, then that very dependence will keep it from engaging in schemes that are offensive to its constituents. On the other hand, if it is not appropriately dependent on the People, it will not possess their confidence, and any attempts on its part to usurp power will be easily defeated by the state governments, who will be supported by the People.

Summing up the thoughts of these last two papers, they both present convincing evidence that the powers that will be delegated to the Federal government will be just as capable of accomplishing the purposes of the Union as they will be incapable of threatening the powers that will remain with the states. They also show that the alarms that have been sounded concerning a gradual annihilation of the state governments by the Federal government are, even with the most generous benefit of the doubt, the result of the irrational and imaginary fears of those who sounded them in the first place.

—Publius

PART FIVE

MINIMUM GOVERNMENT, MAXIMUM FREEDOM

These days it seems as though the federal government is eager to get its hands on just about every aspect of our lives. From the fuel efficiency of our cars to the temperature of our homes and the trans-fat content of our food, the long arm of federal government continues to invade our personal liberty in ways our Founders never imagined.

But it wasn't always this way. In this section of Papers we take a look at Publius's views on limited government—from the proper role of the federal government to the separation of power among its branches to the limited powers of the president. We also look at two of the most counterintuitive arguments made in the Papers: why a bill of rights should be *excluded* while a clause empowering the government to pass any law "necessary and proper" should be *included*. As you'll see, the answers are not as cut-and-dried as many might think.

All Politics Are Local

Beyond the philosophical reasons for opposing federal encroachment into states' rights, Publius hoped to create a central government that could contribute to the people's happiness. They realized, however, that this happiness could never be cultivated through a "one-size-fits-all" approach to local issues. After all, having bureaucrats and decision makers who are far removed from the citizens who are impacted by their decisions can be a recipe for disaster.

The Founders understood that local control of local matters makes for far more responsive and agile government—and far happier people. This should strike most of us as common sense, but perhaps human nature has other ideas. How else can you explain why the power of state governments has been shrinking while the power, size, and reach of the federal government has been expanding?

Hamilton also understood that both tiers of government need to work hand in hand. The federal government, for example, depends on the states to implement national policies at the local level. Whether through the Electoral College, the appointment of senators by states, concurrent jurisdiction with the states regarding internal taxation, or states' ability to commission officers of the militia (even though the militia itself is under federal control), the states should breathe life into the federal government, not the other way around. It stands to reason, therefore, that the states should have a say not only in the policies, but also in the best way to execute them. As President Reagan said, "All of us need to be reminded that the federal government did not create the states; the states created the federal government."

But despite his immense talent and wisdom, Hamilton possibly might have put a bit too much faith in the idea that the states—or the American people themselves—would rise up to stop the federal government from encroaching on their rights. Or perhaps Hamilton simply could not imagine that a majority of voters would one day be conned by an increasingly sophisticated and duplicitous government made up of representatives who, by and large, put party and power above principles.

The Federalist Papers make it clear that Publius strongly believed in the states and federal government balancing out each other's power. Neither would allow the other to become too big or powerful. In fact, Publius surmised, the balance would likely be tipped in favor of the states because they were closest to the people. As Hamilton wrote in Federalist 17: "Upon the same principle that a man is more attached to his family than to his neighborhood, to his neighborhood than to the community at large, the people of each State would be apt to feel a stronger bias towards their local governments than towards the government of the Union . . ."

If a showdown ever occurred, Hamilton believed, the people would likely side with the states over the federal government. The people saw their state politicians every day, and they were impacted by the laws those politicians made and had to abide by the tax rates they set. For the most part, Publius didn't foresee—and could *not* have foreseen—a day in which a debt-laden, money-printing federal government would literally bribe states into agreeing with policies. Whether it's federal highway funds, stimulus grants, or "Race to the Top" money, the federal government routinely uses bribes as a way to spread its influence.

In December 2010, the United States Congress passed the innocuous-sounding "Healthy, Hunger-Free Kids Act of 2010." First Lady Michelle Obama called it a "groundbreaking" bill that would "significantly improve the quality of meals that children receive at school and will play an integral role in our efforts to combat childhood obesity."

Healthy children—what an admirable goal. But the devil is in the details. Among other things, the bill allows the federal government to regulate the kind of foods that can be sold at kids' public school fund-raisers and bake sales. That's right, if the federal government had its way, there'd be no more chocolate bars sold to fund a Little League trip or brownies made to fund new cheerleader uniforms.

But set aside the politics of that idea for a minute, because that forces us into a debate about individual parties and politicians.

Instead, focus on how a bill like that can coexist with the balance of powers set out in the Constitution and passionately defended by Publius. The Founders never foresaw that our federal government would one day have a say in the calories and fat content of our foods, or dictate our health care, or seize our private property. It was obvious, Publius maintained, that the federal government would deal with federal issues and state and local governments would deal with, well, state and local issues.

The idea that some politician in our nation's capital would have an interest in making laws that restrict the choices and freedoms of individuals at the state level was quickly dismissed by Hamilton. "Even if I allowed for the greatest amount of love of power possible for any reasonable man," he wrote in Federalist 17, "I confess that I don't know of any reason why anyone of authority within the General government would ever wish to take for themselves any of the states' powers."

It's kind of funny—the authors of the Federalist Papers readily admitted the fallibility of man and the need for checks and balances yet were somehow unable to fathom why someone would ever attempt to take power from the states. In the minds of Hamilton, Madison, and Jay, the balance of power was such that all sides would have enough, and no side could ever push forward so long as the other two were in place. This was true for both the overall structure behind the government (with power held by the federal government, the state government, and the people) and the structure of the federal government itself.

The Delicate Balance of Power

If you've ever played "rock, paper, scissors" then you know that the game works because no one item can dominate. They each have the power to check the other two. The Founders believed in a similar setup. It wasn't enough to erect "parchment barriers," as Madison dubbed them. No, the Founders realized that the structure would work only if the three branches of government—legislative, executive, and judicial—possessed legitimate and ready powers of defense that would ensure one branch could not run roughshod over the others. Hence the Constitution's separation of powers. Each branch of government possesses separated powers that have the ability to curb the other branches' powers.

When one branch tries to overstep its bounds and lurch into areas outside its scope, the consequences can be unconstitutional and dangerous. Blur the separated powers between the executive and judicial branches, for example, and the judicial branch could selectively enforce the laws they favor and ignore those they don't.

Without a clear separation of powers, the United States would be subject to the negative effects of intergovernmental alliances or encroachments. In Federalist 47, Madison argued that the consequence of commingling powers would be catastrophic. "The accumulation of all powers legislative, executive, and judiciary," he wrote, "in the same hands, whether of one, a few, or many, and whether hereditary, self-appointed, or elective, may justly be pronounced the very definition of tyranny."

But Madison felt strongly that the Constitution provided enough safeguards to ensure that the separation of powers would always remain in place. He used No. 47 to combat critics who argued that the separation should be more absolute, by going constitution to constitution among the existing state documents and pointing out that none of them separate their branches completely; there would always be some overlap.

Aside from concerns over balance of power between the three branches, there was also grave concern that labeling our new leader as a "president" was simply a nicer way of saying "tyrant." Tyranny, of course, was on everyone's mind given what they'd all just been through. Preventing it, therefore, was a top priority.

Hamilton, Madison, and Jay knew they had to allay New Yorkers' fear that the new constitution might carve out a presidential role that could morph into that of a king—so they used Federalist 69 to do just that. Brilliantly written by Hamilton, this essay lines up the constitutional concerns surrounding this point like dominoes and knocks them down one by one through a series of contrasts showing how the Constitution will make a U.S. president anything but a king.

His arguments are convincing, and history has proven that he was mostly correct. But there are, of course, exceptions to every rule. Or, in this case, it might be more accurate to say that there are workarounds for every rule you don't like. Take declaring war, for example. In highlighting the limited power of the president, Hamilton explained that, unlike the British king, our presidents did not have the power to declare war; only to direct the military as commander in chief:

> It would amount to nothing more than the supreme command and direction of the military and naval forces, as first General and admiral of the Confederacy; while that of the British king extends to the declaring of war and to the raising and regulating of fleets and armies—all which, by the Constitution under consideration, would appertain to the legislature.

But look at how that has played out in real life. Congress has not formally declared war since World War II. Instead, one of two things has happened, neither of which is authorized by the Constitution: The president makes a decision to use force all on his own (i.e., Obama in Libya) and Congress sits idly by; or Congress authorizes an action but does not call it a "war" (i.e., Bush in Iraq and Afghanistan).

The Good and Plenty Clause

It's not just the executive branch that has sought to increase its power over the years—the legislative branch has been complicit as well. Instead of laws being contemplated according to their constitutionality, the thinking instead seems to be that Congress should pass whatever laws they like and worry about the courts later.

The basis for this view is almost always the so-called "necessary and proper clause" (I like to call it the "good and plenty clause" because people try to use it to justify all sorts of goodies not called for in the Constitution). Ask many who support universal health care as a basic right just where in the constitution this right is detailed and they almost inevitably point to this clause. So, with the help of Alexander Hamilton, let's set the record straight. Article I, Section 8, clause 18 of the U.S. Constitution states:

> The Congress shall have Power—To make all Laws which shall be necessary and proper for carrying into Execution the foregoing Powers, and all other Powers vested by this Constitution in the Government of the United States, or in any Department or Officer thereof.

Some have used these forty-five words to argue that the federal government can make any law it pleases. In fact, even back during the debate over the ratification, many people feared that this clause would one day be viewed as giving the federal government the power to essentially do whatever it wants. But Hamilton, writing in Federalist 33, begged to differ.

And yet despite all this hollering, strange as it may sound, I can say with perfect confidence that the constitutional operation of the proposed government would be the exact same if these two clauses ["necessary and proper" and "supreme law of the land"] were entirely eliminated as it would if they were repeated in every single article.

In other words, for all the controversy caused by this clause, it had absolutely no meaning. The only reason it was being included was to make it perfectly clear that the federal government had the power to make the laws it needed to enforce the powers it was being given.

Imagine, for example, that you gave your brother the authorization to access your home when you're away. In order for him to utilize that power he might have to do a series of things that you did not specifically mention. He might have to borrow a key, drive to your house, disarm the alarm system, and so on. What the Constitution was merely saying was that all of those things that are necessary and proper for carrying out the powers that had been granted were okay. Without giving Congress that power it would be like giving someone a gun but not telling them where the bullets are. You need both the weapon and the ammunition in order to exert force.

When you read Federalist 33, you can almost picture Alexander Hamilton sitting at his candlelit desk, quill in one hand, with a face like, "Seriously? Do I really even have to explain this? Really?" He even calls the clause "perfectly harmless," and surmises that the entire reason the Convention even included it was to prevent states from later trying to take the lawmaking power away from Congress so they'd be left with nothing but a litany of powers that they couldn't enforce. In other words, the intent of this clause was to ensure that the proposed union would actually happen and that the states would not be able to derail the process after the fact.

The Case Against a Bill of Rights

Is it hard to imagine that someone could actually make a compelling case *against* including a Bill of Rights in the Constitution? After all, principles like freedom of speech, freedom of the press, the right to bear arms, and the right to a speedy trial are synonymous with our freedoms. If you're appalled that someone could be against listing those simple rights, then you might be surprised to find out who was making that case: Alexander Hamilton.

Hamilton's case may be counterintuitive, but it had merit for two main reasons. First, our rights come directly from God. They are *endowed by our Creator*. Listing them as part of a document that lays out the power the people are lending to their government implies that somehow the government has control over these basic rights.

Second, Hamilton argued in Federalist 84, the Constitution's scope was to be so narrow, and the powers it granted government so few, that "a detailed Bill of Rights is not required." By including one, people might interpret that the Framers were intending the Constitution to control "all sorts of personal and private matters." That was obviously not the case.

Hamilton strongly believed that the minute you attempted to create a list of rights, you by default implied that anything *not* on the list was excluded. To think of it another way, it's the difference between telling your kids the five specific things they cannot do while you're away, versus telling them the five specific things they *can* do. Listing what they are restricted from (no alcohol, no driving the car, no playing the stereo loud) implies that anything not on that list is fair game. *Look, Mom and Dad forgot to say that we can't play with the handgun!*

On the other hand, telling them what they *can* do (which is akin to the Constitution granting specific powers to the government) does not allow them to claim that you implied they were allowed to play with the Glock.

Hamilton had another reason for not including a Bill of Rights as well: He worried that some power-lusting politician might "regulate" the rights that were listed, under the guise of "protecting" them. (This, of course, is exactly what has happened in many instances. Yes, FCC, I'm looking at you.)

While Hamilton's argument worked during ratification, the people quickly demanded a Bill of Rights be included. Ironically, it was Hamilton's writing partner, James Madison, who introduced them. They became law, in the form of the Constitution's first ten amendments, just two years later.

NUMBER 17

The True Tendencies of a Federal System

ALEXANDER HAMILTON

For the Independent Journal

The Weaknesses of the Current Confederation

Constitutional References:

Article VI: 2

The idea of directly legislating individual citizens of America, or in other words, passing legislation that would apply to every citizen of this country in every state, is one of the objections raised against the Constitution.[1] It could be argued that such a principle allows the government of the Union to become too powerful, making it possible for it to infringe on the powers that would be best left with the states for local purposes. However, even if I allowed for the greatest amount of love of power possible in a reasonable man, I confess that I don't know of any reason why those in authority within the General government would wish to take for themselves any of the states' powers. It doesn't seem likely to me that anyone would be enticed by the thought of

---

1. United States Constitution: Article VI, clause 2.

FEDERALIST NO. 17

The Message: A new, stronger union is necessary, but the states will still have more power than the federal government and will certainly have the loyalty of the people on their side.

Original Quote: "There is one transcendant advantage belonging to the province of the State governments, which alone suffices to place the matter in a clear and satisfactory light,—I mean the ordinary administration of criminal and civil justice. This, of all others, is the most powerful, most universal, and most attractive source of popular obedience and attachment."

Relevance to Today: Matters related to law and justice were expected to be handled at the local level, thereby creating a strong relationship between the people and their local/state governments. But the federal government has stepped in over time and has increasingly been trying to move issues such as abortion, gay rights, nutrition, and even zoning questions into the federal courts.

Original Quote: "Allowing the utmost latitude to the love of power which any reasonable man can require, I confess I am at a loss to discover what temptation the persons intrusted with the administration of the general government could ever feel to divest the States of the authorities of that description."

Relevance to Today: A power grab by politicians at the federal level was something that our Founders could not really comprehend. Why would a national politician care about taking power from individual states when the good of the union demanded that power be shared along the lines specifically laid out by the Constitution? Today, of course, those lines are constantly shifting, with the federal government playing a more active role than ever in activities, such as transportation and education, that used to be under the sole authority of the states.

controlling the local police of any state. Power over commerce, finance, diplomacy, and war appear to be a complete list of all the things ambitious men wish to control, and the power necessary to control such things ought to belong to the National government in the first place.

On the other hand, things such as the administration of private justice between citizens of the same state, the regulation of agriculture, etc., things that can be taken care of by local legislation, are not things that the General authority would desire to control. Therefore, it is unlikely that the Federal government would have a tendency to take from the states the powers required to manage such things. Any attempt to do so would be as difficult as it would be worthless and possessing those powers would contribute nothing to the dignity, importance, or majesty of the National government.

For the sake of argument, let's say that out of sheer depravity and lust for domination, the Central government desired to possess those powers. Even then it would be safe to say that the wisdom of the National representatives, and thus of the People themselves, would control such an unlimited appetite for power. It will always be easier for the state governments to intrude on the powers of the National government than for the National government to intrude on the powers of the states. This is proven by the great level of influence that the state governments generally have over the People, so long as they govern well. This shows us that there is an inherent weakness in all federal constitutions, so we must be very careful in how we organize it, and provide it with a level of force that is both necessary and compatible with the principles of liberty.

With this said, the state governments would have greater influence partly because of the spread-out nature of the National government, but mostly because of the day-to-day matters that they would administer themselves.

The further away or more spread out something is, the less we tend to care about it. This is a common aspect of human nature. Just as someone is more attached to their family than their neighborhood, and to their neighborhood more than their town or city, the People of each state will most likely have a strong bias in favor of their local governments rather than toward the government of the Union, unless of course the government of the Union was managed much better than their own local governments. Given this powerful tendency of the human heart, the People will likely be more attached to those things that the states will regulate.

The state governments have another advantage: the ordinary and day-to-day administration of criminal and civil justice. More than anything else, this offers nations a universal and attractive source of popular obedience and devotion. Because of its visible protection of life and property (both of which are constantly desired), and its regulation of all the most familiar and personal interests that people care most about, it contributes more than anything else to the love, admiration, and reverence people have toward government. This great cement of society, widespread among all of the states, will also ensure that the state governments have an advantage in gaining their citizens' love and respect. Because of this, the states will end up being an equalizing and frequently dangerous rival to the power of the Union.

The activities of the National government will be less obvious to the majority of citizens, and thus the benefits it provides will mostly be felt by more thinking men. Since their activities will relate more to general interests, the Federal government will be proportionally less likely to "come home," as it were, in the hearts and minds of the People, and will therefore fail to attract as strong a sense of obligation or respect. This opinion is backed up by all the examples of the federal constitutions that we are aware of, as well as by many other examples.

Strictly speaking the ancient feudal systems were not confederacies, but they did share some of the characteristics of a confederacy. There was one common head, the king or sovereign, with authority over the whole nation, several subordinate vassals who had large portions of land given to them were beneath him, and finally, numerous *lesser* vassals who, as long as they showed obedience to their lord, occupied and cultivated their own portion of land. Each major vassal was a sovereign of sorts within his own particular domain. The result of this situation was that the authority of the sovereign was constantly challenged, and there were also numerous wars between the great vassals (sometimes known as barons) themselves. The power of the leader of the nation was often too weak to preserve the public peace or to protect the People against the oppression of their own lords. This period of European history is correctly labeled by historians as the time of feudal anarchy.[1]

Sometimes, the sovereign happened to be an energetic and warlike man with superior abilities (i.e., such as Charlemagne), allowing him to have great personal weight and influence that temporarily makes up for the lack of a more established authority. In general, however, the power of the barons/vassals triumphed over the prince, and in many cases his authority was merely discarded and the great fiefs of his kingdom became independent territories or states. In those cases where the prince triumphed over his vassals, he succeeded because the vassals had used tyranny against their own people. The barons/vassals were just as much the en-

---

1. The time period during which feudalism was the dominant system was the Middle Ages, which lasted from the fifth to the fifteenth century (between the fall of the Western Roman Empire in 476 AD and the Early Modern Era between 1453 and 1789).

emies of the sovereign as they were the oppressors of the People, and were thus feared and hated by both until their mutual dangers and interests forced them to form a union between themselves that ultimately proved fatal to the power of the sovereign. Had the nobles been able to keep the loyalty of their dependents and followers by showing mercy and justice, any conflict between them and the prince would likely have ended in their victory, and in the weakening or overthrow of the royal authority.

This is not a claim based on mere speculation or my own imagination. Scotland provides another good example of its truth and accuracy. The clan-like spirit that existed early in that kingdom united the nobles and their people almost as if they were family and allowed the aristocracy to constantly outmatch the power of the monarch. Only the absorption of Scotland into England[1] restrained this fierce and ungovernable spirit so that it could be ruled over by a more rational and established system of civil politics, as had already existed in England for some time.

The separate states within our Confederacy can be accurately compared with the fiefs of the feudal vassals. Because of the things they administer, and the fact that these things result in obtaining the goodwill and confidence of the People, they will hold an advantage similar to the one held by feudal vassals and will therefore be able to effectively oppose any intrusions by the National government. On the other hand, it would be desirable for the states to be unable to counteract the legitimate and necessary authority of the National government. The main similarity between the states and the fiefs of the vassals is that they both represent a rival to the power of the Central authority, and they both reflect the way that

---

1. This full "absorption" became official on May 1, 1707, with the passage of the "Acts of Union" in both the Scottish and English parliaments, which created the United Kingdom of Great Britain. (Referenced in Federalist 5.)

large amounts of authority are concentrated into certain areas, one for the use of individuals, and the other for the use of political bodies.

A concise historical overview of confederate governments and the results they have had will further illustrate this important principle that has been the source of so many of our political mistakes and confusion, simply because we have not paid attention to it. I will provide this overview in the following papers.

—Publius

FEDERALIST NO. 33

The Message: The "necessary and proper" and "supreme law of the land" clauses are simple and clear and should not incite controversy except by those looking to change their meaning.

———————————

Original Quote: "What is a power, but the ability or faculty of doing a thing? What is the ability to do a thing, but the power of employing the *means* necessary to its execution? What is a LEGISLATIVE power, but a power of making LAWS? What are the *means* to execute a LEGISLATIVE power but LAWS? What is the power of laying and collecting taxes, but a *legislative power,* or a power of *making laws,* to lay and collect taxes? What are the proper means of executing such a power, but *necessary* and *proper* laws?"

Relevance to Today: The "necessary and proper" clause, which is now often used by people to support the idea that the federal government can essentially do anything it wants, was actually very narrow in scope. The intent of the clause was simply to give the federal government the ability to create the laws that would be necessary to enforce the specific powers it was being given. It might be good to remind lawmakers of this the next time they use this clause as justification for some far-reaching policy that has no constitutional basis.

Concerning the General Power of Taxation (Continued)

ALEXANDER HAMILTON

For the Daily Advertiser: Thursday, January 3, 1788

Explanation and Justification of the New Powers of the Union

Constitutional References:
Article I: §8/18 | §10/2—Article VI: 2

The remaining arguments against the taxation provisions in the Constitution are based on the following clauses:

Article I, Section 8, clause 18 authorizes Congress:

To make all laws which shall be *necessary and proper* for carrying into execution *the foregoing powers*, and all other powers vested by this Constitution in the government of the United States, or in any department or officer thereof.

Article VI, clause 2 reads:

This Constitution, and the laws of the United States which shall be made *in pursuance thereof*, and the treaties made . . . under

the authority of the United States, shall be the *supreme law* of
the land, anything in the Constitution or laws of any state to the
contrary notwithstanding.

These two clauses have triggered some of the harshest criticism of the Constitution. Critics have exaggerated, claiming that
their local governments will be destroyed and their liberties ex-
terminated, and represented this clause as if it were some hideous
monster whose hungry jaws will spare no one—no matter their
age, sex, height, or religious convictions. And yet despite all of
these criticisms, strange as it may sound, I can say with perfect
confidence that the proposed constitutional operation of the government would be exactly the same if these two clauses were entirely eliminated as it would if they were repeated in every single
article.

All they amount to is a statement of a truth that is necessary
and unavoidable by the very act of forming a constitutional Federal government and giving it certain powers. The arguments for
these two clauses are so obvious, that it's difficult for me to remain
calm in the face of the exceedingly hysterical rants made against
them.

What is power if not the ability, or the means to do something? What is the ability to do something if not the power of
using the *means* necessary to do it? What is a LEGISLATIVE
power if not the power to make LAWS? What are the *means* of executing a LEGISLATIVE power if not LAWS? What is the power
of imposing and collecting taxes if not a *legislative power*, or the
power of *making laws* to impose and collect taxes? What are the
appropriate means of executing such a power if not *necessary* and
proper laws?

This simple game of deduction allows us to see the true nature
of this clause that has caused so much complaining. It leads us to

an obvious truth: a power to impose and collect taxes must also be a power to pass all of the laws that are *necessary* and *proper* for the execution of that power. And what more does this hated and vilified clause do than simply state the truth, that Congress, which has the power to impose and collect taxes, is granted the right to pass all the laws which are *necessary* and *proper* to put that power into effect?

I have applied this reasoning specifically to the power of taxation because it is the most important authority to be given to the Union. This same line of reasoning will lead to the same result with all of the other powers that are listed in the Constitution, and it is *precisely* in order to execute those powers that the so-called sweeping clause,[1] authorizing Congress to pass all *necessary and proper* laws, was included. If there is anything worthy of criticism, it will be found among the enumerated powers upon which this general statement is based on (i.e., the powers listed in Article I, Section 8, clauses 1–17). The statement itself, although perhaps guilty of being overly repetitious, is perfectly harmless.

If harmless and repetitious, why was it included in the first place? If anything, it could only have been added out of a sense of caution, and to guard against those who might unnecessarily attempt to avoid the legitimate authority of the Union. The Constitutional Convention probably foresaw what has been the primary goal of these papers to communicate: the most threatening danger to our political welfare is state governments completely draining the strength of the Union. Because of this danger, they probably thought it was necessary to leave nothing to chance on such an important point. Whatever the reasoning behind including this clause may have been, the wisdom of its inclusion can be seen in the very objections that have already been raised against it

---

1. Known today simply as the "necessary and proper" clause.

since those objections question the great and essential truth that was obviously the goal of this provision to declare.

Then again, someone could ask, "Just who will judge what laws are *necessary and proper* for the sake of executing the powers of the Union?" This question is based just as much on the granting of those powers as it is upon the clause in question. The Federal government, like any other, will be the first to judge whether its powers are being properly exercised, and its constituents (the citizens of America) will be the last. If the Federal government should ever go beyond its proper boundaries and wield its powers like a tyrant, then the People, its masters, must appeal to their own standards and take whatever actions are appropriate in order to reverse any violations of the Constitution. Whether a law is constitutionally appropriate or not must always be determined by the nature of the powers on which it is based.

Suppose through some purposeful stretch of its authority (an act that is hard to imagine), Congress attempted to change the law of descent[1] in a state. Wouldn't it be obvious that such an attempt would exceed its jurisdiction and invade the rights of the states? Imagine that, because of some supposed interference with its revenues, Congress decided to lift a tax on land that was imposed by a particular state. Wouldn't it be equally obvious that Congress had invaded this concurrent jurisdiction between the Federal and state governments (because land is neither imported nor exported),[2] one that the Constitution clearly implies the states have the authority to tax? If anyone ever doubts such things, then we must give credit to those who, because of their unwise and over-enthusiastic hatred and animosity toward the new Constitu-

---

1. *law of descent:* This refers to the laws by which property/inheritance/estate/etc. was passed on. (Referenced in Federalist 41 as "Course of Descents.")
2. United States Constitution: Article I, Section 10, clause 2.

tion, have obscured the plainest and simplest of truths behind a dark cloud.

"But," some have said, "what about the laws of the Union being labeled the *supreme law* of the land?" Well, what would be the point of those laws, or what would they amount to if they were not supreme? It's obvious: they would amount to nothing. A LAW is, by its very definition, supreme. It is a rule that those to whom it applies are required to follow, all of which is the natural result of every sort of political association (the government and the governed). If individuals exist in a society, then the laws of that society must be the supreme regulator of their conduct and actions. If several political societies (i.e., the states) enter into a larger political society (i.e., the Union) with each other, then the laws of the larger political society that are made according to the powers it has been given in its constitution must necessarily become the supreme laws of the societies which form it, as well as their citizens. If this was not the case, then it would merely be a treaty that bound them together, a treaty which would completely depend on the good faith of the parties involved, and therefore not a government. After all, government is just another word for POLITICAL POWER AND SUPREMACY. However, it wouldn't make any sense if the laws of the larger society violated its constitutional powers and were themselves an invasion of the powers left in the hands of the smaller societies and that these laws would become the supreme law of the land. Laws which fall into this category would simply be unwarranted assumptions of power and should be treated as such.

The clause that declares the laws of the Union supreme, just like the *necessary and proper* clause before it, merely declares a truth that necessarily results from the institution and establishment of a Federal government. I also hope that the wording of the supremacy clause was not missed by anyone: it *explicitly* confines supremacy to those laws made *pursuant to the Constitution* (meaning "according to"). I mention this because, by making it clear what type of laws are to be considered supreme, this clause ensures that this supremacy is understood even though it is implied by the rest of the Constitution—yet another example of abundant caution on the part of the Convention.

Therefore, a law which imposed a tax on behalf of the United States would be considered the supreme law of the land and could not be legally opposed or controlled. On the other hand, a Federal law that ended or interfered with a state tax that was imposed by the authority of that state (except on imports or exports) would not be the supreme law of the land, but a violation of the powers granted by the Constitution. As far as both a Federal and state tax on the same thing are concerned, any improper collection of that tax may be mutually inconvenient, but wouldn't be the result of any superior or misused power on either side, but rather an improper use of it which ended up not being to the advantage of either. However, I would hope that mutual interests between the Federal and state governments will cause both of them to act in a way that avoids any inconvenience for either of them.

What we should ultimately take from all of this is that, under the proposed Constitution, the states will have complete and uncontrollable authority to raise much revenue from whatever source they want via any kind of taxation they wish, except those on imports and exports. I will show in the next paper how this *concurrent jurisdiction* with the Federal government as it relates to taxes was the only possible alternative to giving the proposed Federal government absolute power over the states as far as taxation was concerned.

—Publius

NUMBER 47

The True Meaning of the Principle of Separation of Powers

JAMES MADISON

For the New York Packet: Friday, February 1, 1788
The Constitutional Convention and the New Federalism

Since we've now reviewed both the general form and the general powers of the proposed government, I will now go more in depth on both the structure of this government and how its powers will be distributed between its different Branches.

Some of the more respectable opponents of the Constitution claim it violates the political principle that the Legislative, Executive, and Judicial Branches should be separate and distinct. They have said that no one seemed to care enough to include this essential safeguard of liberty in the structure of the proposed Federal government. The three branches of power are said to have been distributed and blended in such a way that they have lost any sense of balance and form, apparently because they expose very important parts of the government to the much greater weight of other parts.

FEDERALIST NO. 47

The Message: Power has been distributed carefully among the three branches of government. The federal system will, in fact, provide for more independence among the branches than the current state constitutions do.

———————

Original Quote: "The magistrate in whom the whole executive power resides cannot of himself make a law, though he can put a negative on every law; nor administer justice in person, though he has the appointment of those who do administer it. The judges can exercise no executive prerogative, though they are shoots from the executive stock; nor any legislative function, though they may be advised with by the legislative councils. The entire legislature can perform no judiciary act, though by the joint act of two of its branches the judges may be removed from their offices, and though one of its branches is possessed of the judicial power in the last resort. The entire legislature, again, can exercise no executive prerogative, though one of its branches constitutes the supreme executive magistracy, and another, on the impeachment of a third, can try and condemn all the subordinate officers in the executive department."

Relevance to Today: The lines of responsibility as laid out by Publius have been blurred. Judges have created rights and laws, which is really the responsibility of the legislative branch, and the executive branch issues "executive orders" and "signing statements" that in effect create law. In addition, power is also being handed to unelected bureaucrats who are able to circumvent the three-branch system by issuing regulations that do not have to be approved by Congress.

Before I go further, I want to acknowledge that this objection to the Constitution is based on the single most inherently valuable political truth that has ever existed, one which has been approved of by some of the most enlightened supporters of liberty. The very definition of tyranny would indeed be the existence of Legislative, Executive, and Judicial authority all in the same hands, whether it be one, a few, or many hands, and whether those hands are hereditary, self-appointed, or elected. If the Federal Constitution was guilty of putting too much power in one place or another, or mixing those powers in such a way that it could lead to tyranny, then no other arguments could be made to support it. However, I am personally convinced that it will become clear to everyone that this objection can't be supported. While the political idea this objection is based on is correct, it has been misunderstood, and thus misapplied. Therefore, in order to come to the right conclusion on this subject, we must first determine how best to arrange the three Branches of government as separate and distinct powers so that we can preserve liberty as much as possible.

The famous Montesquieu is the political theorist most often cited on this subject. If he is not the author of the principle of separation of powers, he can at least be credited with being its most effective and outspoken supporter, having brought it to the attention of the rest of mankind. Therefore, it's worth trying to understand his basic ideas on this subject. What Homer[1] has been to the didactic writers of epic poetry the British constitution was to Montesquieu. Just as the immortal Homer is considered by many to be the perfect model of the epic poet, the model against which all other epic poets are compared, Montesquieu seems to have

---

1. *Homer:* The legendary eighth-century BC Greek epic poet who wrote the *Iliad* and the *Odyssey*, and is considered to be the first "historian." Didacticism was an artistic philosophy that emphasized the instruction and informative qualities in literature and other art forms. Didactic poets included Aratus (referenced in Federalist No. 18), Ovid, and Virgil.

viewed the British constitution as the standard, or to use his own words, as the "mirror of political liberty," whose characteristic principles exemplified basic truths. So that we don't misunderstand him, let's go to the original source that Montesquieu himself uses as the foundation of his political principles: the British constitution.

Even the quickest and most cursory look at the British constitution will make it clear that the Legislative, Executive, and Judiciary powers are by no means totally separate and distinct from each other. The Executive (the King) forms an integral part of the Legislative authority (Parliament). He alone has the privilege of making treaties with foreign nations which, once made, have the force of law behind them (with a few exceptions). Every single officer in the judicial department is appointed by him and can be removed by him (upon consulting with both houses of Parliament), and can be formed into a constitutional council for the purpose of advising him. One of the houses of Parliament (the House of Lords)[1] also acts as a sort of great constitutional council for the King, in addition to acting as a court in trials of impeachment, and having supreme appellate jurisdiction in all other cases (just as the Supreme Court under the new Constitution). The judges are also extremely involved with the Legislative department (Parliament), so much so that they often attend and participate in its debates, even though they are not allowed to cast votes.

Given these facts about the British constitution that Montesquieu so admired, we can clearly see that when he said "there can be no liberty, where the legislative and executive powers are united in the same person, or body of magistrate" or "if the power of judging, be not separated from the legislative and executive

---

1. *House of Lords:* Referenced in detail in Federalist 39.

powers," that he did *not* mean that the powers of each branch of the government should not be mixed at all with those of any other branch. As his own words tell us, and as his most prized constitutional example conclusively shows us, his intended meaning really means nothing more than this: when the *whole* power of one Branch of government is used by the same hand or hands which possess the *whole* power of another Branch, then the fundamental principles of a free constitution are undermined.

Under the British constitution, this would have been the case if the King, who is the sole Executive, also possessed complete Legislative power, or complete Judicial power; or if the entire Legislative body (Parliament) also had control over every Judicial power, or was also the supreme Executive authority. However, these are not among the defects of the British constitution.

The King, who has complete Executive power, cannot unilaterally make a law, though he can veto any law he wishes. Nor can he administer justice in person, but he can appoint anyone he wishes to do the same thing. The judges have no Executive powers, but they are appointed by the Executive. The judges have no Legislative powers, though the Legislative branch might ask them for advice on laws. The entire Parliament cannot perform any Judicial duties, but if both Houses agree, they can remove a judge from their office, and one of them (the House of Lords) has the final say on all judicial cases (like the Supreme Court). The entire Parliament cannot exercise any Executive powers, but one of its branches (the King) holds supreme Executive powers. Another branch (the House of Lords), if a third of its members vote to do so, can try to condemn every subordinate officer in the Executive branch (impeachment).

The reasons which Montesquieu himself provides us with to back up his political principles make his intentions even more clear:

When the legislative and executive powers are united in the same person or body, there can be no liberty, because apprehensions may arise lest the same monarch or senate should enact tyrannical laws, to execute them in a tyrannical manner . . . were the power of judging joined with the legislative, the life and liberty of the subject would be exposed to arbitrary control, for the judge would then be the legislator. Were it joined to the executive power, the judge might behave with all the violence of an oppressor.[1]

Montesquieu explains some of these things in more detail in other passages, but even from this short passage it is clear what this famous political theorist actually meant when he was discussing the great political principle of separation of powers.

If we examine the constitutions of some of the states, aside from those that emphatically (and sometimes absolutely) establish the principle of separation of powers, there is not a single one in which the separate branches of power are kept absolutely separate and distinct from one another. New Hampshire, the state which has the most recently formed constitution, seems to have been aware that completely avoiding any mixture of these branches whatsoever of government was not only unwise, but impossible. Her constitution has modified this great principle by declaring:

. . . that the legislative, executive, and judiciary powers ought to be kept as separate from, and independent of each other, *as the nature of a free government will admit; or as is consistent with that chain of connection, that binds the whole fabric of the constitution in one indissoluble bond of unity and amity.*[2]

---

1. Montesquieu, *The Spirit of the Laws,* Book 11, Chapter 6. (Referenced in Federalist 78.)
2. New Hampshire Constitution: Part I, Bill of Rights, Article 37.

In keeping with this statement, New Hampshire's constitution does mix some of these branches in several ways. The senate, which is a part of the legislature, also serves as a court for the trial of impeachments. The president, who is the head of the executive department, is also the presiding member of the senate, and besides being able to cast a vote in all cases, he can also cast his vote to break a tie. The president himself is annually voted into power by the members of the legislature, who also vote on who will be part of his executive council (his advisors). Several other state officials are appointed by the legislature, while members of the judicial branch are appointed by the executive branch.

The Massachusetts constitution is less explicit than New Hampshire's, but it also includes the principle of separation of powers. It declares:

> ... that the legislative department shall never exercise the executive and judicial powers, or either of them: the executive shall never exercise the legislative and judicial powers, or either of them: the judicial shall never exercise the legislative and executive powers, or either of them.[1]

This declaration matches up perfectly with what Montesquieu said, and this principle is not in any way violated by the new Constitution. The Massachusetts constitution goes no further than prohibiting each branch of government from exercising the powers of one of the other branches. This particular passage is simply part of the introduction to the Massachusetts constitution, but in the body of the constitution itself, the separate branches of government are partially mixed together. The executive has partial

---

1. Massachusetts Constitution: Part I, "A Declaration of the Rights of the Inhabitants of the Commonwealth of Massachusetts," Article XXX.

veto power over the legislature, while the senate, which is part of the legislature, acts as a trial of impeachment for both executive and judicial officials. Once again, judicial officials are appointed and can be removed by the executive branch, so long as both houses of the legislature agree. Lastly, a number of government officials are annually appointed by the legislature. Since by its very nature the appointment of government officials is primarily a duty of the executive branch, those who drafted the Massachusetts constitution actually violated their own principle on that last point.

I am not going to examine the constitutions of Rhode Island or Connecticut because they were formed before the Revolution, and even before the idea of separation of powers became a widespread and important political principle.

The constitution of New York includes no declarations on this principle, but it appears that those who framed it were well aware of the dangers of improperly mixing the different branches of government. It does, however, give the executive partial control over the legislature, a power which the judicial branch also has. The executive and judicial branches are even partially mixed together in their exercise of this power over the legislature. Members of both the executive and legislative branches are involved in the appointment of government officials, both executive and judicial. Additionally, its court for the trial of impeachments and "correction of errors" is contained in one house of the legislature but also includes the most important members of the judicial branch.

The New Jersey constitution has blended the powers of government more than any of the other constitutions we've examined. The governor, who is the executive and appointed by the legislature, is not only Chancellor and Ordinary surrogate of the state, and a member of the supreme court of appeals, but president of one of the houses of the legislature with the ability to cast a vote, as well. The same house of the legislature acts as an executive council to the governor (his advisors), and, along with the governor, makes up the supreme court of appeals. Members of the judicial branch are appointed by the legislative branch, and can also be removed by one of the houses of the legislature so long as the other house impeaches them first.

According to the constitution of Pennsylvania,[1] the president (the head of the executive branch) is annually elected by the legislature. In conjunction with an executive council, the president appoints the members of the judicial branch, and also forms a court of impeachments for both executive and judicial officials. It also seems as if the legislature is able to remove the judges of that state's supreme court from office, as well as ordinary justices of the peace; the executive power of pardoning also requires the approval of the legislature in some cases. The members of the executive council are made EX OFFICIO[2] justices of the peace throughout the state.

In Delaware,[3] the executive is also elected annually by the legislature. The speakers of each house of the legislature are also Vice Presidents in the executive branch. The executive, along with six others (three of whom are appointed by the legislative branch), make up the supreme court of appeals; furthermore, the executive, along with the legislature, appoints all the other judges in the state. Throughout the states, it appears that members of the legislature can also act as justices of the peace. In New York, the members of one house of the legislature are EX OFFICIO justices of the peace, as are the members of the executive council. The primary executive officers are appointed by the legislature, while one house of the same legislature acts as the court for trials

---

1. This constitution has since been changed.

2. *EX OFFICIO:* Latin, *ex officio,* meaning "By right of office."

3. This constitution has since been changed.

of impeachment. Any government official can be removed by the legislative branch.

Maryland has incorporated separation of powers into its constitution in the most absolute terms, declaring that the legislative, executive, and judicial powers of government ought to be forever separate and distinct from each other. However, despite this declaration, her constitution still requires that the executive be appointed by the legislature, and that the executive appoint members of the judiciary.

The language of the constitution of Virginia is even more direct on this subject, and declares:

> ... that the legislative, executive, and judicial departments, shall be separate and distinct; so that neither exercise the powers properly belonging to the others; nor shall any person exercise the powers of more than one of them at the same time; except that the justices of county courts shall be eligible to either house of the assembly.[1]

And yet, despite this requirement, the legislature is responsible for appointing the executive, his executive council, and also the judges of the lower courts. Two members of the executive council are replaced every three years at the discretion of the legislature, while all the primary executive and judicial officers are also appointed by the legislature. The power of the executive to issue pardons is also given to the legislature in one case.

The constitution of North Carolina, which also declares "that the legislative, executive, and supreme judicial powers of government, ought to be forever separate and distinct from each other,"[2]

---

1. Virginia Constitution: Article III, Section 1.
2. North Carolina Constitution (1776): "Declaration of Rights" (this constitution has since been changed).

also gives the legislature the power to appoint not just the executive, but also the principal officers of both the executive and judicial branches.

Likewise, in South Carolina, the constitution requires that the executive be appointed by the legislature. The legislature is also responsible for appointing the members of the judicial branch, even including justices of the peace and sheriffs. It also gives the legislature the power to appoint all the officers in the executive branch, right down to the captains in the state's army and navy.

The constitution of Georgia declares "that the legislative, executive, and judiciary departments, shall be separate and distinct, so that neither exercise the powers properly belonging to the other."[1] Yet the legislature is responsible for appointing the officers of the executive branch, and must also approve all of the pardons issued by the executive. It even appoints justices of the peace.

By providing all of these examples in the state constitutions where the Legislative, Executive, and Judicial Branches have not all been kept entirely separate, I am not trying to advocate one constitution over the other. While I am fully aware of their many excellent characteristics, I am also aware that many of them show signs of both the inexperience, as well as the undue haste of those who framed them. It is obvious that, in some instances, the principle of separation of powers was violated by some of the powers being mixed together too much, while in others the powers of government were consolidated in one branch or another. Additionally, not one of the state constitutions has made it realistically possible to put into practice the separation of powers that is outlined on the paper of their constitutions.

I'm primarily trying to illustrate that the accusation brought against the new Constitution, namely, that it violates the sacred

---

1. Georgia Constitution (1777): Article I (this constitution has since been changed).

principle of free government, is unwarranted according to both the real meaning of separation of powers (as intended by Montesquieu), and how it is, in this day, understood in America. I will continue to examine this very interesting topic in the next paper.

—Publius

NUMBER 69

The President Compared with a King of Great Britain and the Governor of the State of New York (Continued)

ALEXANDER HAMILTON

For the New York Packet: Friday, March 14, 1788
The Executive Branch

Constitutional References:
Article I: §3/7 | §4 | §7/2–3 | §8/5, 11–16 | §9/8 |
§10/1—Article II: §1/1 | §2/1 | §3 | §4
Article III: §3/1–2

I will now discuss the true characteristics of the Executive Branch as outlined in the proposed Constitution. By doing so, I hope to show just how unfairly this Branch has been misrepresented by the Constitution's opponents.

The first thing that catches our attention is Executive authority, which, with few exceptions, will be delegated to a single individual.[1] This is hardly a point that should be used as a basis of

---

1. United States Constitution: Article II, Section 1, clause 1.

FEDERALIST NO. 69

The Message: The president will be the top executive of the nation and the commander in chief of our armed forces, but his powers will be clearly defined and limited.

———

Original Quote: "The person of the king of Britain is sacred and inviolable; there is no constitutional tribunal to which he is amendable; no punishment to which he can be subjected without involving the crisis or a national revolution. In this delicate and important circumstance of personal responsibility, the President of Confederated America would stand upon no better ground than a governor of New York . . ."

Relevance to Today: As we saw in the dramatic cases of President Richard Nixon and Bill Clinton, the president is not above the law. Congress, and by association, the people, have the right, even the duty, to prosecute the president, or force his resignation, if they believe he has acted above the law. Our freedoms completely depend on the public holding our leaders responsible and ensuring that the concept of having two different sets of rules, which are so prevalent in most countries, never gets a foothold here.

———

Original Quote: "The President of the United States is to have power to return a bill, which shall have passed the two branches of the legislature, for reconsideration; and the bill so returned is to become a law, if, upon that reconsideration, it be approved by two thirds of both houses."

Relevance to Today: Constitutional experts trace the usage of "signing statements"—a statement that changes or bypasses the meaning of legislation—back to James Monroe. That may be true, but one thing is for sure: Presidents Barack Obama (breaking a campaign promise) and George W. Bush, regularly relied on signing statements to get around legislation they didn't like. Obama, for example, used a signing statement to overrule Congress's defunding of his "czars." This is just one small example of the growth of executive power that our Founders—and many anti-Federalists—were concerned about. And we should be as well.

comparison, for if the President seems similar to the King of Great Britain in this regard, then he must also be similar to the Grand Signor,[1] the Khan of Tartary,[2] the man of the seven mountains, or the governor of New York.

This President will be elected for *four years*, and he will be able to serve for as long as the People of the United States believe he is worthy of their approval.[3] In this regard, he is completely different than the King of Great Britain, who is a *hereditary* monarch with a crown received from patrimony[4] and passed on to his heirs forever. However, there is a great similarity between the President and a governor of New York, who is elected for *three* years, and is eligible to be elected for an unlimited number of terms. If we take into account how much time it would take to establish a danger-

---

1. *Grand Signor:* The term used by Europeans to refer to the Ottoman *Padishah* (Persian title meaning "Lord of Kings"), a title that was first adopted by Sultan Mehmed II (1432–81; reigned 1444–46 and 1451–81). The term "Grand Turk" was used interchangeably with "Grand Signor."

2. *Khan of Tartary:* Tartary, or Great Tartary, was a term used by Europeans from the Middle Ages to the twentieth century to refer to a large area of land in northern and central Asia that stretched from the Caspian Sea and the Ural Mountains to the Pacific Ocean, and which was inhabited by Turkic and Mongol people. *Khan* is a Turkic/Mongol word for a sovereign or military ruler.

3. This was changed with the addition of the Twenty-Second Amendment in 1951, which reads:

1. "No person shall be elected to the office of the President more than twice, and no person who has held the office of President, or acted as President, for more than two years of a term to which some other person was elected President shall be elected to the office of the President more than once. But this Article shall not apply to any person holding the office of President, when this Article was proposed by the Congress, and shall not prevent any person who may be holding the office of President, as acting as President, during the term within which this Article becomes operative from holding the office of President or acting as President during the remainder of such term.

2. This Article shall be inoperative unless it shall have been ratified as an Amendment to the Constitution by the legislatures of three-fourths of the several States within seven years from the date of its submission to the States by the Congress."

4. *patrimony:* An estate or piece of property that is inherited from one's father or ancestors; a heritage.

ous influence or tyranny in a single state, let alone throughout the entire United States, we must conclude that a term of only *four* years for the President of the Union should be quite a bit less frightening than a term of *three* years in the corresponding office of a single state (governor).

The President of the United States will at all times be able to be impeached, tried, and, upon being convicted of treason, bribery, or other high crimes and misdemeanors, removed from office, after which time he could still be prosecuted and punished through the normal legal process.[1] The very person of the King of Great Britain is sacred and untouchable, there is no constitutional court that he must submit to, and if he were to be punished for anything, it would bring about the crisis of a national revolution. As far as the touchy, yet important idea of personal responsibility is concerned, the President of the United States would be held accountable just as much as a governor of New York, and even more than the governors of Virginia and Delaware.

The President of the United States will have the power to return any bill that passes both Houses of Congress so that they can reconsider it, and this bill will not become law unless it is then approved by two-thirds of both Houses.[2] The King of Great Britain, alternatively, can veto any act of both houses of Parliament. Even if he does not use this power for long periods of time it by no means implies that he doesn't have it. This power exists because the Crown has been able to substitute raw authority in place of personal influence. In other words, the Crown has found a way to utilize a power that, if used, could cause national unrest, for the hard work of gaining a majority in one or the other houses of Par-

---

1. United States Constitution: Article I, Section 4; Article I, Section 3, clause 7.
2. United States Constitution: Article I, Section 7, clauses 2–3.

liament. The President's veto power, conversely, is a limited power, one that is different from the British King's absolute veto power. In fact, it is almost exactly the same as the authority that the Council of Revision[1] has in New York, where the governor plays an important role. In this respect, the power of the President would be greater than the governor of New York, because the President would have a power all to himself that the governor shares with the chancellor and judges of this state. But the President's power would be exactly the same as the governor of Massachusetts. It was likely, in fact, that this part of the proposed Constitution was emulating the Massachusetts constitution.

The President is to be:

> ... Commander in Chief of the Army and Navy of the United
> States, and of the militia of the several states, when called into
> the actual service of the United States ... He is to have power
> to grant reprieves and pardons for offences against the United
> States, except in cases of impeachment ... [to] recommend
> to their consideration [Congress's] such measures as he shall
> judge necessary and expedient; he may, on extraordinary oc-
> casions, convene both Houses [of Congress], or either of them,
> and in case of disagreement between them, with respect to the
> time of adjournment, he may adjourn them to such time as he
> shall think proper ... to take care that the laws be faithfully
> executed, and shall commission all the officers of the United
> States.[2]

---

1. *Council of Revision:* The legal body under the 1777 New York state constitution that revised all new legislation made by the New York state legislature. It was made up of the governor, the chancellor, and the justices of the supreme court, or any two of them.
2. United States Constitution: Article II, Section 2, clause 1; Section 3.

In most of these details, the powers of the President will be very similar to the powers of both the King of Great Britain and the governor of New York. The biggest differences are these . . . *First*, the President will only occasionally command whatever part of the militia is actually mobilized by Congress. Both the King of Great Britain and the governor of New York have all to themselves the power to command the militia of their territories whenever they want. As far as this is concerned, the power of the President would be less than both the monarch and the governor.

Second, the President will be the commander in chief of the army and navy of the United States. In this respect, his authority would be nominally the same as that of the King of Great Britain, but in reality much less. His authority would amount to nothing more than the supreme command and direction of the military and naval forces as the first general and admiral of the Union. The power of the British King includes *declaring* war, and also *raising* and *regulating* fleets and armies, both of which would be the powers of Congress under the Constitution we are currently discussing.[1] In contrast, according to the constitution of this state, the governor of New York only has the authority to *command* its militia and navy (similar to the President's authority). But the constitutions of several of the states explicitly declare that their governors are to be the commanders in chief of both the army and navy. Given this, it is certainly justifiable for me to ask whether the constitutions of New Hampshire and Massachusetts in particular confer on their governors larger powers than the President of the United States will have.

Third, the power of the President to grant pardons will extend to all cases, *except those of impeachment*. The governor of New York may pardon whomever he wishes, even those who have been

---

1. United States Constitution: Article I, Section 8, clauses 11–16.

impeached. He just can't pardon in cases of either treason or murder. As far as political consequences are concerned, isn't the power of the governor greater than that of the President? Because of the governor's pardoning powers, he would be capable of protecting, and thus preventing the punishment of anyone who was engaged in any conspiracy against the government that may not have yet festered into full-blown treason.

Given that fact, if the governor himself was the leader of such a conspiracy, he would be able to legally protect any and all of his accomplices right up until they actually put their plot into action. Although he could pardon treason if it was prosecuted through the normal legal process, a President of the Union would be completely unable to shelter anyone from impeachment and conviction. Wouldn't it be more tempting to engage in treason if it was possible to go unpunished for all of your preparations (as in New York), as opposed to if you only had a very small chance of avoiding the death penalty or a prison sentence after actually committing the crime (as with the President)? Would the latter scenario be influenced at all if it was likely that the one who could grant the pardon (the President) in the first place would be politically affected by that decision, and thus would probably be politically incapable of granting it? We should also keep in mind that the proposed Constitution limits treason to ". . . levying war against them [the United States], or in adhering to their enemies, giving them aid and comfort [sic]," [1] and that the laws of the state of New York limit it in a similar way.

Fourth, the President can adjourn Congress only if there is a disagreement between the two Houses of Congress about when they should adjourn. The British monarch may adjourn or even dissolve Parliament. The governor of New York may also adjourn

---

1. United States Constitution: Article III, Section 3, clauses 1–2.

the state legislature for a limited time, a power which, in certain situations, can be used for very important purposes.

The President will have the power, with the advice and consent of the Senate, to make treaties, so long as two-thirds of the Senators present concur.[1] The King of Great Britain is the sole and absolute representative of the nation in all foreign negotiations, and can negotiate treaties of peace, commerce, alliance, and every other sort of treaty based solely on his own authority. Some have implied that the King's authority in this regard is not final, and that his negotiations with foreign powers can be revised by, and require the ratification of, Parliament, but I don't believe that anyone has ever heard of that idea before now. Every jurist[2] of that kingdom, and everyone else who is familiar with its constitution, knows that it is an established fact that the monarch has complete freedom to make treaties, and that every treaty that is concluded by the royal authority is completely, perfectly, and legally valid—independent of any other legal sanction.

It is true that Parliament sometimes alters existing laws so that they conform to the stipulations found within any new treaty. This is what may have caused some to falsely believe that Parliament's approval was required for a treaty to go into effect. But Parliament is required to do such things simply to adjust the extremely complicated and intricate system of revenue, commerce, and all other laws of that Kingdom so that they are in line with any new treaty.

---

1. United States Constitution: Article II, Section 2, clause 2.
2. A reference to the English jurist William Blackstone's (1723–80) *Commentaries on the Laws of England*, Volume I, Chapter 7, in which he writes: "The constitution of the kingdom hath entrusted him [the monarch] with the whole executive power of the laws . . . what is done by the royal authority, with regard to foreign powers, is the act of the whole nation: what is done without the king's concurrence is the act only of private men." (Referenced in Federalist 84.)

Additionally, occasionally Parliament must pass new laws that are necessary and appropriate when government must adjust to new circumstances. Therefore, in this respect, there is absolutely no comparison between the power of the President and the power of the British monarch. The monarch can do by himself what the President can only do with the agreement of the Senate. Obviously the President's power in this regard would be greater than that of any state governor, but that is only because it is the exclusive right of the Union to negotiate and conclude treaties with foreign nations.[1] If the Union did in fact fall apart, I believe that the governors of each state would end up being fully vested with this delicate and important power.

The President will also be authorized to receive ambassadors and other public officials.[2] Even though this has been heavily criticized, it is actually more a matter of dignity than of authority. This authority will not affect how the government is run. However, it will be much more convenient than requiring that Congress, or one of its Houses, convenes every single time a new foreign official arrives, especially if it was only to replace a predecessor.

The President will have the power to nominate, and with *the advice and consent of the Senate*, to appoint ambassadors and other public officials, judges of the Supreme Court, and in general, all of the officers of the United States that are established by law, as well as those that are not specifically called for in the Constitution.[3] The King of Great Britain absolutely and beyond any doubt has this power for himself, since he can not only appoint officers, but can create entirely new offices. He can confer titles of nobility

---

1. United States Constitution: Article I, Section 10, clause 1.
2. United States Constitution: Article II, Section 3.
3. United States Constitution: Article II, Section 2, clause 2.

at his pleasure, and he can appoint an enormous number of lucrative church positions as well.

Obviously, the President's power in this regard is far less than the British King's. It's not even equal to the power of the governor of New York, at least if we are to interpret New York's constitution according to common practice in that state. In New York, the power of appointment belongs to a council made up of the governor and four members of the senate, who are chosen by the assembly. The governor *claims*, and has frequently *exercised* the right to nominate whomever he wishes to any particular office, and he is also *entitled* to cast a vote in the confirmation of that nomination. If, as he claims, he really has the right of nomination, then his authority is equal to the President's in this regard, and even exceeds it as far as confirming the nomination is concerned. In the Federal government, if the Senate was divided, then the appointment would not be confirmed; but in the government of New York, if the council was divided, the governor could turn the tables and confirm his own nomination if he so desired.[1]

If we compare the great amount of publicity that would inevitably surround any appointment made by the President and an entire House of Congress (the Senate), with the privacy surrounding an appointment by the governor of New York, who is closeted away with four other people (and more often than not, just two), and if we also consider how much easier it would be to influence this smaller group of people than it would be to influence all of the Senators of the United States Senate, plus the President, then

---

1. "Candor requires that I acknowledge that I do not think that the governor's claim to the right of nomination is well founded. Yet, it is always justified to base one's reasoning on the practice of a government, at least until the appropriateness of its actions becomes constitutionally questionable. Independent of this claim however, when we take into account all other considerations and examine their consequences, we shall be inclined to draw pretty much the same conclusion."

we cannot hesitate to conclude that the New York governor's power of appointment is far greater than the President's as it is outlined in the Constitution.

Except for the concurrent authority that the President will have with regard to treaties, it's hard to tell whether the President would possess more or less power than the governor of New York. Further, it's absurd to draw any comparison between the President and the King of Great Britain. But, in order to make the contrast between the two even more obvious, I will lay out their main differences side by side.

The President of the United States will be elected by the People for *four* years.[1] The King of Great Britain is an eternal and *hereditary* prince. It will be possible to personally punish and disgrace the first, while the second is sacred and untouchable.

The first would have a *partial* veto power over the Legislative Branch, while the second has an *absolute* veto power.

The first will have the right to command the military and naval forces of the nation, while the other, in addition to this right, also has the power to *declare* war, and to *raise* and *regulate* fleets and armies by his own authority.

The first would share the power of making treaties with the Senate, while the other has the power of making treaties all to himself.

The first would have a similarly shared authority to appoint officers, while the other has the sole power to make all appointments.

The first can bestow on no one any private privileges, favors, or Titles of Nobility,[2] while the other can, of his own authority, declare illegal aliens to be residents, commoners noblemen, and

---

1. United States Constitution: Article II, Section 1, clause 1.
2. United States Constitution: Article I, Section 9, clause 8.

he can even form corporations with all the rights of corporate entities, all by himself.

The first cannot dictate any rules concerning the commerce
or currency of the nation (a power given to Congress),[1] while the
other has absolute authority over commerce in several different
ways, including the authority to establish markets and fairs, regulate weights and measures, impose embargos for a limited time,
coin money, and either authorize or prohibit the circulation of
foreign coin.

The first has absolutely no spiritual authority whatsoever,
while the other is the supreme head and governor of the national
church!

What answer should we give to those who try to convince
us that two things which are so different actually resemble each
other? We should give the same answer we give to those who tell
us that a government whose power is completed based on the
elected and temporary servants of the People is an aristocracy, a
monarchy, and a tyranny.

—Publius

---

1. United States Constitution: Article I, Section 8, clause 5.

NUMBER 84

Concerning Several Miscellaneous Objections

ALEXANDER HAMILTON
Miscellaneous Objections and Conclusion

Constitutional References:
Article I: §1/7 | §9/2–3, 8—Article II: §2/2—
Article III: §1 | §2/3 | §3/1–2

Throughout the course of these papers I have endeavored to answer most of the objections made against the Constitution. However, there are still a few more that I have not yet answered because they did not fall under any particular category and/or because I forgot to mention them. I will now discuss these as concisely as I can, since this discussion has already become very long.

The most significant objection that remains is that the new Constitution contains no Bill of Rights. In addition to the answers I have provided on this issue, it has been mentioned that many of the state constitutions lack the same thing—including New York's. And yet, the People in this state who are most critical of the new system are the very same people who express immense

FEDERALIST NO. 84

The Message: Our God-given rights to liberty and happiness are so self-evident that a bill of rights could prove dangerous because it may imply to people that those rights not specifically listed are not held by the people.

Original Text: "[A bill of rights,] in a sense and to the extent in which they are contended for, are not only unnecessary in the proposed Constitution, but would even be dangerous."

Relevance to Today: Almost all of the rights detailed in the Bill of Rights have come under attack at one time or another. From the grammar of the Second Amendment, to the limits of free speech, it's not hard to make the case the rights *not* listed are sometimes easier to maintain than those that are. A right listed in the Bill does not invite itself to be regulated or restricted.

Original Text: ". . . there will be a considerable saving of expense from the differences between the constant session of the present and the temporary session of the future congress."

Relevance to Today: The business of being a politician has consumed many of those who take up what can now only be called a "profession." They go native in Washington and raise millions as they spend much of their time focused on elections and special-interest causes rather than on the people. The Founders thought a professional political class would be disconnected from their home states and prone to giving in to the temptations of power. They were right.

admiration for the constitution of New York. They justify their position by claiming two things: first, that even though the New York constitution has no bill of rights, it has various provisions in it that favor and protect specific privileges and rights that amount to the same thing; and second, that it fully adopts the Common[1] and Statute Law[2] of Great Britain, which also secures many rights that are not explicitly written down.

To the first reason they give, I answer that the proposed Constitution has a number of the same types of provisions. Independent of the structure of government, we find the following in the proposed Constitution:

Article I, Section 3, clause 7: "Judgment in cases of impeachment shall not extend further than to removal from office, and disqualification to hold and enjoy any office of honor, trust or profit under the United States; but the party convicted shall, nevertheless, be liable and subject to indictment, trial, judgment and punishment, according to law."

Article I, Section 9, clause 2: "The privilege of the writ of *habeas corpus*[3] shall not be suspended, unless when in cases of rebellion or invasion the public safety may require it."

---

1. *Common Law:* Referenced and defined in Federalist 37.

2. *Statute Law:* Referenced and defined in Federalist 37.

3. *habeas corpus:* Habeas corpus (Latin) means "That you have the body [the person being detained]." This writ requires that a person be brought before a judge or a court, especially for investigations related to a restraint on the liberty of that person; used as a protection against illegal imprisonment. It has its origins in the Magna Carta of 1215, signed by King John of England, which reads: "No Freeman shall be taken or imprisoned, or be disseised [dispossessed] of his Freehold, or Liberties, or free Customs, or be outlawed, or exiled, or any other wise destroyed; nor will We not pass upon him, nor condemn him, but by lawful judgment of his Peers, or by the Law of the land."

Article I, Section 9, clause 3: "No bill of attainder[1] or *ex post facto*[2] law shall be passed."

Article I, Section 9, clause 8: "No title of nobility shall be granted by the United States; and no person holding any office of profit or trust under them, shall, without the consent of the Congress, accept of any present, emolument, office, or title, of any kind whatever, from any King, Prince, or foreign state."

Article III, Section 2, clause 3: "The trial of all crimes, except in cases of impeachment, shall be by jury; and such trial shall be held in the state where the said crimes shall have been committed; but when not committed within any state, the trial shall be at such place or places as the Congress may by law have directed."

Article III, Section 3, clause 1: "Treason against the United States shall consist only in levying war against them, or in adhering to their enemies, giving them aid and comfort. No person shall be convicted of treason, unless on the testimony of two witnesses to the same overt act, or on confession in open court."

Article III, Section 3, clause 2: "The Congress shall have power to declare the punishment of treason; but no attainder of treason shall work corruption of blood, or forfeiture, except during the life of the person attained."

Aren't these provisions, on the whole, just as important as the ones found in the New York state constitution? In fact, the Consti-

---

1. *bill of attainder:* Refer to Federalist 44 for the definition.
2. *ex post facto:* Latin, meaning "after the fact"; refer to Federalist 44 for the definition.

tution provides greater security for liberty by establishing the writ of *habeas corpus*, prohibiting *ex post facto* laws, and also TITLES OF NOBILITY, for which there are no such provisions in the New York constitution. Throughout the ages, the most powerful instruments of tyranny have been the act of arbitrarily imprisoning someone, as well as creating crimes after the fact, or, in other words, punishing men for things they have done that, at the time, were not against any law (*ex post facto* laws). The wise observations of William Blackstone[1] on arbitrary imprisonment deserve to be repeated:

> To bereave a man of life or by violence confiscate his estate, without accusation or trial, would be so gross and notorious an act of despotism, as must at once convey the alarm of tyranny throughout the whole nation; but confinement of the person, by secretly hurrying him to jail, where his sufferings are unknown or forgotten, is a less public, a less striking, and therefore *a more dangerous engine* of arbitrary government.[2]

Blackstone goes on to provide a cure for this fatal evil by giving high praise to the *Habeas Corpus* Act,[3] calling it "the BULWARK of the British constitution."

---

1. *William Blackstone:* An English judge, jurist, and professor who lived from 1723 to 1780 and wrote the classic treatise on English common law, *Commentaries on the Laws of England,* which was published in four volumes between 1765 and 1769. (Referenced in Federalist 69.)

2. Blackstone, *Commentaries on the Laws of England,* Volume I.

3. *Habeas Corpus* Act: An act of the Parliament of England (before the United Kingdom was formed in 1707) passed in 1679, during the reign of Charles II (1630–85; reigned 1660–85). While the right of *habeas corpus* had existed in England for at least three centuries, this act is the one most remembered for strengthening that right. It declared that a command of the king or his Privy Council (the king's governing council) was not a valid answer to a petition of *habeas corpus* from a court.

No one needs to remind us about the importance of not allowing titles of nobility. This one principle can truly be called the cornerstone of republican government because, as long as such titles are not allowed, there can never be anything that seriously threatens the government from being one of the People.

As far as the so-called protection of the common and statute law by the New York constitution, I reply that both are explicitly subject "to such alterations and provisions as the legislature shall from time to time make concerning the same."[1] Therefore, both can be repealed at any moment by the legislature, and, consequently, have no guaranteed protection under the state constitution. The only reason "protections" for common and statute law were put in was to recognize the ancient laws (pre-Revolution) and remove any doubts that people had about them as a result of the Revolution. These can, therefore, not be considered as part of a declaration or bill of rights, which must always be understood in our constitutions as *limits*[2] placed on the power of government.

It has been accurately noted that bills of rights began as an agreement between a king and his subjects that limited the king's powers in favor of the privileges of his subjects; or in other words, they were a defense of the rights which had not been surrendered to the prince. The MAGNA CARTA[3] was just such a document that the barons (nobles), with swords in their hands,

---

1. Constitution of New York, Article I (Bill of Rights), Section 14; formerly Section 16 before it was amended and renumbered in 1938.

2. Emphasis added.

3. *MAGNA CARTA:* The Magna Carta, whose name means "Greater Charter" in Latin, is a document that the barons of England forced King John (1167–1216; reigned 1199–1216) to sign in 1215. It declared certain liberties for the barons and their subjects, and was the first major effort to make sure that the king's will was not merely arbitrary but had appropriate checks placed on it. It was reissued in smaller versions several times during the thirteenth century.

succeeded in obtaining from King John.[1] This was proven by the fact that successive princes obeyed it. Another example is the Petition of Right[2] agreed to by Charles I[3] at the beginning of his reign. Also, the Declaration of Right[4] presented to the Prince of Orange (William III) in 1688 by the lords and commons was later made into an act of Parliament called the Bill of Rights. This makes it clear that these people had no power to refer to a constitution founded upon the power of the People and which was enforced by their representatives.

In this country, the People surrender nothing, and since they retain everything, they have no need for a Bill of Rights. "We the People of the United States, to secure the blessings of liberty to

---

1. *King John:* John lived from 1167 to 1216 and was king of England from 1199 to 1216. He is most famous for having signed the Magna Carta.

2. *Petition of Right:* A significant English constitutional document that was drawn up by the English Parliament in the run-up to the English Civil War (1642–51), and given the royal assent of Charles I (referenced in the next footnote) in 1628. It was ratified on June 7, 1628. Among other things, this document affirmed the principle that only Parliament could impose taxes, that martial law could not be imposed in times of peace, and that prisoners must be allowed to contest the legitimacy of their detention via the writ of *habeas corpus*. It also prohibited the "billeting" of troops (requiring private citizens to house them), which is reflected in the Third Amendment to the U.S. Constitution: "No Soldier shall, in time of peace be quartered in any house, without the consent of the owner, nor in time of war, but in a manner to be prescribed by law."

3. *Charles I:* Charles I lived from 1600 to 1649 and was king of England from 1625 to 1649. He was executed on January 30, 1649, by Parliament for his continuous attempts to curb their authority. There were also many religious conflicts during his reign, including his refusal to assist the Protestant forces during the Thirty Years' War (1618–48), as well as his marriage to a Catholic princess (Henrietta Maria of France). The last part of his reign was marked by the English Civil War (1642–51), which was primarily between those who supported Parliament ("Parliamentarians") and the king ("Royalists"). The war ended with the Parliamentary victory at the Battle of Worcester on September 3, 1651.

4. *Declaration of Right:* An act of the Parliament of England that put into statutory form (refer to Statute Law in Federalist 37) the rights of subjects and permanent residents of a constitutional monarchy, such as existed in England. It was submitted to William and Mary (William III and Mary II) in March 1689 and invited them to become the joint sovereigns of England.

ourselves and our posterity, do *ordain* and *establish* this Constitution for the United States of America": this is a better recognition of popular rights than all the many truths which represent the bulk of our state bills of rights, all of which sound like they should be in a treatise on ethics rather than a constitution of government.

Since the proposed Constitution is merely meant to regulate our general political interests, a detailed Bill of Rights is not required, as it would be for a constitution that regulated all sorts of personal and private matters. Therefore, if the criticism of the Constitution on this point is valid, then there should be just as much criticism for the constitution of the state of New York. The truth, though, is that both contain all that is necessary and reasonably desirable for carrying out their purposes.

As far as a bill of rights that is as extensive as the one argued for by the Constitution's opponents, I would go even further and say that such a thing would not only be unnecessary, but even dangerous. It would contain several exceptions to powers that are currently not even granted to the Federal government by the Constitution, and because of this, it would allow some colorful excuse to be made up as a pretext to claim un-granted powers. Why should we declare that the government should not do things that it has no power to do in the first place? For example, why should a bill of rights include the right of freedom of the press when no power exists in the Constitution to restrict freedom of the press? I am not saying that such a right would give the Federal government the ability to regulate the press, but that such a right may provide devious men with a reasonable excuse for claiming that power. They might reasonably argue that it is ridiculous that the Constitution would be given the responsibility of not abusing an authority which it does not have, *except for the fact that* the existence of the right to freedom of the press in the Constitution clearly implies that it was intended that the Federal government have the right to properly regulate it. This is but a small example of the legitimacy that would be given to the doctrine of constructive powers (granting new powers to the Federal government) by an unwise and overly enthusiastic desire for a Bill of Rights.

On the subject of freedom of the press, I must say one or two things. First, there is not a single word about it in the constitution of New York, and second, everything that has been said about it in the other states amounts to nothing. What does "the freedom of the press shall always be preserved" mean? What is "freedom of the press"? Who can define it in such a way that it would be impossible to stretch its meaning?

I believe that defining freedom of the press would be impractical, and that, despite all the declarations we place in any constitution to protect it, its protection will in the end completely depend on the spirit of the People and government, as well as the public opinion of the time.[1] It is on these things, after all, that we

---

1. "To show that there is a power in the Constitution by which the liberty of the press could be affected, the power of taxation has been referred to. It is said that taxes may be imposed upon publications which are so high, that it would basically amount to a prohibition being placed on that publication. I am not aware of any logic by which it could be maintained that the declarations in the state constitutions in favor of the freedom of the press would act as a constitutional obstacle to the imposition of taxes on publications by the state legislatures. It certainly cannot be pretended that any amount of taxes, however low, would amount to an abridgement of the liberty of the press. We know that newspapers are taxed in Great Britain, and yet it is notorious that the press nowhere else enjoys greater liberty than in that country. And if taxes of any kind could be imposed without violating that liberty, then it is evident that the extent of those taxes must depend on the discretion of the legislature, as it is regulated itself by public opinion, making it so that any general declarations in favor of the freedom of the press would provide no greater security than would have been provided without them. The very same invasions could be carried out under the state constitutions (which contain those general declarations in favor of the freedom of the press through taxation) just as much as under the proposed Constitution, which has nothing of the kind. It would be just as insignificant to declare that government ought to be free, that taxes ought not be excessive, etc. as that the liberty of the press ought not to be restrained."

must seek the only foundation firm enough to place all our rights upon.

Before I move on, there is one more viewpoint to consider. Despite all the criticism of it, the truth is that the Constitution, in every rational sense and for every useful purpose, *is* a BILL OF RIGHTS. The constitution of Great Britain is made up of the several bills of rights, and conversely the bill of rights in each state (county) makes up the British constitution. Similarly, if adopted, the Constitution will be the Bill of Rights of the Union. Isn't something that declares and specifies the political privileges of citizens as it relates to the structure and administration of the government a Bill of Rights? The Constitution formed by the Convention does just that in the most sufficient and precise way—something which cannot be found in any of the state constitutions.

Isn't another goal of a Bill of Rights to define certain freedoms/immunities and ways of going about things that are relevant to personal and private matters? That has also been taken care of in a variety of ways by the same Constitution. It is absurd to claim that the meaning and purpose of a bill of rights can't be found in the work of the Convention. You may say that the Constitution does not go far enough (though this is not easy to back up), but it cannot be accurately claimed that a bill of rights isn't there at all. It would be like grasping for the wind to discover the purpose of declaring the rights of citizens when they are provided for and protected by the mechanisms of government itself. Therefore, the criticisms that have been made on this subject amount to nothing but meaningless distinctions that completely lack any substance.

Another objection frequently repeated is this: It is improper to grant the National government such large powers because the National Capital (the seat of government) will be too far away from many of the states for the everyday citizen to have a good idea of what is going on in Congress. This argument, if it proves anything, proves that there should be no National government at all, for the powers that everyone seems to agree the Union should have cannot be entrusted to any political body that is not properly controlled. There are good reasons to show that this criticism is not a good one.

In most of the arguments regarding distance, there is an almost visible delusion of imagination taking place. What sources of information should the People in a distant county trust in order to judge what their state representatives in their own state legislature are doing? They cannot observe them personally, since only the citizens who are there can do that. They must therefore trust in intelligent men to provide them with information. But how do these men get their information? Obviously from what is contained in new laws, the press, from correspondence with their representatives, and from people who are present at their deliberations.

It is equally obvious that similar sources of information would be available to the People concerning the actions of the Federal government, and that any barriers to quick communication would be compensated for by the alertness of the state legislatures because of their own close observations of the Federal government. The executive and legislative powers in each state will serve as the lookouts of every person employed by the Federal government in every capacity, and, since they will have the ability to regularly and effectively obtain intelligence, they will never lack for information. They can then pass this information on to their citizens concerning their representatives in the National government.

The rivalry between the state and central governments for power will make it likely that the state governments will keep their citizens up to date. Because of this, we can be assured that the People will be better informed about the actions of the National government than perhaps even their own state governments.

We must also remember that the citizens who live in or

near the Capital will care about the liberty and prosperity of our country just as much as those who live far away from it. They will always be ready to sound the alarm if there is any harmful plot coming out of the National government. The press will also quickly spread any such news to the most remote and distant parts of the Union.

Among all of the strange objections being made against the proposed Constitution, the most extraordinary and least legitimate is that the Constitution provides no way of making sure that the debts owed *to* the United States are paid. This has been painted as some wicked plot to abandon those debts that are owed to us, and to protect public defaulters. The newspapers have been full of heated rants about this accusation, despite the fact that it is baseless, and either extremely ignorant or extremely dishonest.

In addition to the points I have made in previous papers, I will only say that both common sense and established political principles plainly conclude: ". . . states neither lose any of their rights, nor are discharged from any of their obligations, by a change in the form of their civil government."[1]

The last objection of any importance (which I remember) is related to the question of how expensive the establishment of this new government will be. Even if it were true that adopting the proposed government would greatly increase our expenses, this should not count against the Plan. The great majority of the People of America are convinced that the Union is the foundation of their political happiness. Nearly everyone with common sense in both parties agrees that this happiness cannot be preserved under the current system without radical changes,

---

1. A reference to *Institutes of Natural Law; Being the Substance of a Course of Lectures on Grotius de Jure Belli et Pacis,* Volume II, Book 2, Chapter 10, sections 14–15 (1774), by Thomas Rutherforth, and *De Jure Belli et Pacis* (On the Law of War and Peace), Book 2, Chapter 9, section 5 (1625), by Hugo Grotius (1583–1645).

that new and extensive powers should be given to the National government, and that these new powers will require a different organization for the Federal government, since so much power existing in any one place would be unsafe. In admitting all of this, the question of how expensive it will be becomes irrelevant because it would be impossible to safely decrease the size of the foundation that this new system will stand on.

The two Houses of Congress will initially have a combined total of sixty-five representatives, the same number of people in the current congress under the Confederation. It is true that this number will increase, but that will only be to keep up with our growing population and resources. Any number less than this would be unsafe, but if we kept the same number even as our population continued to grow, it would not provide adequate representation for the People. So what will cause this dreaded increase in expenses? Some have said the increase in government positions will be the cause, so let's examine that a bit.

It is obvious that the main departments of the administration of the current government will also be required under the new one. Right now there is a Secretary of War, Secretary of Foreign Affairs, Secretary for Domestic Affairs, and a Treasury Department consisting of three positions: a treasurer, assistants, and clerks. These offices are absolutely necessary for any government, and will be sufficient for the new as well as the old. As to ambassadors and other diplomats in foreign countries, the new Constitution can do nothing but make their offices more respectable and their services more useful. It is clearly true that there will be many new government positions created in order to employ people who will collect revenue, but this does not necessarily mean that this will increase public expenses. In most cases, this will amount to nothing more than switching state and national officers. For instance, for the collection of taxes, nearly everyone employed will have formerly been an employee of a state, since none of the states will need anyone for this purpose any longer. How would it increase public expense to have the United States, rather than the states, employ customs officers?

Where else will our expenses dramatically rise, as some have said will happen? The main possibility, as far as I can see, is in supporting the judges of the United States. I am not including the President, because there is now a president of the congress whose expenses will no doubt be almost equal to those of the President of the United States. It is certain that supporting the judges of the United States will be an additional expense, but we do not know how much this will be yet because it will depend very much on how the Judicial Branch will be organized.[1] But no reasonable organization of the Judiciary would incur expenses which would have any great impact on the Treasury.

Let's now look at those things that would allow us to make up for extra expenses that may result from establishing the proposed government with savings.

The first thing will be the great amount of business that will be performed by the President—business which currently keeps congress busy year round. All foreign diplomacy will naturally become his responsibility, along with the Senate, whose final approval will be required for all treaties.[2] It will therefore be possible for Congress to be in session and accomplish its work during a much smaller portion of the year, perhaps a quarter of a year for the House of Representatives, and a third or half of a year for the Senate, although the extra business of treaties and appointments may require more time for the Senate. From this, we may conclude that, until the number of Representatives in the House of

---

1. United States Constitution: Article III, Section 1.
2. United States Constitution: Article II, Section 2, clause 2.

Representatives is greatly increased beyond its current number, a great amount of money will be saved by Congress being in session for only a portion of the year compared with the current congress, which is in session year round.

There is yet another very important thing to consider with respect to the financial utility of this new system. The business of the United States has up until now occupied both the state legislatures and congress, with congress requiring certain things from the state legislatures that they then had to provide. This has forced the state legislatures to stay in session much longer simply to take care of local business, since more than half of their time has been taken up for the sake of issues related to the Union. There are now upwards of 2,000 representatives in the state legislatures who have performed what, under the new system, will be done by sixty-five people, and probably no more than 400–500 in the future.[1] Under the new government, Congress will conduct the business of the United States themselves without the intervention of the state legislatures, who will then only have to manage their own affairs and not stay in session nearly as long as they currently do. The simple fact that the state legislatures will have to be in session much less under the new system will make up for any additional expenses that will be incurred by the establishment of the new system.

The result of all of this is that any expenses which result from the establishment of the proposed Constitution will be much less than previously imagined, and they will be balanced out by significant savings. While it is not certain exactly where our expenses or our savings will be increased, it is certain that a government any less expensive would be unable to fulfill the purposes of the Union.

—Publius

---

1. There are currently 535 representatives in Congress: 435 representatives and 100 senators.

PART SIX

TAXATION WITH
REPRESENTATION

Taxes. The mere mention of the word evokes strong reactions in most people today, just as it did when the nation was formed. Who has the power to collect taxes? What will the tax rates be? Who will get special tax breaks? Where does the money go? Those questions were on the minds of Americans during the constitutional debate just as much as they are today.

Federalist 12 was Publius's first attempt at answering them.

Instead of getting into the minutiae of policy, Alexander Hamilton, who wrote No. 12, focused on the ways government could increase "the number of paths to prosperity." After all, the tax base is ultimately a function of a country's wealth, and wealth is a function of commerce—not government regulation. "The diligent merchant, the hardworking farmer, the active mechanic, the industrious manufacturer, and indeed all men," Hamilton wrote, "look forward with great and growing anticipation to reaping the rewards of their hard work."

Reaping the rewards of their hard work, what a concept! Hamilton didn't promise handouts or equality of outcome; he wrote about rewarding hard work—and he believed that the government's role should be to encourage that effort. There was no mention of using taxation as a tool for social engineering or redistributing wealth to create equality or fairness.

Fortunately for America, Providence seemed to have once again put the right person in the right place at the right time. Hamilton, who so keenly understood taxes and economics that he would go on to become America's first treasury secretary, explained that the velocity with which money moves through the system affects *everything*, including citizens' ability to pay taxes. The key was to ensure that government did not, through regulations, bureaucracy, and stifling taxes, handcuff banks or individuals from keeping commerce moving. Taxes were meant to grow prosperity—not government.

On the other hand, Hamilton was not a fool. He understood that the new government would have certain expenses related to it, and he also knew, based on their experience in the Revolution, that a country is only as strong as its bank account. A country with no money may as well be a country with no army. Therefore, he reasoned, nothing should be off the table when it came to national emergencies.

But that didn't mean Hamilton was a fan of all taxes. His papers on taxes made it clear that he favored the narrow application of excise taxes, which are basically taxes on consumption. The notion of an "income tax" was not even in the discussion back then. It wasn't until the Sixteenth Amendment, ratified in 1913, that the federal government officially had the power to directly tax citizens. Hamilton viewed direct taxation as a cumbersome, ineffective means of collecting revenue and, in a section that could easily have been written yesterday, explained why higher taxes don't mean more money for the government.

> It is evident from the state of the country, from the habits of the people, from the experience we have had on the point itself, that it is impracticable to raise any very considerable sums by direct taxation. Tax laws have in vain been multiplied; new methods to enforce the collection have in vain been tried; the public expectation has been uniformly disappointed, and the treasuries of the States have remained empty.

Simply put, an increase in tax laws or rates doesn't result in an increase in tax revenue. It's an economic fact that was as true then as it is now. For evidence, just take a look at the current statistics. While our tax rates have been all over the board in the last few decades, the amount of revenue we take in is consistently right around 18 percent of gross domestic product. It's not the *rates* that matter; it's the amount of economic activity that can be generated. Hamilton, and many of the other Founders, understood that, and believed that direct taxation and higher rates punished hard work, discouraged entrepreneurship, and ultimately slowed down economic growth.

But while those arguments were made by Hamilton as a matter of philosophy, they weren't part of the Constitution itself. The federal government would be able to tax citizens who were already being taxed by the states and would also have the power to collect taxes. That led many to express concerns that the federal government might simply overpower the states—a concern that Hamilton addressed in Federalist 32.

His basic argument was that while, yes, the federal government would have a lot of power, the people would never allow them to encroach on their state's rights. "I am persuaded," he wrote, "that the sense of the people, the extreme hazard of provoking the resentments of the State governments, and a conviction of the utility and necessity of local administrations for local purposes, would be a complete barrier against the oppressive use of such a power . . ."

I don't think that worked out exactly the way Hamilton thought it might. I'm not sure how things work in the state where you live, but I'm guessing that it's a lot like it is in New York: The state is to the federal government what an ant is to a steamroller. The federal government has often used its oppressive power without so much as a peep from the states. Or, if the states do try to stand up (i.e., as happened in some cases during the debate over the recent health-care bill), the government often resorts to financial penalties.

Understanding the authors' thoughts on taxation goes a long way in helping to explain today's mess in Washington. Remember, the Founders were all about an "efficient" government, not one that takes in an ever-increasing amount of revenue in order to fund an ever-increasing set of laws and regulations.

The rest of No. 32 was focused on the issues that arise by having two different taxing authorities. Hamilton again put a lot of faith into the system, assuming that, except for some very specific circumstances that the constitution addressed, the federal and state governments would just figure it out. If that was his standard, I guess he turned out to be right. They *did* figure it out, but unfortunately the solution was that everyone should tax everything.

In Federalist 36, Hamilton took on a few more of the objections that had been raised by critics over giving the federal government the power to tax. While he made a great case—Washington obviously needs to fund a number of necessary governmental functions—it's also clear that he did not envision just how large and powerful the federal government would eventually become.

One of the specific objections was that a national government would not have enough knowledge of local conditions to set proper tax rates and policy. Hamilton argued that it would because it could leverage local assets, like state representatives. In retrospect, I think what Hamilton could not have known was that there would come a time when the federal government simply *didn't care* about local conditions. (In fact, federal government often uses the local conditions of states to expand power, as they did with the stimulus funds.) Having information available is one thing; actually using it is another.

To ensure that all direct taxes were fair and equal, Hamilton explained that the Constitution required that citizens would be taxed by the same set of universal rules. The Rule of Apportionment (Article I, Section 2, clause 3 of the Constitution) would determine how much tax revenue should be collected from each state, based on its population. This rule, according to Hamilton, would ensure that, because the direct taxes were based on a mathematical formula, they could not be abused. As a state's population grew, not only would its representation in Congress increase, but so would its tax burden.

Hamilton also returned to the objection about possible interference between the states and the feds that he addressed earlier in No. 32. He reiterated that he felt this argument had been overblown—though his logic does not seem to have held up over time. He believed, simply, that each side (state and federal) would not tax the things that the other side already was. "An effectual expedient for this purpose will be," he wrote, "mutually, to abstain from those objects which either side may have first had recourse to." In other words, if gas is already being taxed by the state, then the federal government wouldn't add their own tax to it.

We all know how that turned out.

But let's be honest: Hamilton in no way argued that the federal or state government would not have the power to tax. In fact, he believed that even taxes that he did not support, like a poll tax, should not be specifically banned, because they one day might be necessary. In emergencies, Hamilton claimed, the government would need every asset at its disposal. As he explained:

> There may exist certain critical and tempestuous conjunctures of the State, in which a poll tax may become an inestimable resource. And as I know nothing to exempt this portion of the globe from the common calamities that have befallen other

parts of it, I acknowledge my aversion to every project that is calculated to disarm the government of a single weapon, which in any possible contingency might be usefully employed for the general defense and security.

In other words, since every country eventually faces its share of emergencies, it would be shortsighted to take away anything that could generate revenue in times of need. It makes sense from a logical perspective—but I think what Hamilton failed to realize was that the government might one day consider *every* day to be an emergency.

To put into context just how different our current tax system is from the one our Founders envisioned, consider this prediction from Hamilton (our translation):

> Once each state's debt is done away with, and their expenses are limited to their natural levels, then any possibility of interference between the laws of the states and the Union will almost completely disappear. A small tax on land will fulfill the needs of the states and will turn out to be their most simple and appropriate resource.

I may be mistaken, but I haven't noticed any headlines recently about state debt being "done away with" and I certainly haven't heard any politicians propose that we revert to "small taxes" on land only. These days the discussion is all about how high the top rates should go, what the appropriate definition of "rich" really is, or whether the "AMT patch" should be extended for another year.

Now, I know you may be thinking that none of this really matters. We live in different times, we face different issues, and we have different economic needs, right? But maybe that's how things have gone wrong. Maybe our willingness to stray from the limited-government, limited-tax ideas of our Founders is exactly the reason *why* things are so different now. Is it really a surprise that those who advocate for the endless expansion of government, for stifling regulations on businesses, for greater redistribution of wealth, and for ever-expanding control over the activities of citizens also almost always support higher taxation, as well?

Taxes are, after all, one of the most effective weapons that government has in managing the economy and its people. Taxes can be used to target, to reward, to dissuade, and, of course, to penalize and punish. How a tax system is devised not only impacts prosperity, but also impacts the two reasons the government exists in the first place: freedom and happiness.

It's obvious that our Founders understood this. It's also clear that our modern leaders do not.

FEDERALIST NO. 12

The Message: Prosperity comes from the energies of the people, not from the government. The faster that money circulates through the economy, the more the government will have available to it through taxes.

Original Quote: "The prosperity of commerce is now perceived and acknowledged by all enlightened statesmen to be the most useful as well as the most productive source of national wealth, and has accordingly become a primary object of their political cares."

Relevance to Today: Private commercial activity was the primary driver of national wealth back then, and it's still the primary driver today. But political elites want us to believe that the government can create this wealth itself by "creating jobs" or tweaking tax policy to punish or reward various groups. The truth is that creative, motivated, and energized people are responsible for creating jobs—not politicians.

Original Quote: "It is evident from the state of the country, from the habits of the people, from the experience we have had on the point itself, that it is impracticable to raise any very considerable sums by direct taxation. Tax laws have in vain been multiplied; new methods to enforce the collection have in vain been tried; the public expectation has been uniformly disappointed, and the treasuries of the States have remained empty."

Relevance to Today: It's kind of funny that this logic was so clear 225 years ago but is so muddy today. Raising tax rates on direct taxes simply does not result in more government wealth. That's why the percentage of revenue when compared to the size of our economy stays consistent no matter what the top tax rates are, and it's one reason why the "treasuries of the States" are still empty today.

NUMBER 12

How the Union Will Foster the Collection of Revenue

ALEXANDER HAMILTON

For the New York Packet: Tuesday, November 20, 1787

The Importance of a Strong Union to Our Safety and Prosperity

Constitutional References:

Article I: §8/1, 3, 5, 10

The effect of the Union on each state's economic prosperity has already been sufficiently outlined, so we'll now turn to looking at how the Union would generate revenue.[1]

All enlightened citizens now recognize and acknowledge that a well-functioning economy is the most useful, as well as the most productive, source of national wealth, and as such, has become one of our primary concerns. By increasing the number of paths to prosperity, and by circulating precious metals,[2] which are valued objects of human greed and enterprise, all segments of

---

1. United States Constitution: Article I, Section 8, clauses 1, 3, 5, and 10.
2. United States Constitution: Article I, Section 8, clause 5.

industry become energized and produce not only more products, but also a greater variety of them.

The diligent merchant, the hardworking farmer, the active mechanic, the industrious manufacturer, and indeed all men look forward with great anticipation to reaping the rewards of their hard work. Undeniable experience has decided the long-standing debate between agriculture and commerce, silencing the rivalry between both, and proving that their interests are intimately linked. It has been found in numerous countries that the value of land increases as commerce flourishes—and how could it be any other way? Since commerce allows for the free circulation of all the products made around the world, provides land cultivators with new incentives, is the greatest source of increasing money in a state, and is the faithful servant of both labor and industry, is it any wonder that it would also increase the value of land, which is the source of nearly all products and goods? It is amazing that something so simple could have so many opponents. This is just one of many examples of how misinformed jealousy and too much intellectualizing get in the way of common sense and conviction.

The ability of a country to pay taxes is almost always determined by the quantity of money in circulation, and the speed with which it circulates. Commerce facilitates both of these, making it easier to pay taxes and providing the treasury with all that it requires.

The German emperor's hereditary lands contain a large amount of fertile, cultivated, and populous territory, most of which has excellent and mild climates. In addition, some of the best silver and gold mines of Europe are in these territories, and yet the German emperor hardly profits from all of this because that country lacks any developed commerce. Several times he has been forced to go to foreign nations for financial assistance in order to preserve his most basic and important interests, and he is incapable, via his own resources, of sustaining a long war.

But it is not just this aspect of revenue that the Union will be useful for. There are other ways its influence will be felt more immediately and decisively. It is obvious from the current state of the country, the habits of the People, and our own experience, that it is impractical to raise a large amount of money by direct taxation. The number of tax laws has increased in vain, new methods of enforcing collection have been tried, and yet the public has been consistently disappointed with the results as the treasuries of the states remain empty. The system of administration that results from popularly elected governments, as well as a real lack of money resulting from a sluggish and broken state of trade, has defeated every attempt by the legislatures to increase revenues.

No one who is aware of what goes on in other countries will be surprised by this. Even in a nation as rich as Great Britain, where direct taxes on the wealthy might be more tolerated and, because of the strength of their central government, more feasible, most tax revenues come from indirect taxes, such as customs duties and excise taxes.[1] Taxes on imported goods form the majority of the customs duties. It is evident that, here in America, we will have to depend on those types of taxes for revenue for a long time.

For the most part, excise taxes must be narrowly applied, since the People will not easily accept their intrusive and authoritative nature for very long. On the other hand, only a small amount of revenues will be collected from taxes on the homes and lands of farmers, as personal property is too difficult to tax in any other way than by unseen taxes on consumption.

The things that best enable us to utilize such a valuable resource must be adapted to our political welfare; and this will

---

1. *excise taxes:* Referenced and defined in Federalist 21.

clearly mean the existence of a general Union. As helpful as this will be to commerce, it will be just as useful to collecting revenues from that commerce. Also, as helpful as the Union will be to making tax collecting regulations more simple and effective, it will be just as useful at making the same tax rate more productive, as well as giving government the power to increase the rate without damaging trade.

The relative geography of these states, the number of rivers that run through them, the bays along their shores, the ease of communication that exists in every direction, and the shared language and culture of their people would make it easy to engage in illegal trade if they were disunited. That would result in the commercial regulations of each state being frequently ignored. Each state or confederacy would be driven by mutual jealousy to avoid this situation by ensuring low taxes. Our governments would not accept the rigorous precautions used by European nations to protect both the land and sea routes into their countries, precautions that, by the way, have been proven insufficient to guard against the greedy schemes of others.

France has an army of patrols that are constantly on duty to make sure that her economic regulations are enforced so that contraband dealers are not allowed to make any inroads into their economy. Mr. Necker[1] has estimated that there are upwards of twenty thousand men in these patrols. This clearly proves that if the states end the Union and find themselves in a situation similar to that of France with respect to her neighbors, they will face immense difficulties in attempting to prevent illegal trade in a land that is very well connected, and will, therefore, be at a disadvantage in collecting taxes. Besides, the arbitrary and overbearing

---

1. *Mr. Necker:* Jacques Necker (1732–1804) was a French statesman and the finance minister of Louis XVI (1754–93; reigned 1774–91).

powers required by those patrols would be intolerable in a free country.

If, however, we had one national government there would only be one border for us to guard with respect to our commerce: the ATLANTIC COAST. Ships arriving directly from foreign countries with valuable cargo on board would rarely choose to go through the complicated and hazardous process of unloading their illegal cargo before coming into port since they would have to face both the dangers of the coast, and of being detected before and after arriving at their final destination. Only an ordinary amount of vigilance would be required to prevent any violation of the laws concerning our right to revenue from customs duties.[1] A few armed vessels, wisely placed and correctly utilized, could prove to be an effective system of law enforcement at very little expense.

Since the government would have the cooperation of the states, and also an interest in enforcing the laws equally everywhere, such a naval force would more than likely be effective. As the United States are[2] far away from Europe, and even further away from all the other places that we trade with, we should take advantage of this gift from nature by preserving the Union rather than giving it up by remaining disunited.

The time it takes to travel between us and Europe is impractical compared with only the few hours or a single night it would take to travel between the coasts of France and Britain. That provides an extraordinary level of security to us against contraband coming directly from foreign countries, whereas a roundabout route to one state through another would be both easy and safe. Any perceptive person can recognize the difference between a

---

1. United States Constitution: Article I, Section 8, clause 10.
2. Not "is" until after the Civil War.

direct import from abroad, and the indirect importation of small packages at the right time via the medium of another bordering state—something that would be made even easier by the level of communication between the states themselves.

It is clear that one National government would be able to extend the duties on imports further than would be practical by the states or any partial confederacy, and at much less expense; and I feel safe in asserting that these duties have, I believe, never exceeded an average of 3% in any state. In France they are estimated to be approximately 15%, and they are even higher in Britain. In this country, there doesn't seem to be anything that would prevent the current rate from at least being tripled. If regulated by the Federal government, alcohol alone might be able to provide considerable revenues. If the entire amount of alcohol imported into the United States was proportional to the amount imported into New York, then there would be approximately four million gallons imported, which, at a shilling per gallon, would produce two hundred thousand pounds in revenue. This tax rate on alcohol would be easily accepted, but even if it lowered consumption, such an effect would be helpful to agriculture, the economy, and also to the morals and health of society. Alcohol is, after all, perhaps the most overconsumed commodity in this country today.

Since a nation cannot exist for very long without revenue, what will the consequences be if we are not able to utilize revenue to its fullest extent, as commerce would allow us to do? Without this single resource, we must give away our independence and sink to the despised level of a mere province. No nation will willingly accept this, so we must bring in revenue whenever and however we can.

In this country, if most revenue does not come from commerce, it must be oppressively taken from land. It has already been concluded that excise taxes are not supported by the People, and are therefore not a very useful way to collect tax revenue. Also, in states where agriculture is the primary occupation, there are an insufficient number of goods that can be taxed in such a way, and therefore these taxes wouldn't provide much revenue in those states anyway.

Personal property, as I mentioned earlier, is too difficult to trace in order to provide any significant amount of revenue—other than through taxes on consumption. In large cities it may be possible to oppress individuals in this way without much benefit to the state, but it would almost certainly escape the eye of the tax collector outside of the cities. However, since the necessities of the state must somehow be met, most of the public burden must necessarily be placed on landowners because of the inability to acquire revenue from other sources. On the other hand, since the requirements of government can never find any adequate supply of revenue unless all the sources of revenue are open to its demands, the public finances will never be respectable or secure unless this is so. Therefore, even if we did utilize these taxes, we wouldn't even have the consolation of a full treasury to make up for the oppression of those who work the land. But public and private distress will keep pace with each other, and when they eventually unite, they will reject the foolish idea that we should not form a union.

—Publius

FEDERALIST NO. 32

The Message: While all levels of government must have the power of taxation, the states and the people must be on guard to ensure that it is used justly.

―――――――――――

Original Quote: "Although I am of opinion that there would be no real danger of the consequences which seem to be apprehended to the State governments from a power in the Union to control them in the levies of money, because I am persuaded that the sense of the people, the extreme hazard of provoking the resentments of the State governments, and a conviction of the utility and necessity of local administrations for local purposes, would be a complete barrier against the oppressive use of such a power; yet I am willing here to allow, in its full extent, the justness of the reasoning which requires that the individual States should possess an independent and uncontrollable authority to raise their own revenues for the supply of their own wants."

Relevance to Today: The federal government and state governments should collect taxes only to carry out their individual, constitutionally supported mandates. Unfortunately, the federal government has taken over in areas such as local education, so that our tax dollars take a very expensive vacation in Washington, D.C., and come back to us without local control.

NUMBER 32

Taxation (Continued)

ALEXANDER HAMILTON

For the Daily Advertiser: Thursday, January 3, 1788

Explanation and Justification of the New Powers of the Union

Constitutional References:

Article I: §8/1, 4 | §9/5 | §10/2

I believe that the power of the Union to control the states with regard to collecting revenue will not present any real dangers to the state governments.[1] I believe this because I am convinced that the sense of the People, the extreme hazards associated with provoking the state governments, as well as the general awareness of the usefulness and necessity of local governments for local purposes, will all act as complete barriers to the oppressive use of this power.

However, for the sake of argument, let's assume there is a good reason for state governments to have an independent and uncontrollable power to raise their own revenues for their own desires. Even if you make that assumption it's clear that, with the

---

1. United States Constitution: Article I, Section 10, clause 2.

exception of taxes on imports and exports, the states would retain the complete and absolute authority to raise their own revenues. Any attempt on the part of the Federal government to infringe on those rights would be a violent assumption of power, unwarranted by any Article or clause in the Constitution.

Consolidating all of the states into one nation would imply that each state would lose its national sovereignty and that whatever power remained in the parts would be entirely dependent on the National will. But since the new Constitution aims to only create a partial Union or consolidation, the state governments will retain all the sovereign rights that they had before, and that were not *exclusively* delegated to the United States by the Constitution.[1] This *exclusively* delegated sovereignty would only occur in three cases:

1. Where the Constitution explicitly granted an exclusive authority to the Union;
2. Where the Constitution granted an authority to the Union and prohibited the states from exercising the same authority;
3. Where the Constitution granted an authority to the Union which would be absolutely and totally *contradictory* and *repugnant* if it existed in a similar form in the states.

I have used the terms "contradictory" and "repugnant" in order to distinguish between this case and one that might appear to resemble it, but it is, in fact, entirely different. An example of

---

1. This principle was eventually codified in the Tenth Amendment of the Bill of Rights (found in the Appendix of this work), which was passed by the 1st Congress of the United States in 1789, and reads: "The powers not delegated to the United States by the Constitution, nor prohibited by it to the States, are reserved to the States respectively, or to the people." (Referenced in Federalist 40, 81–82.)

this would be any shared jurisdiction between the Federal and state governments that might occasionally interfere with the policy of any Branch of government, but would not imply any direct contradiction or repugnancy in relation to Constitutional authority.

These three cases of exclusive Federal jurisdiction can be exemplified by the following examples: Article I, Section 8, clause 17 explicitly says that Congress shall exercise *"exclusive legislation"* over the district that will become the seat of government.[1] This is an example of the first case. Clause 1 of the same section gives Congress the power *"to lay and collect taxes, duties, imposts, and excises,"* while Article I, Section 10, clause 2 declares that *"no state shall,* without the consent of Congress, *lay any imposts or duties on imports or exports,* except for the purpose of executing its inspection laws." Therefore, the Union will have the exclusive power to lay taxes (duties) on imports and exports (assuming Congress has not granted that power to any state). Another clause declares that Congress will not be able to impose a tax or duty on goods exported from any state,[2] which means that the allowable exception can now only extend to *taxes* (duties) *on imports.* This is an example of the second case.

An example of the third case can be found in the clause that declares that Congress shall have power "to establish a UNIFORM RULE of naturalization throughout the United States."[3] This must necessarily be an exclusive power, since if each state could set its own rule of naturalization, then there would be no UNIFORM RULE.

A case that some may think is very similar to the one just

---

1. The future Washington, D.C.
2. United States Constitution: Article I, Section 9, clause 5.
3. United States Constitution: Article I, Section 8, clause 4.

mentioned, but that is in fact entirely different, revolves around the power to impose taxes on all goods that are neither imports nor exports. I believe that this power has concurrent and co-equal authority in both the United States and in the individual states. There is clearly no phrase in the Constitution that makes this power *exclusive* to the Union, and there is no phrase that prevents the states from exercising it either. It's so clear that this language does not exist in the Constitution that a persuasive contrary argument could be made given the states' restriction on taxing imports and exports.

The very fact that this restriction was inserted implies that the states would possess all the powers that the restriction does not include, and going even further, that the states' authority over all other taxes would remain undiminished. Any other view of this power would be both unnecessary and dangerous. Unnecessary because if giving the Union the power to impose taxes on imported and exported goods implied that the states could not impose their own taxes on the very same goods, or that they had to be submissive to the Federal government on that issue, then the restriction would be completely irrelevant. And dangerous because including this power in the Constitution would lead to something that was never intended: the states having a concurrent power of taxation with the Union on all goods not specifically restricted.

In reality, this restriction is an example of what lawyers call a NEGATIVE PREGNANT, meaning a *negation* of one thing and an *affirmation* of another. The negation of the state's authority to impose taxes on imported and exported goods is an affirmation of its authority to impose taxes on all other goods. It would be bad reasoning to argue that this clause means that the states are *absolutely* excluded from taxing other goods, and that all such taxes were *under the control* of Congress. The restraint placed on the states only says that they cannot, *without the consent of Congress*, impose such taxes. So, if we were to interpret this with the same bad reasoning that the opponents of the Constitution use, it would amount to a very formal provision in the Constitution being inserted for the sake of a very absurd conclusion: that the states, *with the consent of Congress*, could tax imports and exports, or, for that matter, tax every other type of good *unless they were controlled* by the same Congress. If that was the intention, then why wasn't it placed in the original clause that allegedly gives the general power of taxation completely to the Union?[1] Obviously this could not have been the intention, so that reasoning can't be supported.

The supposed contradiction between a concurrent power to tax some good existing in both the states and the Union, however, cannot be supported by the same reasoning. It is possible that a state might impose a tax on a certain good, which might make it unwise for the Union to also tax the same good—but that by no means implies that the Union wouldn't have a constitutional ability to do so. How much the tax should be, and how wise it would be to impose would both be questions of prudence, but would not involve any direct conflict of powers. The financial policies of both the Union and the state governments might, from time to time, not coincide exactly, and therefore might require mutual restraint on both sides. However, it would require an obvious constitutional contradiction, and not merely an inconvenience in the exercise of a power, to imply the destruction of a preexisting sovereign right.

The division of sovereign power between the Union and the states makes a concurrent jurisdiction between the two necessary in certain cases, and also leads to the theory that all powers that are not explicitly taken away from the states in order to be given

---

1. United States Constitution: Article I, Section 8, clause 1.

to the Union shall fully remain theirs. The very nature of the Constitution makes this clear. Notwithstanding the powers that are explicitly given to the Union, it's obvious that a lot of care was taken to specifically forbid the states from exercising certain powers in cases where it was deemed inappropriate for the states to exercise the same powers as the Union. Article I, Section 10 includes all such clauses.

These facts are a clear indication of how the Convention dealt with these issues and serve to provide us with a reliable method of interpreting the Constitution. These interpretations justify the arguments I have made and refute all those made to the contrary.

—Publius

NUMBER 36

Taxation (Continued)

ALEXANDER HAMILTON

For the New York Packet: Tuesday, January 8, 1788
Explanation and Justification of the New Powers of the Union

Constitutional References:
Article I: §8/1

The previous papers have shown that, whether or not there are more or less members in Congress, they will consist almost entirely of landowners, merchants, and professionals. Some may point out that other types of citizens can be found in the state legislatures, and they're right—there are some exceptions to this rule, but not enough to greatly affect the general character of the government. There are strong minds in every walk of life who can rise above the disadvantages of their situation, and whose reputation can command the respect of those not only from their own class, but from society in general. The door to elected office ought to be open to all, and I trust, because of human nature, that we will see examples of determined and gifted plants taking root in the soil of both the Federal and state legis-

FEDERALIST NO. 36

The Message: Our tax system benefits from being closest to the people because it will spur competition between the states and make taxes lower and more efficiently collected.

Original Quote: "When the particular debts of the States are done away, and their expenses come to be limited within their natural compass, the possibility almost of interference will vanish. A small land tax will answer the purpose of the States, and will be their most simple and most fit resource."

Relevance to Today: States should remain debt-free and should obtain their revenue through reasonable taxes on land. Today we see states not only dependent on the federal government to balance their budgets, but also constantly expanding the scope of items that fall in their domain. The states will never be able to exercise their sovereignty as long as they are dependent on Washington.

Original Quote: "As to the suggestion of double taxation, the answer is plain. The wants of the Union are to be supplied in one way or another; if to be done by the authority of the federal government, it will not be to be done by that of the State government."

Relevance to Today: While the Founders argued in favor of the federal and state governments' each having the power to tax, they were convinced that neither would tax the same thing at the same time. But now? Plenty of items, from gasoline to alcohol to tobacco, have federal excise taxes along with state sales taxes. In addition, of course, there's income tax, which is often charged at the federal, state, and sometimes even local level. These concurrent taxes were never part of the Founders' plan.

latures. But these occasional examples don't render my general point on this subject any less valid.

While this subject can be looked at from several other viewpoints, they would all lead to the same conclusion. In particular, I would ask whether there is a greater affinity or common interest between the carpenter and the blacksmith and the linen manufacturer or stocking weaver, or between a merchant and any of them? It is well known that there are often as many rivalries between the different branches of the mechanical and manufacturing trades as there are between any of the branches of labor and industry. So, unless there were so many representatives in Congress that its deliberations would be devoid of all sense of wisdom, then it would be impossible for what seems to be the spirit of this objection to ever take place in practice. But I will avoid dwelling on this objection any longer since the arguments being made against it are so vague that they are impossible to respond to.

There is, however, a specific objection that is worth discussing. It's been asserted that Congress's power of internal taxation[1] could never be effectively used because those who exercise it would lack sufficient knowledge of local circumstances, and because of the interference between the tax laws of the Union and the states. The claim that Congress would not have sufficient knowledge in this regard seems to be entirely baseless. If a state legislature requires knowledge and details about any particular county in the state, how does it go about getting it? From the representatives of that county, of course! Isn't it possible that Congress could obtain similar knowledge from the representatives of each state? And isn't it safe to assume that the members elected to Congress will be intelligent enough to be able to communicate that information? Does "knowledge of local circumstances" mean a detailed knowledge

---

1. United States Constitution: Article I, Section 8, clause 1.

of the topography of each state, its mountains, rivers, streams, highways, back roads, and all? Or does it simply mean a general awareness of a state's situation and resources, the condition of its agriculture, commerce, and manufacturing, the nature of its products and what it consumes, and the different degrees and kinds of its wealth, property, and industry?

Nations in general, even under popular governments, usually delegate the administration of their finances to a single individual, or to committees of just a few individuals who prepare a plan of taxation that is subsequently passed into law. Inquisitive and enlightened statesmen are generally considered to be the best qualified to decide what things should be taxed. This, in and of itself, is a clear indication of the type of knowledge of local circumstances that is required for the purposes of taxation.

The taxes that are intended to fall under the general category of internal taxes can be further divided into two groups, *direct* and *indirect* internal taxes. Although both are objected to, it seems that the arguments are mostly confined to direct internal taxes. Indirect taxes, which are understood to be taxes and excises on consumable goods, rarely encounter any difficulties. Any knowledge related to them will be based on the nature of the good itself, or would be easy to obtain from any well-informed person, especially from the merchant class.

The circumstances that may distinguish these types of taxes from one state to another would be few, simple, and easy to comprehend. The biggest thing to avoid would be taxing those goods that are primarily used in only a single state—but this could easily be determined by examining the system of revenue in each state. That, in turn, could always be done by examining the respective laws of each state, as well as the information provided by the representatives of each of those states in Congress.

The objection to direct taxes seems to have more credibility when applied to real property, or to houses or land. But even that view does not stand up to closer inspection. Land taxes are commonly imposed in one of two ways: either by an *actual* appraisal of the value of the land (whether this is permanent or periodical), or by occasional assessments of the value of the property at the discretion of, or according to the best judgment of, the public officials who are in charge of doing such things. In either case, the actual EXECUTION of that duty, which, of course, requires knowledge of local details, must be carried out by discreet people who act as commissioners or assessors, and who are either elected by the People or appointed by the government for that purpose. All the law can do is name the People who will do this job, or prescribe the process of their election or appointment, to determine how many people will do that job, and their qualifications, and to draw a general outline of their powers and duties. Is there anything in this process that can't be performed by Congress just as well as by the state legislatures? The attention of both can only go so far as general principles, while the local details, as they are already observed, must be referred to those who will actually put the plan into action.

Fortunately, there is a simple point of view that can be taken to satisfy all sides: Congress can simply use the *system of each state within that particular state*. Whatever method that is already being used to impose and collect this type of tax in each state can be adopted and employed by the Federal government.

Remember, the amount of these taxes will not be left up to Congress, but will be determined by the population of each state as described in Article I, Section 2, clause 3 of the Constitution ("Rule of Apportionment").[1] An actual census, or counting of the People, will allow this rule to be created, which will then ef-

---

1. *Rule of Apportionment*: Referenced and defined in Federalist 15.

fectively shut the door to the possibility of bias or oppression. Therefore, the Constitution provides security against this power of taxation being abused. In addition to this security, there is a provision in the Constitution that says that "all duties imposts and excises, shall be UNIFORM throughout the United States."[1]

Different speakers and writers who support the Constitution have appropriately observed that if exercising this internal power of taxation by the Union proves to be inconvenient, either through debate or actual experience, then the Federal government can instead resort to a system of requisitions and quotas (similar to the one currently in place under the Articles of Confederation).

Those who oppose the Constitution have triumphantly responded by asking why not omit that ambiguous power in the first place and rely on requisitions instead? Two solid answers can be given to this question. First, the actual use of this new power may be found both *convenient* and *necessary*, since it would be impossible to prove theoretically that it could not be used advantageously, except by experimenting with it. In fact, the opposite seems more likely. Second, such a power in the Constitution will prove to be very useful in making a system of requisitions effective. If the states know that the Union can supply itself without using them then they'll have a powerful motive to act.

As to the interference between the revenue laws of the Union and the states, we have already seen that there can't be any clash of authority. Therefore, the laws of each cannot, in a legal sense, interfere with the other. It is quite possible, in fact, to avoid any interference between the policies of each system. An effective solution to this problem would be for each side to mutually abstain from taxing those things that the other side may have begun to tax first. As neither side can *control* the other, each will have an obvi-

---

1. United States Constitution: Article I, Section 8, clause 1.

ous interest in this reciprocal self-control, and where there is an *immediate* common interest between the two, we can safely count on it being utilized.

Either way, once each state's debt is done away with, and their expenses are limited to their natural levels, then any possibility of interference between the laws of the states and the Union will almost completely disappear. A small tax on land will fulfill the needs of the states and will turn out to be their most simple and appropriate resource.

Many terrifying ghosts have been made out of this power of internal taxation in order to arouse the fears of the People—double sets of revenue officials (Federal and state), the doubling of the burdens of the People by double taxations, and of course the frightening idea of some type of horrifying, oppressive poll tax. All have been ingenuously played off with all of the dexterity of political trickery.

As to there being double sets of revenue officials, there are at least two cases where it would be impossible for this to happen. The first is when the right to impose a certain tax is exclusive with the Union, such as taxes on imports, and the second is anything that had not yet fallen under any state regulations, and this could apply to a variety of things. In all other cases it's likely that the United States will completely abstain from taxing those things that are already primarily taxed for local purposes, or will make use of state officials and state regulations for the sake of collecting any additional Federal tax. That would be the best solution to collecting revenue, since it would be more cost-effective and would avoid any anger on the part of the state governments or the People being directed toward the Federal government. In any event, this would be a practical way to avoid any inconveniences, and there's nothing more we can do other than to show that the predicted evils do not necessarily result from the Plan.

With regard to arguments over the supposed inappropriate use of influence, it should be enough to say that inappropriate influence can't be assumed—but this argument can be answered more specifically. If this kind of influence existed in the government of the Union, then the best way to accomplish its goal would be to utilize state officials as much as possible, and to win them over to the Union by augmenting their salaries. This would help change the tide of state influence toward the direction of the Union, instead of forcing Federal influence to flow in a contrary and choppy current. But arguments like this are offensive, and should be banished from the debate on the great question now before the People. They accomplish no other purpose than to cast doubt over the truth.

As to double taxation, or being taxed twice for the same thing, the answer is plain: The needs of the Union will be supplied in one way or another, and if that is by the authority of the Federal government, then it will not be left to the state governments. The amount of taxes that will be paid by the community will be the same in either case, except that there will be an advantage if the taxes are collected by the Union: The all-important resource of commercial taxes (which are the most convenient source of revenue) can be more efficiently managed under Federal, rather than state regulation. That will, of course, help avoid the possibility of having to use more inconvenient methods to collect them in the first place. There will also be another advantage: Should there be any problem in exercising the power of internal taxation, it will force the government to take greater care in the choice and arrangement of the method of collection. This will tend to make it a permanent policy of the Federal government to push as far as possible toward making the luxury of the rich subservient to the public treasury in order to avoid the possibility of having to impose taxes that might arouse dissatisfaction among the poorer and more numerous classes of society. It's wonderful when the government's interest in preserving its own power coincides with a proper distribution of public burdens and tends to prevent the least wealthy part of the community from being oppressed!

As far as poll taxes are concerned, I don't hesitate in making it clear that I disapprove of them. While they have existed for a long time in those states that have been the most uniformly protective of their freedom,[1] I would regret seeing them used by the Federal government. But just because they have the power to impose them, does that mean that they necessarily *will* be imposed? Every state in the Union has the power to impose this type of a tax, and yet some states have not implemented it. Should the states be characterized as tyrannies simply because they possess this power? If they aren't characterized as such, then how can the existence of the same power be used as an objection to the proposed Federal government, or claimed to be an obstacle to the Constitution's adoption?

As much as I dislike this type of tax, I am still thoroughly convinced that the Federal government should have the power to resort to it if necessary. There are certain national emergencies during which certain actions that are avoided during ordinary times may become essential to the public well-being. Because of the possibility of such emergencies, the government ought to have the option of resorting to these contingencies. In fact, the lack of things that, if taxed, could actually be productive sources of revenues is one particular reason why the options left open to the Federal government should not be restricted. There may come emergencies and stormy seasons for the nation during which a poll tax may be absolutely essential. And since I know of nothing

---

1. The New England states: New Hampshire, Massachusetts, Connecticut, Rhode Island (Maine and Vermont were not yet states at this time).

that exempts this part of the globe from the problems and disasters which have occurred on other parts of it, I freely acknowledge my hatred toward any and all attempts to disarm the government of a single weapon which, in any possible contingency, could be used to protect our common defense and security.

I've examined the powers that have been proposed for the new Federal government and that specifically deal with its resources and its ability to effectively fulfill the great and essential goals of the Union. There are other powers that, for the time being, have not yet been examined, but that will be covered in the next group of papers in order to provide a more complete view of the subject.

I flatter myself that the progress we have made so far has satisfactorily answered the concerns of those who are candid and fair. I also hope that we have shown that some of the most passionate objections that have been tirelessly made against the Constitution and which, at first glance, appear to be valid, are not only baseless, but, if they had actually been considered during the formation of the Constitution, would have rendered it unable to satisfy the great goals of public happiness and national prosperity. I equally flatter myself that a more complete and critical investigation of this new system will end up convincing even more of the sincere and objective advocates of good government that it would be, beyond any doubt, proper and wise to adopt it. How happy we will be, and how honorable it would be for human nature, if we have enough wisdom and virtue to set such a glorious example for mankind.

—Publius

PART SEVEN

TRUTH, JUSTICE,
AND THE AMERICAN WAY

Do not separate text from historical background. If you do, you will have perverted and subverted the Constitution, which can only end in a distorted, bastardized form of illegitimate government.

—James Madison

The Founding Fathers spent a lot of time wrestling with words. They knew that the specific words they chose mattered. They struggled over the language in the Constitution and they labored over their sentences in the Federalist Papers to ensure that their intent would be understood by the regular citizens who would read them.

British prime minister William Gladstone described the Constitution as "the most wonderful work ever struck off at a given time by the brain and purpose of man." [1] I share his opinion—but a lot of the Constitution's guardians, our federal and Supreme Court judges, apparently don't. Too many of them believe in what they call a "living constitution"—meaning a document whose

---

1. Derek H. Davis, *Religion and the Continental Congress: 1774–1789: Contributions to Original Intent* (New York: Oxford University Press, 2000), p. 4.

original intent is irrelevant because the interpretation of the words needs to change with the times.

Some, like Supreme Court justice Stephen Breyer, have argued that the United States should use international law as an authority in some of its decisions.[1] Supreme Court justice William J. Brennan actually argued that it is "arrogant to pretend that from our vantage we can gauge accurately the intent of the Framers on application of principle to specific, contemporary questions."[2] But somehow it's less arrogant to claim that you know better than the Founders?

Other influential people argue that the Constitution is basically out of date. Former Service Employees International Union president Andy Stern, for example, recently claimed that checks and balances in the Constitution had become an "impediment to making the changes necessary to keep America competitive in the world economy." And as one legal analyst put it, "We live on the threshold of the twenty-first century and must solve today's problems in accordance with today's perspectives and values."[3]

In my mind, this is an American tragedy. It's as if someone has taken a Rembrandt and started writing on it with crayons in an effort to "improve it."

Ironically, Publius seemed to understand that this sort of thing might one day happen. "Until the people have," Hamilton wrote in Federalist 78, "by some solemn and authoritative act, annulled or changed the established form, it is binding upon themselves collectively, as well as individually; and no presumption, or

1. Transcript of Discussion Between Antonin Scalia and Stephen Breyer, American University Washington College of Law, January 13, 2005, and Deborah Pearlstein, "Who's Afraid of International Law," American Prospect Online, April 5, 2005.

2. Quoted in Davis, Religion and the Continental Congress, p. 7.

3. Herman Schwartz, "Meese's Original Intent: A Constitutional Shell Game," Nation, December 7, 1985, p. 607.

even knowledge, of their sentiments, can warrant their representatives in a departure from it, prior to such an act."

In other words, if people at some point in the future don't like what the Constitution says, then they can amend it or annul it. Until then, it's the supreme law of the land and no judge can deviate from it.

But what about precedent, you may be thinking. Judges make decisions all the time that are then used as the basis for other decisions, and so on. Case law and precedent are widely used legal principles. Well, Hamilton addressed that, too:

> The rule which has obtained in the courts for determining their relative validity is, that the last in order of time shall be preferred to the first ... But in regard to the interfering acts of a superior and subordinate authority, of an original and derivative power, the nature and reason of the thing indicate the converse of that rule as proper to be followed. They teach us that the prior act of a superior ought to be preferred to the subsequent act of an inferior and subordinate authority; and that accordingly, whenever a particular statute contravenes the Constitution, it will be the duty of the judicial tribunals to adhere to the latter and disregard the former.

Sure, precedent is fine in most circumstances, but when it comes to the Constitution, there is no such thing. The Constitution always prevails. Always.

Because of the light they shed on the Founders' intent, the Federalist Papers are often used by the courts. In fact, the Papers are by far the most cited source for Supreme Court decisions in modern American history.[1] That should be great news, except that

---

1. Pamela C. Corley, Robert M. Howard, and David C. Nixon, "The Supreme Court and Opinion Content: The Use of the Federalist Papers," *Political Research Quarterly*, 2005.

judges too often pull excerpts to justify their own personal views, rather than the view of our Founders. Consider, for example, the 1997 Supreme Court case *Printz v. United States.*

In his dissent, Justice David Souter wrote, "In deciding these cases, which I have found closer than anticipated, it is the Federalist [Papers] that finally determines my position." He cited Federalist 27 as the justification for his dissent. Justice Antonin Scalia, who sided with the majority in the case, cited the exact same Paper to justify his decision.

They were fighting over the meaning of phrases such as "will be incorporated into operations of the national government" and "will be rendered auxiliary in the enforcement of the laws." Souter argued that those phrases meant the federal government could compel state governments to take certain actions. Scalia, however, argued that the phrase simply meant that state officials owe a duty to the federal government.

Who's right? Beats the heck out of me—I'm not an attorney— but that's not what matters. The point is that the Papers have turned into a political football, which, to anyone who reads them, should be pretty ironic since they really weren't written to be open to interpretation.

A Lifetime Sentence

Publius also used the Federalist Papers to explain exactly how the judicial branch would fit within the newly proposed government. The judiciary branch, Hamilton wrote, "has no influence over either the sword or the purse; no direction either of the strength or of the wealth of the society; and can take no active resolution whatever. It may truly be said to have neither FORCE nor WILL, but merely judgment."

As Publius made clear throughout the Papers, the roles of the legislative and judicial branches would be very different. The legislature makes laws; the judiciary makes sure those laws conform to the Constitution. Publius was very clear that the judicial branch was intended to be the weakest among the three. Why? Because judges would not be directly accountable to the voters. After being appointed by the president and confirmed by the Senate, a federal judge would then have a lifetime tenure.

As guardians of the Constitution, judges need to be insulated from the short-term sways in opinion that politicians often take advantage of. That gives them the independence they need to make decisions without regard to elections—but it also gives them a level of power not available to others in government. Barring gross misconduct, judges can stay in office as long as they want.

Because of that, Publius placed a great emphasis on their character. They can hold their offices only "during good behavior," Hamilton wrote in Federalist 78—meaning not just good behavior relative to their personal character, but also relative to their loyalty to the Constitution.

He went on to talk about how difficult it would be to find people suitable to be judges for life, saying that the "ordinary depravity" of human nature would preclude many people from qualifying. While certainly true, it's an interesting choice of words and once again illustrates one of the overarching principles that our Founders used in drafting the Constitution: the fallibility of man. By admitting that men aren't perfect, that we're sinners and depraved, it's possible to devise a system that helps find those who can rise above the crowd.

Power to the . . .

In explaining the balance of power between the legislature and judiciary, Hamilton made sure that people understood that one group would still be above them both: the people. Whenever a law stood in contrast to the Constitution, judges were to side with the Constitution since it was directly representative of the will of the people.

But is that what really happens in practice? In modern America the judicial system has gained a surprising amount of power. Some would argue that, contrary to our Founders' wishes, it has even become the most powerful branch of our government. One man is supposed to mean one vote. But today one judge can equal one million votes, which, when that happens, throws the entire balance of power out of whack.

When political forces can't get their agenda through the legislative process, they turn to judges who will literally legislate from the bench. The Constitution, for example, says nothing about "gay rights." It speaks about the rights of individuals *as Americans*, not their sexual orientation. The right to an abortion is mentioned nowhere in the Constitution, but a majority of the Supreme Court justices thought it would be a good idea in *Roe v. Wade,* so they proclaimed this to be a new "right." Judges have invented "rights" for welfare, micromanaging schools, prisons, and the hiring practices of companies.

The reality is that the delicate balance of power between the branches isn't so delicately balanced anymore. These days, anyone craving the power to make laws and effect real change in this country is almost better off switching from campaigning for office to lobbying for a nomination to the bench.

The Judicial Branch: The Tenure of Judges During Good Behavior

ALEXANDER HAMILTON
The Judicial Branch

Constitutional References:
Article I: §7/1 | §9/3—Article II: §2/2—Article III: §1—Article VI: 2

We will now examine the Judicial Branch of the proposed government. Throughout the process of describing all of the defects of the existing Confederation, it has become all too clear that a Federal Judiciary would not only be useful, but necessary. However, it won't be necessary to repeat all of those points, since no one disputes that a Federal Judiciary, at least in theory, is completely appropriate. The only relevant questions that have been raised are related to how such a Judiciary would be structured, and how extensive it will be, so I will confine my comments to those points.

The way in which the Judicial Branch will be structured seems to fall into these three categories:

FEDERALIST NO. 78

The Message: The Constitution creates a judicial branch that will be strong and independent, but this requires that judges have lifetime tenures.

Original Quote: "Whoever attentively considers the different departments of power must perceive, that, in a government in which they are separated from each other, the judiciary, from the nature of its functions, will always be the least dangerous to the political rights of the Constitution; because it will be least in a capacity to annoy or injure them."

Relevance to Today: The Founders may have put a bit too much faith in the judiciary's ability to remain independent interpreters of the law, as there are countless examples of activist judges attempting to create law or impose their own ideological bent on the Constitution. Take the Commerce Clause, for example, which has over recent years allowed the Federal government to involve itself in everything from limiting state gun rights (because crime is bad for commerce) to involving itself in state medical marijuana laws (because growing pot in one state involves all states).

Original Quote: "No legislative act, therefore, contrary to the Constitution, can be valid. To deny this, would be to affirm, that the deputy is greater than his principal; that the servant is above his master; that the representatives of the people are superior to the people themselves; that men acting by virtue of powers, may do not only what their powers do not authorize, but what they forbid."

Relevance to Today: The Founders' message was simple: a law that violates the Constitution is invalid on its face. The judiciary's role is simply to make it official. But as the new Federal health-care reform law—which would force American citizens to purchase health insurance—wound its way to the Supreme Court, many legal experts pointed out that it was unlikely the court would rule the law unconstitutional. Why? Because the Court does like to overturn the will of Congress—exactly the kind of thing Federalist 78 warned against.

1. The method of appointing judges
2. The length of their tenure in office
3. The division of judicial authority between different courts,
   and how they will relate to each other

First, regarding the method of appointing judges. This will be done in the same way that all the other officials of the Union will be appointed,[1] and has been so thoroughly discussed in the last two papers (Nos. 76–77) that, if I discussed it here, I'd simply be repeating the same information.

Second, regarding the length of the judges' tenure in office. This primarily deals with how long they will hold their office, the provisions which will be in place to support them (i.e., salary), and the precautions that are taken to ensure that they show good behavior.

According to the new Constitution, all judges who are appointed by the United States will continue to hold their offices *during good behavior*, which is in keeping with the most respected state constitutions, including New York's.[2] The fact that the Constitution's critics have used even *this* provision to attack it is no doubt symptomatic of some sort of delirious imagination or judgment on their part. Requiring that judges maintain a standard of good behavior in order to remain in office represents one of the most valuable advances in the practice of government that has been made in the modern age. In a monarchy, such a requirement provides an excellent barrier to the tyranny of a prince, and in a republic, it provides just as excellent of a barrier to any sort of legislative tyranny on the part of the representative body. It is the best

---

1. United States Constitution: Article II, Section 2, clause 2.
2. United States Constitution: Article III, Section 1.

method that can be used in any government to ensure a steady, honorable, and impartial administration of the laws.

If you think carefully about the different Branches of power in a government in which the Branches are separate from each other, you must recognize that, from the nature of its function, the Judicial Branch will always be the least dangerous to the political rights of the Constitution because it will be the Branch least capable of interfering with or endangering those rights. The Executive not only enforces the laws, but he also holds the sword of the nation, and the Legislature not only controls the public treasury,[1] but also lays down the rules that regulate the rights and responsibilities of every citizen. The Judiciary, on the other hand, has no control over the sword or the treasury, it can neither direct the strength nor the wealth of society, and it is absolutely incapable of making laws that would go into effect immediately. It can truly be said that it has neither FORCE nor WILL, but merely judgment, and even then, it must ultimately depend on the Executive in order for its judgments to be carried out.

This very basic look at the subject suggests several important things. It proves beyond any doubt that the Judiciary is absolutely the weakest Branch of the three Branches of power,[2] since it cannot successfully attack either of the other two. Because of this, we must ensure that it is capable of defending itself against their attacks. It also proves that while the courts may from time to time be individually oppressive, they can never threaten the general liberty of the People so long as the Judiciary remains truly distinct from both the Legislative and Executive Branches. I agree with the statement "There is no liberty, if the power of judging be not sepa-

---

1. United States Constitution: Article I, Section 7, clause 1.

2. Montesquieu, *The Spirit of the Laws*, Book 11, Chapter 6 (referenced in Federalist 9). The celebrated Montesquieu says, "of the three powers above mentioned, the JUDICIARY is next to nothing." (Referenced in Federalist 47.)

rated from the legislative and executive powers."[1] It proves that since liberty can have nothing to fear from the Judiciary alone, and because it is naturally weak as a result of its dependence on the other two co-equal Branches of power and thus always in danger of being overpowered or influenced by them, the most important guarantee of the Judiciary's power and independence would be a permanent tenure in office for judges who show good behavior. This should be regarded as an absolutely essential ingredient for the Judiciary, and could even be regarded as the fortress that will ultimately protect public justice and security.

The complete independence of the court system is uniquely essential to a limited constitution. By "limited constitution," I mean one that contains certain restrictions on the Legislative authority, such as that it shall pass no Bills of Attainder, no *ex post facto* laws, etc.[2] Practically speaking, restrictions like these can be preserved in no other way but through the courts of justice since it's their duty to declare all laws that obviously contradict the spirit of the Constitution as void. Without this power, any attempt to preserve specific rights and privileges would amount to nothing.

There has been some confusion with regard to the right of the courts to pronounce legislative acts void. Some have said, contrary to the Constitution, that this right implies that the Judiciary would be superior to the Legislative Branch. They argue that an authority that can declare the actions of another authority void must necessarily mean that it is superior to the one whose actions it voided. Since this political principle is very important in all of the constitutions of America, it is appropriate to briefly discuss the foundation it's based on.

The idea itself is based on a very clear principle: Every act

---

1. Ibid.; also quoted by James Madison in Federalist 47.
2. United States Constitution: Article I, Section 9, clause 3.

of an authority that is contrary to the mandate that allows it to exercise that power is void. Therefore, no act of Congress that is contrary to the Constitution can be valid. To deny that would be the same as saying a deputy is greater than his superior, that a servant is above his master, that the representatives of the People are superior to the People themselves, and that men who utilize the powers they have been given may not only do what their mandate does not authorize, but what it forbids.

Some claim that Congress can act as the judge of its own constitutional powers, and that whatever it decides is final and applies to all the other Branches of government, but this would definitely not be the case if their actions weren't based on the Constitution. It is not possible to claim that the Constitution could ever intend to allow the representatives of the People to substitute *their will* for the will of their constituents. It is far more reasonable to believe that the courts were designed to be an intermediate body between the People and the Legislature so that, among other things, they could keep Congress within the limits of its authority. The interpretation of the law is the unique duty of courts and a constitution must be regarded by the judges as the fundamental law.[1] It is, therefore, the responsibility of the judges to determine not just the meaning of the law, but also the meaning of any particular act of Congress. If there is an irreconcilable difference between the two, then the Constitution should be preferred over the law, and the intention of the People over the intention of their representatives.

This conclusion in no way implies that the judicial authority is superior to the Legislative power. It only assumes that the power of the People is superior to both, and that wherever the will of the Legislature as declared in laws stands in opposition to that of the

---

1. United States Constitution: Article VI, clause 2.

People as declared in the Constitution, then judges ought to make their decisions according to the Constitution rather than the Legislature. They ought to conduct themselves according to the standard of fundamental laws, not those which are not fundamental.

There are some familiar examples that show how courts come to a decision between two contradictory laws. It is rather common for two statutes to exist at the same time and also contradict each other in whole or in part. In these cases, neither of them contains any sort of repealing clause.[1] In situations like these it is the responsibility of the courts to make a determination and establish their meaning and function. If it's at all possible to fairly reconcile the two laws, then both reason and the law require that this be done. However, if this is impractical, then it becomes necessary to rule in favor of one law to the exclusion of the other. The rule by which courts commonly determine the validity of two such laws is that the most recent law is typically preferred to the less recent one. But this is merely a preference, and is not required by any law, but rather by the nature of the court system itself. It is a rule that is not based on law, but is rooted in common sense. It is a rule not dictated by legislative process, but instead adopted by the courts themselves in order to support their role as interpreters of the law. They have acted based on the opinion that, when confronted with two contradictory laws enacted by two *equal* authorities, it is reasonable to prefer the more recent law, since it is the most recent indicator of the will of that authority.

With regard to contradictory laws passed by two *unequal* authorities, the exact opposite of this "rule" is more appropriate. This "rule" says that the past acts of a superior authority should be preferred over the subsequent, more recent acts of a lesser and

---

1. A clause in a law that repeals a previously enacted law that it may contradict or interfere with.

subordinate authority. Therefore, whenever a particular law or statute contradicts the Constitution, it will be the duty of the courts to
adhere to the Constitution, and to disregard the new law.

It would be disingenuous to claim that the courts would substitute their own desires for the constitutional intentions of the
legislature. If that were the case, then it would happen in a case
involving two contradictory laws just as often as it would in a case
involving only a single law. The courts must declare the sense of
the law, and if they're prone to exercise their own WILL instead
of JUDGMENT, then the consequence would be the substitution
of their own will over that of the entire Congress. If that were true
then why even have judges who are independent from the Legislature in the first place?

If the courts are supposed to defend a limited Constitution
against legislative violations, then the idea of a permanent tenure
of office for judges who show good behavior is a strong one considering that no other idea would help encourage an independent
spirit in the judges. This spirit is absolutely essential for them to
faithfully execute their duty.

The judicial independence that is required to guard the Constitution itself is just as necessary to protect the rights of individuals against the emotions that are sometimes spread throughout
the population by conniving men and major crises. While such
emotions typically calm down once people have access to better
information and have had more time to reflect on the situation,
they sometimes have the short-term tendency to compel the
government to take dangerous actions, including oppressing the
minority. I trust that the friends of the Constitution will never
agree with its enemies,[1] some of whom question the fundamen-

---

1. A reference to the "Protest of the Minority of the Convention of Pennsylvania," which
was a speech by Luther Martin (1744–1826), who was an Anti-Federalist who walked out of

tal principle of republican government, which is simply that the People have the right to alter or abolish the established Constitution whenever they find it to be inconsistent with their happiness.[1] However, it can't be inferred that whenever some momentary passion that is contrary to the Constitution takes hold over the majority of the People, that the representatives of the People are justified in violating the Constitution, or that the judges would be under some sort of obligation to secretly cooperate with these violations. Such violations would be the result of political schemers in Congress in the first place anyway. Unless the People, by a solemn and authoritative act, abolish or change the established Constitution, it is binding on them both individually and collectively. Therefore, their representatives would have no excuse whatsoever, based on some assumption about the current feelings of the People, to violate or depart from the Constitution before any such formal changes were made. But it is easy to see how, in such a situation as that, the judges would have to show a remarkable amount of determination in order to carry out their duties as faithful guardians of the Constitution, especially when the voices of a majority of the People themselves had called for the Legislative Branch to violate it.

This independence will also prove to be an essential defense whenever society's emotions get worked up over things not related to violations of the Constitution. These things will often go no further than the violation of the individual rights of certain groups

the Constitutional Convention in protest. He subsequently delivered the speech *Protest of the Convention of Pennsylvania* during the ratification debate of the Maryland Constitutional Convention on November 29, 1787, and it was also printed in the *Maryland Gazette* on December 28, 1787.

1. Declaration of Independence: "*But when a long train of abuses and usurpations, pursuing invariably the same Object evinces a design to reduce them under absolute Despotism, it is their right, it is their duty, to throw off such Government, and to provide new Guards for their future security.*" (Thomas Jefferson)

of citizens by unjust and biased laws. The strength of the Judiciary will be extremely important in restricting the use and severity of these laws. Such strength will not only help control the immediate problems caused by laws that have already been passed, but will also act as a check on the legislative body that passed those laws in the first place.

Once a body like Congress realizes that any shameful intentions on their part will face the obstacles put in place by the courts, those motives will in one way or another force them to change their approach. This restraining influence of the Judicial Branch was intended to influence the leaders of our governments more than most people may imagine. More than one state has already experienced the benefits of a moderate and honorable Judiciary. Even though the Judiciary likely angered those whose shameful plots it interfered with, it has, nonetheless, commanded the respect and applause of every honest and objective citizen.

Every thoughtful person should value and cherish anything that tends to promote a just temperament in the courts. Even if they may not have benefited from justice today, there's no telling if they will become the victim of injustice tomorrow. Additionally, everyone must now be aware of the fact that the presence of an unjust spirit in the courts would inevitably drain the foundation of public and private confidence, and replace it with universal distrust and misery.

However, if judges only held their offices temporarily, then we could certainly not expect that the rights of the Constitution and individuals would be as stubbornly and uniformly adhered to as they should be. Temporary appointments, no matter who made them or how they were carried out, would be fatal to the necessary independence of the Judiciary. If the power to appoint judges existed either in the Executive *or* the Legislative Branch, then there would be a danger that whichever Branch possessed that power would become complacent with it. If the power existed in both of these Branches (as it does under the Constitution), then either Branch would be unwilling to risk the displeasure of the other one. If this power belonged to the People, or to those who had been specially selected by the People for this purpose, there would be too much of a temptation to rely on popularity, when what would really matter would be whether or not the judge would use anything but the Constitution and the laws to make a determination.

There is yet another more important reason to support permanent judicial offices, and it is based on the qualifications that are required to be a judge. As many have appropriately and frequently observed, a result of a free government is an enormous number of laws. In order to avoid arbitrary decisions and rulings, it is absolutely necessary that the courts should be bound by strict rules and precedents that will help define and clarify their duty in every sort of case that comes before them.

Given the foolishness and wickedness of mankind, it's easy to imagine that the records of all the cases that had come before the courts in the past would naturally swell to a large size. Therefore, in order to acquire a thorough and competent knowledge of these records, many long and difficult hours of study would be required. As a result, there will be very few people in society who will have the legal skills which would qualify them to be a judge. Also, taking into account just the ordinary corruption of human nature, the number of people who would have both the required knowledge *and* integrity to be a judge would certainly be even smaller.

These considerations make it clear that the government won't have many suitable people to choose from to be judges. Given this, it would be less likely that judges would carry out their duties with the appropriate effectiveness and dignity if they only held their offices temporarily, since they wouldn't have many good reasons to leave a lucrative legal practice in order to take a seat at the bench. Ultimately, the administration of justice would be placed in less capable and less qualified hands. Given our current national situation (which will likely remain the same for a long time), awarding judges with only temporary terms in office would result in many more disadvantages than it may appear at first.

Overall, there can be no doubt that the Convention acted wisely when it copied from those constitutions a requirement that judges hold life terms during *good behavior*. Far from being blamed for this, their Plan would have actually been inexcusably defective if it had lacked this important feature of good government. The experience of Great Britain provides an excellent example of the wisdom and appropriateness of this practice.

—Publius

The Extent of the Judicial Branch's Power (Continued)

ALEXANDER HAMILTON
The Judicial Branch

Constitutional References:
Article I: §10—Article III: §2/1–2—Article IV: §2/1

In order to accurately determine what would fall under the jurisdiction of the Federal Courts, we should first consider the things that its powers should appropriately apply to. It doesn't seem to be controversial to say that the judicial authority of the Union should apply in the following cases:[1]

1. All cases which involve the laws of the United States which were justly and constitutionally passed by Congress
2. All cases which involve the execution of all the requirements of the Constitution
3. All cases in which the United States is one of the parties
4. All cases which involve the PEACE OF THE UNION,

1. United States Constitution: Article III, Section 2, clause 1.

FEDERALIST NO. 80

The Message: Unlike politicians, judges must be insulated from the ever-shifting emotional state of the electorate so that they have total reverence for the Constitution rather than for the popular sentiment of the day.

Original Quote: "Controversies between the nation and its members and citizens can only be properly referred to the national tribunal. Any other plan would be contrary to reason to precedent, and to decorum."

Relevance to Today: As with the debate surrounding the health-care reform law signed by President Barack Obama, states will often feel as if federal law infringes on the rights of individuals and undermines the independence of states. It would, of course, be impossible to settle these important matters without a supreme court of the land. Allowing for a final arbiter to determine the constitutionality of legislation is one of the vital ways to ensure that our individual liberties endure.

Original Quote: "The additional securities to republican government, to liberty, and to property, to be derived from the adoption of the plan under consideration, consist chiefly in the restrain which the preservation of the Union will impose on local factions. . . ."

Relevance to Today: Just as there was back during the debate over the Constitution, there is still a geographical divide that gives America its unique political and cultural views. Those who live in Iowa often don't share the worldview of New Yorkers. But though we may look at the world differently and butt heads when it comes to political ideology, the way we interpret the doctrines of the Constitution must be consistent if we are to remain united. All states must have a uniform understanding of the Constitution so that citizens have one interpretation of the Constitution, rather than fifty.

whether related to foreign nations or peace between the states themselves

5. All cases which originate on the high seas, and thus fall under admiralty or maritime jurisdiction

6. Lastly, all those cases in which the state courts cannot be expected to be impartial and unbiased

The first point is obvious, since there must always be a constitutional way to enforce constitutional laws. For example, what would be the point of restricting the authority of the state legislatures if there was no way to constitutionally enforce such a restriction? The new Constitution prohibits the states from doing certain things that are contrary to either the interests of the Union, or the principles of good government.[1] Taxing imported goods and printing paper money are examples of each. Nobody would ever think that such restrictions would be carefully followed if there wasn't some sort of power in the government capable of punishing those who break them. This power must either exist in the form of the ability to veto state laws, or by the Federal Courts having the ability to overrule any law that obviously violates any portion of the Constitution. There is no third option that I can think of. Giving Federal Courts the power to overrule unconstitutional state laws seems to have been the preferred choice of the Convention, as well as, I would think, most of the states.

As for the second point, it is impossible to make it any clearer. If there was ever such a thing as good political principles, one of them would be the necessity of making sure the judicial power of the government extended as far as its legislative power. The absolute necessity of Federal laws being interpreted uniformly makes this clear. Thirteen independent supreme courts that all

---

1. United States Constitution: Article I, Section 10.

make their own decisions based on the same laws would make the government akin to the mythical hydra,[1] from which nothing but contradiction and confusion would come.

Even less needs to be said regarding the third point. Any controversies between the nation and either its states or its citizens can be properly resolved only in the National, or Federal Courts. Any other plan would be contrary to reason, precedent, and order.

The very basic idea behind the fourth point is simply that the peace of the WHOLE should not be left up to the decision of the PART. The Union will no doubt be held responsible by foreign nations for the conduct of the states, so because of this responsibility, the Union should also have the ability to prevent such wrongs from ever happening in the first place. Since one of the just causes of war would be the denial or perversion of justice by a court, it makes sense that the Federal Judicial Branch should have jurisdiction over all cases involving citizens of foreign countries. This is not only essential to preserving the public faith, but also to ensuring the public peace.

There may eventually end up being a distinction between cases based on treaties and international laws and those that merely involve municipal laws. Those that fall under international law would be appropriate for the Federal Courts, while the others can fall under state jurisdiction. But it is realistic to expect that an unjust sentence against a foreigner based entirely on the *lex loci*[2] would, if left uncorrected, be interpreted as some sort of aggression against that person's king, or a violation of a treaty requirement, or of international law. An even bigger problem with distinguishing between cases involving our own domestic laws,

---

1. *Hydra:* An ancient Greek serpent-like mythological monster that had seven heads, and whenever a head was cut off, two heads grew in its place.
2. *lex loci*: Latin, meaning "Law of the Place" (local laws).

and those involving international law, would be the immense difficulty, if not impossibility, of being able to practically tell the difference between the two. Since an overwhelming majority of the cases involving foreigners are related to national laws, it would be safer, and also more efficient, to refer all of them to National Courts.

Continuing with the fourth point, the power of deciding cases between two different states, between one state and the citizens of another, or between the citizens of different states, is perhaps just as important to maintaining the peace of the Union as those cases related to foreign nations. History provides us with many horrible examples of the conflicts and private wars that distracted and desolated Germany prior to the creation of the IMPERIAL CHAMBER by Maximilian[1] toward the end of the 15th century. The same history also shows us how important that institution was in resolving the problems and establishing the peace of that empire. This was a court which had the final say on all the differences between the different members/states of the German nation. Even under the extremely flawed Articles of Confederation, there was a method put in place for the federal government to settle territorial disputes between the states. There are, however, other potential sources of conflict between the states besides just territorial disputes, some of which we have already experienced in the past. I am, of course, referring to the many fraudulent laws that have been passed in too many of the states. Although the new Constitution provides a way to avoid these types of things, it's possible that the spirit that created them in the first place will take a new form

---

1. Maximilian I (1459–1519) reigned as Holy Roman Emperor from 1508 to 1519. He was significantly involved in the *Reichsreform* ("Imperial Reform"; referenced in Federalist 19), and led the Reichstag at Worms in 1495, which concluded the *Reichsreform*, which ultimately reshaped a significant portion of the constitution of the Holy Roman Empire. (Referenced in Federalist 6 and 19.)

that can neither be foreseen nor guarded against. In the end, whatever actions tend to disturb the peace between the states should fall under the jurisdiction of Federal regulation and control.

It can be said that the basis of the Union is that "the citizens of each state shall be entitled to all the privileges and immunities of citizens of the several states."[1] So, if it is true that every government *should possess the means of executing its own laws by its own authority*, it follows that the Federal Courts ought to have jurisdiction over all cases between one state or its citizens and another state or its citizens, in order to maintain the equal privileges and immunities of every citizen of the Union. In order to make sure that this most fundamental provision is protected against any abuse or evasion, it is necessary that these types of cases should be judged by a court system that does not have any local biases, and will thus act as an objective umpire between the different states and their citizens. Also, since this court system will owe its official existence to the Union, it will most likely never act against the principles upon which it is founded.

The fifth point will receive hardly any criticism at all. Even the most passionate supporters and idolizers of state authority have not shown any sign that they would deny the National Judiciary jurisdiction over maritime cases. Generally, these cases so frequently involve international law and affect the rights of foreigners that they also fall under that category of cases which involve the public peace. Even under the present Confederation, the most important cases that fall under this category are submitted to federal jurisdiction.

As to the sixth point, the reasonableness of using Federal Courts in cases where the state courts cannot be expected to be entirely fair speaks for itself. No one should be a judge in his own

---

1. United States Constitution: Article IV, Section 2, clause 1.

case, or for that matter, in any case in which he has any interest or bias whatsoever. This principle is the primary reason Federal Courts should be used in cases between different states and their citizens, as well as some cases between citizens of the same state. Also, land claims that are based on the grants of different states (some of whom have borders in dispute), should be decided by Federal Courts, since the courts of either of the states that made the grants in the first place cannot be expected to remain objective. The laws of each of the states may also have tied the hands of the judges before the case even came to trial, requiring them to decide in favor of their respective states before anything even happened. Where this isn't the case, the judges would most likely feel biased in favor of their own state government regardless, since they are human beings after all.

Since we have now laid out the principles that will form the basis of the Federal Judicial Branch, we can now test and see how appropriate the powers that the new Constitution will give to it are. They are laid out this way in the Constitution:

> All cases in law and equity arising under the Constitution, the laws of the United States, and treaties made, or which shall be made, under their authority; to all cases affecting ambassadors, other public ministers and consuls; to all cases of admiralty and maritime jurisdiction; to controversies to which the United States shall be a party; to controversies between two or more states; between the state and citizens of another state; between citizens of different states; between citizens of the same state; claiming lands under grants of different states; and between a state or the citizens thereof, and foreign states, citizens and subjects.[1]

---

1. United States Constitution: Article III, Section 2, clause 1.

This makes up the entire power of the Judicial Branch of the Union. Let's now review them in detail. The powers will extend:[1]

First, to all cases in law and equity *arising under the Constitution and the laws of the United States*. This fits into the first two types of cases (Points 1–2) that will appropriately fall under the jurisdiction of the United States. Some have asked what the difference is between "cases arising under the Constitution" and those "arising under the laws of the United States." The difference has already been explained if you consider as examples all the restrictions placed upon the authority of the state legislatures. For example, the states do not have the power to print money, but this would be a violation of the Constitution, not any particular law of the United States. Regardless, should paper money end up being printed by one of the states, the ensuing legal case would originate from and be carried out under the Constitution and not any particular law of the United States. This is a clear example of the difference between the two phrases.

It has also been asked why the word "equity" was included. What equitable cases[2] could possibly arise out of the Constitution and the laws of the United States? There are hardly any examples of litigation between individuals not containing at least one of these things: *fraud, accident, trust,* or *hardship*, all of which make the case a matter of equity rather than legal jurisdiction, insofar as these terms are understood and established in several of the states. For example, it is the unique duty of a Court of Equity to provide relief from what are called "hard bargains." These are contracts which, while there may not have been any direct fraud or deceit (which would invalidate them in a court of law), there may have been some unwarranted or unconscionable abuse of the

---

1. Ibid.

2. *equitable cases:* Referenced in Federalist 37 under the footnote "Court of Equity."

needs or misfortunes of one of the parties, both of which would be unacceptable in a Court of Equity. In such cases, if foreigners were involved on either side, it would be impossible for the Federal Courts to do justice without an equitable, as well as a legal juris- diction (given the fact that a foreigner would likely be ignorant of the laws of the United States). Agreements that transfer the own- ership of lands which may be claimed by different grants in differ- ent states are yet another example of why it would be necessary for the Federal Courts to have an equitable jurisdiction. However, in those states where the formal and technical distinction between LAW and EQUITY either doesn't exist, or doesn't make its way into everyday practice as it does in New York, this reasoning may not be as acceptable.

Moving on, the authority of the Judicial Branch of the Union shall also extend to:

Second, to treaties made, or which shall be made, under the authority of the United States, and to all cases involving ambas- sadors or other public ministers and consuls. These obviously be- long to the fourth category of cases (Point 4), since it involves the preservation of national peace.

Third, to cases of admiralty and maritime jurisdiction. These make up the fifth category of cases (Point 5) which belong under the jurisdiction of the Federal Courts.

Fourth, to cases in which the United States is a party. These are part of the third category (Point 3).

Fifth, to controversies between two or more states, between a state and citizens of another state, and between citizens of differ- ent states. These belong to the fourth category (Point 4), and also to the sixth category (Point 6) in some cases.

Sixth, to cases between citizens of the same state who are claiming lands under the grants of different states. These fall into the last category (Point 6), and are also the only situations that the proposed Constitution explicitly anticipated that Federal jurisdiction would include disputes between citizens of the same state.

Seventh, to cases between a state (and its citizens) and foreign states, citizens, or subjects. I have already explained how these belong to the fourth category of cases (Point 4), and how they should also fall under Federal jurisdiction.

Based on this review of the powers given to the Federal Judicial Branch by the new Constitution, it appears that they all conform to the principles (Points 1–6) that are not only necessary to perfect our system, but also ought to have been the foundation of this Branch in the first place. If there appear to be small problems with how these principles were adapted into the new Constitution, then just remember that Congress will have the authority to make such *exceptions* and regulations that it deems appropriate to remove these problems.[1] The possibility that there might be specific problems that come up under this system should never cause a well-informed mind to object to principles that were intended to avoid larger, more general problems, but at the same time provide many large and general advantages.

—Publius

---

1. United States Constitution: Article III, Section 2, clause 2.

The Text of the Constitution of the United States as Originally Ratified, Cross-Referenced with *The Federalist Papers*

Preamble

We the People of the United States, in order to form a more perfect Union, establish Justice, insure domestic Tranquility, provide for the common defense, promote the general Welfare, and secure the Blessings of Liberty to ourselves and our Posterity, do ordain and establish this Constitution for the United States of America. [*Nos. 22, 53*]

Article I

Section 1
All legislative Powers herein granted shall be vested in a Congress of the United States, which shall consist of a Senate and House of Representatives. [Congress: *Nos. 52–66*]

Section 2
1. The House of Representatives shall be composed of Members chosen every second Year by the people of the several States, and the Electors in each State shall have the Qualifications requisite for Electors of the most numerous Branch of the State Legislature. [*Nos. 24, 39, 41, 45, 52–54, 57, 59*]
2. No Person shall be a Representative who shall not have attained to

the Age of twenty-five Years, and been seven Years a Citizen of the United States, and who shall not, when elected, be an Inhabitant of that State in which he shall be chosen. [*No. 52*]

3. Representatives and direct taxes shall be apportioned among the several States which may be included within this Union, according to their respective numbers, which shall be determined by adding to the whole number of free persons, including those bound to service for a term of years, and excluding Indians not taxes, three-fifths of all other persons. The actual enumeration shall be made within three years after the first meeting of the Congress of the United States, and within every subsequent term of ten years, in such manner as they shall by law direct. The number of Representatives shall not exceed one for every thirty thousand, but each State shall have at least one Representative, and until such enumeration shall be made, the State of New Hampshire shall be entitled to choose three, Massachusetts eight, Rhode Island and Providence Plantations one, Connecticut five, New York six, New Jersey four, Pennsylvania eight, Delaware one, Maryland six, Virginia ten, North Carolina five, South Carolina five, and Georgia three. [*Nos. 21, 35–36, 38–39, 54–56, 58*]

4. When vacancies happen in the representation from any State, the Executive Authority thereof shall issue Writs of Election to fill such vacancies. [*No. 67*]

5. The House of Representatives shall choose their Speaker and other officers; and shall have the sole power of impeachment. [*Nos. 65–66, 79, 81*]

Section 3

1. The Senate of the United States shall be composed of two Senators from each State (chosen by the legislature thereof) for six years; and each Senator shall have one vote. [*Nos. 9, 38–40, 43–45, 52, 55, 59, 62, 64, 67*]

2. Immediately after they shall be assembled in consequence of the first election, they shall be divided as equally as may be into three classes. The seats of the Senators of the first class shall be vacated

at the expiration of the second year, and of the third class at the expiration of the sixth year, so that one third may be chosen every second year; (and if vacancies happen by resignation, or otherwise, during the recess of the legislature of any State, the executive thereof may make temporary appointments until the next meeting of the legislature, which shall then fill such vacancies). [*Nos. 59, 61, 63–64, 67*]

3. No person shall be a Senator who shall not have attained to the age of thirty years, and been nine years a citizen of the United States, and who shall not, when elected, be an inhabitant of that State for which he shall be chosen. [*Nos. 62, 64*]

4. The Vice President of the United States, shall be President of the Senate, but shall have no vote, unless they be equally divided.

5. The Senate shall choose their other officers, and also a President Pro Tempore, in the absence of the Vice President, or when he shall exercise the office of President of the United States. [*No. 68*]

6. The Senate shall have the sole power to try all impeachments. When sitting for that purpose, they shall be on Oath of Affirmation. When the President of the United States is tried, the Chief Justice shall preside: and no person shall be convicted without the concurrence of two-thirds of the members present. [*Nos. 38, 64–66, 79, 81*]

7. Judgment in cases of impeachment shall not extend further than to removal from office, and disqualification to hold and enjoy any office of honor, trust or profit under the United States; but the party convicted shall nevertheless be liable and subject to indictment, trial, judgment and punishment, according to law. [*Nos. 64–66, 69, 77, 79, 84*]

Section 4

1. The times, places and manner of holding elections for Senators and Representatives, shall be prescribed in each State by the legislature thereof; but the Congress may at any time by law make or alter such regulation, except as to the places of choosing Senators. [*Nos. 38, 59–60*]

2. The Congress shall assemble at least once in every year, and such meeting shall (be on the first Monday in December), unless they shall by law appoint a different day. [*No. 61*]

Section 5

1. Each House shall be the judge of the elections, returns and qualifications of its own members, and a majority of each shall constitute a quorum to do business; but a small number may adjourn from day to day, and may be authorized to compel the attendance of absent members, in such manner, and under such penalties as each House may provide. [*No. 53*]

2. Each House may determine the rules of its proceedings, punish its members for disorderly behavior, and, with the concurrence of two thirds, expel a member. [*No. 53*]

3. Each House shall keep a journal of its proceedings, and from time to time publish the same, excepting such parts as may in their judgment require secrecy; and the yeas and nays of the members of either House on any question shall, at the desire of one-fifth of those present, be entered on the journal. [*No. 53*]

4. Neither House, during the session of Congress, shall, without the consent of each other, adjourn for more than three days, nor to any other place than that in which the two Houses shall be sitting. [*No. 53*]

Section 6

1. The Senators and Representatives shall receive a compensation for the services, to be ascertained by law, and paid out of the Treasury of the United States. They shall in all cases, except treason, felony and breach of the peace, be privileged from arrest during their attendance at the session of their respective Houses, and in going to and returning from the same; and for any speech or debate in either House, they shall not be questioned in any other place.

2. No Senator or Representative shall, during the time for which he was elected, be appointed by any civil office under the authority of the United States, which shall have been created, or the emoluments whereof shall have been increased during such time; and no person

holding any office under the United States, shall be a member of either House during his continuance in office. [*Nos. 52, 55, 76*]

Section 7

1. All bills for raising revenue shall originate in the House of Representatives; but the Senate may propose or concur with amendments as on other bills. [*Nos. 38, 58, 66, 78*]

2. Every bill which shall have passed the House of Representatives and the Senate, shall, before it becomes a law, be presented to the President of the United States. If he approves, he shall sign it, but if not he shall return it, with his objections to that House in which it shall have originated, who shall enter the objections at large on their journal, and proceed to reconsider it. If, after such reconsideration two-thirds of that House shall agree to pass the bill, it shall be sent, together with the objections, to the other House, by which it shall likewise be reconsidered, and if approved by two-thirds of that House, it shall become a law. But in all such cases the votes of both Houses shall be determined by yeas and nays, and the names of the persons voting for and against the bill shall be entered on the journal of each House respectively. If any bill shall not be returned by the President within ten days (Sundays excepted) and after it shall have been presented to him, the same shall be a law, in like manner as if he had signed it, unless the Congress, by their adjournment prevent its return, in which case it shall not be a law. [*Nos. 62, 64, 69, 73*]

3. Every order, resolution, or vote, to which the concurrence of the Senate and House of Representatives may be necessary (except on a question of adjournment) shall be presented to the President of the United States; and before the same shall take effect, shall be approved by him, or being disapproved by him, shall be re-passed by two-thirds of the Senate and House of Representatives, according to the rules and limitations prescribed in the case of a bill. [*Nos. 64, 66, 69, 73*]

Section 8 [No. 83]
The Congress shall have power:

1. To lay and collect taxes, duties, imposts and excises, to pay the debts and provide for the common defense and general welfare of the United States; but all duties, imposts and excises shall be uniform throughout the United States; [Nos. 12, 21, 30–32, 35–36, 38, 41, 45, 53]
2. To borrow money on the credit of the United States; [No. 41]
3. To regulate commerce with foreign nations, and among the several States, and with the Indian Tribes; [Nos. 11–12, 22, 40, 42, 44, 53, 56]
4. To establish an uniform Rule of Naturalization, and uniform laws on the subject of bankruptcies throughout the United States; [Nos. 32, 42]
5. To coin money, regulate the value thereof, and of foreign coin, and fix the standard of weights and measures; [Nos. 12, 42, 69]
6. To provide for the punishment of counterfeiting the securities and current coin of the United States; [No. 42]
7. To establish Post Offices and post roads; [Nos. 14, 42]
8. To promote the progress of Science and useful arts, by securing for limited times to authors and inventors the exclusive right to their respective writings and discoveries; [No. 43]
9. To constitute tribunals inferior to the Supreme Court; [No. 82]
10. To define and punish piracies and felonies committed on the high seas, and offenses against the law of nations; [Nos. 12, 42]
11. To declare war, grant letters of marquee and reprisal, and make rules concerning the captures on land and water; [Nos. 41, 69]
12. To raise and support armies, but no appropriation of money to that use shall be for a longer term than two years; [Nos. 23–26, 28, 30, 38, 41, 69]
13. To provide and maintain a navy; [Nos. 11, 23, 30, 38, 41, 69]
14. To makes rules for the government and regulation of the land and naval forces; [Nos. 23, 38, 56, 69]
15. To provide for calling forth the Militia to execute the laws of the Union, suppress insurrections, and repel invasions; [Nos. 21, 23, 28, 38, 56, 69]

16. To provide for organizing, arming, and disciplining, the Militia, and for governing such part of them as may be employed in the service of the United States, reserving to the States respectively the appointment of the officers, and the authority of training the Militia according to the discipline prescribed by Congress; [*Nos. 4, 23, 29, 38, 41, 46, 53, 56, 69*]

17. To exercise exclusive legislation in all cases whatsoever, over such District (not exceeding ten miles square) as may, by cession of particular States, and the acceptance of Congress, become the Seat of the Government of the United States, and to exercise like authority over all places purchased by the consent of the legislature of the State in which the same shall be, for the erection of forts, magazines, arsenals, dock-yards, and other needful buildings—and [*Nos. 32, 43*]

18. To make all laws which shall be necessary and proper for carrying into execution the foregoing powers, and all other powers vested by this Constitution in the Government of the United States, or in any department or officer thereof. [*Nos. 29, 31, 33, 44*]

Section 9

1. The migration or importation of such persons as any of the States now existing shall think proper to admit shall not be prohibited by the Congress prior to the year one thousand eight hundred and eight, but a tax or duty may be imposed on such importation, not exceeding ten dollars for each person. [*Nos. 38, 42*]

2. The privilege of the Writ of *Habeas Corpus* shall not be suspended, unless when in cases of rebellion or invasion the public safety may require it. [*Nos. 83–84*]

3. No Bill of Attainder or *Ex Post Facto* Law shall be passed. [*Nos. 44, 78, 84*]

4. No capitation, or other direct, tax shall be laid, unless in proportion to the Census or enumeration herein before directed to be taken. [*Nos. 21, 38*]

5. No tax or duty shall be laid on articles exported from any State. [*No. 32*]

6. No preference shall be given by any regulation of commerce or revenue to the ports of one State over those of another: nor shall vessels bound to, or from, one State, be obliged to enter, clear, or pay duties in another.

7. No money shall be drawn from the Treasury, but in consequence of appropriations made by law; and a regular statement and account of the receipts and expenditures of all public money shall be published from time to time. [*No. 72*]

8. No Title of Nobility shall be granted by the United States: and no person holding any office of profit or trust under them shall, without the consent of the Congress, accept of any present, emolument, office, or title, of any kind whatever, from any King, Prince, or foreign state. [*Nos. 39, 69, 84*]

Section 10 [Nos. 32, 37, 41, 80]

1. No State shall enter into any treaty, alliance, or confederation; grant Letters of Marque and Reprisal; coin money; emit bills of credit; make anything but gold and silver coin a tender in payment of debts; pass any Bill of Attainder, *Ex Post Facto* Law, or law impairing the obligation of contracts, or grant any Title of Nobility. [*Nos. 44, 69*]

2. No State shall, without the consent of the Congress, lay any imposts or duties on imports or exports, except what may be absolutely necessary for executing its inspection law: and the net produce of all duties and imposts, laid by any State on imports or exports, shall be for the use of the Treasury of the United States; and all such laws shall be subject to the revision and control of Congress. [*Nos. 32–33, 44*]

3. No State shall, without the consent of Congress, lay any duty of tonnage, keep troops, or ships of war in time of peace, enter into any agreement or compact with another state, or with a foreign power, or engage in war, unless actually invaded, or in such imminent danger as will not admit of delay. [*No. 44*]

Article II

Section 1

1. The executive power shall be vested in a President of the United States of America. He shall hold his office during the term of four years, and, together with the Vice President, chosen for the same term, be elected, as follows: [The Executive Branch: *Nos. 67–77; Nos. 39, 69, 71, 73, 75, 77*]

2. Each State shall appoint, in such manner as the legislature thereof may direct, a number of Electors, equal to the whole number of Senators and Representatives to which the State may be entitled in the Congress; but no Senator or Representatives, or person holding an office of trust or profit under the United States, shall be appointed an Elector. [*Nos. 39, 44–45, 59, 64, 68, 71, 77*]

3. (The Electors shall meet in their respective States, and vote by ballot for two persons, of whom one at least shall not be an inhabitant of the same State with themselves. And they shall make a list of all the persons voted for, and of the number of votes for each; which list they shall sign and certify, and transmit sealed to the Seat of the Government of the United States, directed to the President of the Senate. The President of the Senate shall, in the presence of the Senate and House of Representatives, open all the certificates, and the votes shall then be counted. The person having the greatest number of votes shall be the President, if such number be a majority of the whole number of Electors appointed; and if there be more than one who have such majority and have an equal number of votes, then the House of Representatives shall immediately choose by ballot one of them for President; and if no person have a majority, then from the five highest on the list the said House shall in like manner choose the President. But in choosing the President, the votes shall be taken by States, the representation from each State having one vote; a quorum for this purpose shall consist of a member or members from two-thirds of the States, and a majority of all the States shall be necessary to a choice. In every case, after the choice of the President, the person having the greatest number of votes of the

Electors shall be the Vice President. But if there should remain two or more who have equal votes, the Senate shall choose from them by ballot the Vice President.) [*Nos. 59, 66, 68, 77*]

4. The Congress may determine the time of choosing the Electors, and the day on which they shall give their votes; which day shall be the same throughout the United States. [*Nos. 59, 68, 77*]

5. No person, except a natural-born citizen, or a citizen of the United States at the time of the adoption of this Constitution, shall be eligible to that office of President; neither shall any person be eligible to that office who shall not have attained to the age of thirty-five years, and been fourteen years a resident within the United States. [*No. 64*]

6. In case of the removal of the President from office, or of his death, resignation, or inability to discharge the powers and duties of the said office, the same shall devolve on the Vice President, and the Congress may by law provide for the case of removal, death, resignation, or inability, both the President and Vice President, declaring what officer shall then act as President, and such officer shall act accordingly, until the disability be removed, or a President shall be elected. [*No. 68*]

7. The President shall, at stated times, receive for his services, a compensation, which shall neither be increased nor diminished during the period for which he shall have been elected, and he shall not receive within that period any other emolument from the United States, or any of them. [*Nos. 73, 79*]

8. Before he enter on the execution of his office, he shall take the following Oath or Affirmation: "I do solemnly swear (or affirm) that I will faithfully execute the office of President of the United States, and will, to the best of my ability, preserve, protect, and defend the Constitution of the United States." [*No. 44*]

Section 2 [No. 71]

1. The President shall be Commander in Chief of the Army and Navy of the United States, and of the Militia of the several States, when called in the actual service of the United States; he may require the opinion, in writing, of the principal officer in each of the executive

departments, upon any subject relating to the duties of their respective offices, and he shall have power to grant reprieves and pardons for offences against the United States, except in cases of impeachment. [*Nos. 4, 29, 38, 69–70, 74*]

2. He shall have power, by and with the advice and consent of the Senate, to make treaties, provided two-thirds of the Senators present concur; and he shall nominate, and by and with the advice and consent of the Senate, shall appoint, ambassadors, other public ministers, and consuls, judges of the Supreme Court, and all other officers of the United States, whose appointments are not herein otherwise provided for, and which shall be established by law; but the Congress may by law vest the appointment of such inferior officers, as they think proper, in the President alone, in the Courts of Law, or in the heads of departments. [*Nos. 38, 42, 55, 62, 64–67, 69, 72, 75–78, 84*]

3. The President shall have power to fill up all vacancies that may happen during the recess of the Senate, by granting commissions which shall expire at the end of their next session. [*Nos. 67, 76–77*]

Section 3 [Nos. 64, 69, 71, 77]

He shall from time to time give to the Congress information of the State of the Union, and recommend to their consideration such measures as he shall judge necessary and expedient; he may, on extraordinary occasions, convene both Houses, or either of them, and in cases of disagreement between them, with respect to the time of adjournment, he may adjourn them to such time as he shall think proper; he shall receive ambassadors and other public ministers; he shall take care that the laws be faithfully executed, and shall commission all the officers of the United States.

Section 4 [Nos. 39, 69–70, 77]

The President, Vice President and all civil officers of the United States, shall be removed from office on impeachment for, and conviction of, treason, bribery, or other high crimes and misdemeanors.

Article III

Section 1 [Nos. 22, 39, 79, 81–82]

The Judicial power of the United States, shall be vested in one Supreme Court, and in such inferior courts as the Congress may from time to time ordain and establish. The Judges, both of the Supreme and inferior courts, shall hold their offices during good behavior, and shall, at stated times, receive for their services, a compensation, which shall not be diminished during their continuance in office. [Nos. 78–83]

Section 2

1. The Judicial power shall extend to all cases in law and equity, arising under this Constitution, the laws of the United States, and treaties made, or which shall be made, under their authority—to all cases affecting ambassadors, other public ministers, and consuls—to all cases of admiralty and maritime jurisdiction—to controversies to which the United States shall be a party—to controversies between two or more States—between a State and citizens of another State—between citizens of different States—between citizens of the same State claiming lands under grants of different States, and between a State, or the citizens thereof, and foreign states, citizens or subjects. [Nos. 3, 39, 80, 82–83]

2. In all cases affecting ambassadors, other public ministers, and consuls, and those in which a State shall be party, the Supreme Court shall have original jurisdiction. In all the other cases before mentioned, the Supreme Court shall have appellate jurisdiction, both as to law and fact, with such exceptions, and under such regulations as the Congress shall make. [Nos. 3, 39, 80–84]

3. The Trial of all crimes, except in cases of impeachment, shall be by jury; and such trial shall be held in the State where the said crimes shall have been committed; but, when not committed within any State, the trial shall be at such place or places as the Congress may by law have directed. [Nos. 83–84]

Section 3 [Nos. 74, 84]

1. Treason against the United States, shall consist only in levying war against them, or in adhering to their enemies, giving them aid and comfort. No person shall be convicted of treason unless on the testimony of two witnesses to the same overt act, or on confession in open court. [*No. 69*]

2. The Congress shall have power to declare the punishment of treason, but no attainder of treason shall work corruption of blood, or forfeiture except during the life of the person attained. [*No. 43*]

Article IV

Section 1 [No. 42]

Full faith and credit shall be given in each State to the public acts, records, and judicial proceedings of every other State. And the Congress may by general laws prescribe the manner in which such acts, records and proceedings shall be proved, and the effect thereof.

Section 2

1. The citizens of each State shall be entitled to all privileges and immunities of citizens in the several States. [*No. 80*]

2. A person charged in any State with treason, felony, or other crime, who shall flee from justice, and be found in another State, shall on demand of the executive authority of the State from which he fled, be delivered up, to be removed to the State having jurisdiction of the crime.

3. (No person held to service or labor in one State, under the laws thereof, escaping into another, shall, in consequence of any law or regulation therein, be discharged from such service or labor, but shall be delivered up on claim of the party to whom such service or labor may be due.)

Section 3

1. New States may be admitted by the Congress into this Union; but no new State shall be formed or erected within the jurisdiction of any other State; nor any State be formed by the junction of two or

more States, or parts of States, without the consent of the legislatures of the States concerned, as well as of the Congress. [*Nos. 14,
43, 75*]

2. The Congress shall have power to dispose of and make all needful
   rules and regulations respecting the territory or other property belonging to the United States; and nothing in this Constitution shall
   be so construed as to prejudice any claims of the United States, or
   of any particular State. [*No. 43*]

Section 4 [Nos. 21, 39, 43, 85]

The United States shall guarantee to every State in this Union a Republican Form of Government, and shall protect each of them against invasion; and on application of the legislature, or of the executive (when the
legislature cannot be convened), against domestic violence.

Article V

The Congress, whenever two-thirds of both Houses shall deem it necessary, shall propose Amendments to this Constitution, or, on the application of the legislatures of two-thirds of the several States, shall call
a Convention for proposing Amendments, which, in either case, shall
be valid to all intents and purposes, as part of this Constitution, when
ratified by the legislatures of three-fourths of the several States, or by
Conventions in three-fourths thereof, as the one or the other mode of
ratification may be proposed by the Congress; provided that no Amendment which may be made prior to the year one thousand eight hundred
and eight shall in any manner affect the first and fourth clauses in the
Ninth Section of the First Article; and that no State, without its consent,
shall be deprived of its equal suffrage in the Senate. [*Nos. 37, 39–40, 43,
49, 85*]

Article VI

1. All debts contracted and engagement entered into, before the adoption of this Constitution, shall be as valid against the United States
   under this Constitution, as under the Confederation. [*No. 43*]

2. This Constitution, and the laws of the United States which shall be made in pursuance thereof; and all treaties made, or which shall be made, under the authority of the United States, shall be the Supreme Law of the Land; and the Judges in every State shall be bound thereby, anything in the Constitution or laws of any State to the contrary notwithstanding. [*Nos. 15–17, 22, 27, 31, 33, 38, 44, 64, 78*]

3. The Senators and Representatives before mentioned, and the members of the several State legislatures, and all executive and judicial officers, both of the United States and of the several States, shall be bound by Oath or Affirmation to support this Constitution; but no religious test shall ever be required as a qualification to any office or public trust under the United States. [*Nos. 27, 44*]

———————

The Articles of Confederation and Perpetual Union

To all whom these Presents shall come, we the undersigned Delegates of the States affixed to our names send greeting.

Between the states of New Hampshire, Massachusetts-bay, Rhode Island and Providence Plantations, Connecticut, New York, New Jersey, Pennsylvania, Delaware, Maryland, Virginia, North Carolina, South Carolina and Georgia

Article I

The Stile of this Confederacy shall be "The United States of America."

Article II

Each state retains its sovereignty, freedom, and independence, and every power, jurisdiction, and right, which is not by this Confederation expressly delegated to the United States, in Congress assembled.

Article III

The said States hereby severally enter into a firm league of friendship with each other, for their common defense, the security of their liberties, and their mutual and general welfare, binding themselves to assist each other, against all force offered to, or attacks made upon them, or any of them, on account of religion, sovereignty, trade, or any other pretense whatever.

Article IV

The better to secure and perpetuate mutual friendship and intercourse among the people of the different States in this Union, the free inhabitants of each of these States, paupers, vagabonds, and fugitives from justice excepted, shall be entitled to all privileges and immunities of free citizens in the several States; and the people of each State shall have free ingress and regress to and from any other State, and shall enjoy therein all the privileges of trade and commerce, subject to the same duties, impositions, and restrictions as the inhabitants thereof respectively, provided that such restrictions shall not extend so far as to prevent the removal of property imported into any State, to any other State, of which the owner is an inhabitant; provided also that no imposition, duties or restriction shall be laid by any State, on the property of the United States, or either of them.

If any person guilty of, or charged with, treason, felony, or other high misdemeanor in any State, shall flee from justice, and be found in any of the United States, he shall, upon demand of the Governor or executive power of the State from which he fled, be delivered up and removed to the State having jurisdiction of his offense.

Full faith and credit shall be given in each of these States to the records, acts, and judicial proceedings of the courts and magistrates of every other State.

Article V

For the most convenient management of the general interests of the United States, delegates shall be annually appointed in such manner as the legislatures of each State shall direct, to meet in Congress on the first Monday in November, in every year, with a power reserved to each State to recall its delegates, or any of them, at any time within the year, and to send others in their stead for the remainder of the year.

No State shall be represented in Congress by less than two, nor more than seven members; and no person shall be capable of being a delegate for more than three years in any term of six years; nor shall any person, being a delegate, be capable of holding any office under the United States, for which he, or another for his benefit, receives any salary, fees or emolument of any kind.

Each State shall maintain its own delegates in a meeting of the States, and while they act as members of the committee of the States.

In determining questions in the United States in Congress assembled, each State shall have one vote.

Freedom of speech and debate in Congress shall not be impeached or questioned in any court or place out of Congress, and the members of Congress shall be protected in their persons from arrests or imprisonments, during the time of their going to and from, and attendance on Congress, except for treason, felony, or breach of the peace.

Article VI

No State, without the consent of the United States in Congress assembled, shall send any embassy to, or receive any embassy from, or enter into any conference, agreement, alliance or treaty with any King, Prince or State; nor shall any person holding any office of profit or trust under the United States, or any of them, accept any present, emolument, office or title of any kind whatever from any King, Prince or foreign State; nor shall the United States in Congress assembled, or any of them, grant any title of nobility.

No two or more States shall enter into any treaty, confederation or alliance whatever between them, without the consent of the United States in Congress assembled, specifying accurately the purposes for which the same is to be entered into, and how long it shall continue.

No State shall lay any imposts or duties, which may interfere with any stipulations in treaties, entered into by the United States in Congress assembled, with any King, Prince or State, in pursuance of any treaties already proposed by Congress, to the courts of France and Spain.

No vessel of war shall be kept up in time of peace by any State, except such number only, as shall be deemed necessary by the United States in Congress assembled, for the defense of such State, or its trade; nor shall any body of forces be kept up by any State in time of peace, except such number only, as in the judgment of the United States in Congress assembled, shall be deemed requisite to garrison the forts necessary for the defense of such State; but every State shall always keep up a well-regulated and disciplined militia, sufficiently armed and accoutered, and shall provide and constantly have ready for use, in public stores, a due number of filed pieces and tents, and a proper quantity of arms, ammunition and camp equipage.

No State shall engage in any war without the consent of the United States in Congress assembled, unless such State be actually invaded by enemies, or shall have received certain advice of a resolution being formed by some nation of Indians to invade such State, and the danger is so imminent as not to admit of a delay till the United States in Congress assembled can be consulted; nor shall any State grant commissions to any ships or vessels of war, nor letters of marquee or reprisal, except it be after a declaration of war by the United States in Congress assembled, and then only against the Kingdom or State and the subjects thereof, against which war has been so declared, and under such regulations as shall be established by the United States in Congress assembled, unless such State be infested by pirates, in which case vessels of war may be fitted out for that occasion, and kept so long as the danger shall continue, or until the United States in Congress assembled shall determine otherwise.

Article VII

When land forces are raised by any State for the common defense, all officers of or under the rank of colonel, shall be appointed by the legislature of each State respectively, by whom such forces shall be raised, or in such manner as such State shall direct, and all vacancies shall be filled up by the State which first made the appointment.

Article VIII

All charges of war, and all other expenses that shall be incurred for the common defense or general welfare, and allowed by the United States in Congress assembled, shall be defrayed out of a common treasury, which shall be supplied by the several States in proportion to the value of all land within each State, granted or surveyed for any person, as such land and the buildings and improvements thereon shall be estimated according to such mode as the United States in Congress assembled, shall from time to time direct and appoint.

The taxes for paying that proportion shall be laid and levied by the authority and direction of the legislatures of the several States within the time agreed upon by the United States in Congress assembled.

Article IX

The United States in Congress assembled, shall have the sole and exclusive right and power of determining on peace and war, except in the cases mentioned in the sixth article—of sending and receiving ambassadors—entering into treaties and alliances, provided that no treaty of commerce shall be made whereby the legislative power of the respective States shall be restrained from imposing such imposts and duties on foreigners, as their own people are subjected to, or from prohibiting the exportation or importation of any species of goods or commodities whatsoever—of establishing rules for deciding in all cases, what captures on land or water shall be legal, and in what manner prizes taken by land or naval forces in the service of the United States shall be divided or appropriated—of granting letters of marquee and reprisal in times of peace—appointing courts for the trial of piracies and felonies committed on the high seas and establishing courts for receiving and determining finally appeals in all cases of captures, provided that no member of Congress shall be appointed a judge of any of the said courts.

The United States in Congress assembled shall also be the last resort on appeal in all disputes and differences now subsisting or that hereafter may arise between two or more States concerning boundary, jurisdiction or any other causes whatever; which authority shall always be exercised in the manner following. Whenever the legislative or executive authority or lawful agent of any State in controversy with another shall present a petition to Congress stating the matter in question and praying for a hearing, notice thereof shall be given by order of Congress to the legislative or executive authority of the other State in controversy, and a day assigned for the appearance of the parties by their lawful agents, who shall then be directed to appoint by joint consent, commissioners or judges to constitute a court for hearing and determining the matter in question: but if they cannot agree, Congress shall name three persons out of each of the United States, and from the list of such persons each party shall alternately strike out one, the petitioners beginning, until the number shall be reduced to thirteen; and from that number not less than seven, nor more than nine names as Congress shall direct, shall in the presence of Congress be drawn out by lot, and the persons whose names shall be so drawn or any five of them, shall be commissioners or judges, to hear and finally determine the controversy, so always as a major part of the judges who shall hear the cause shall agree in the determination: and if either party shall neglect to attend at the day appointed, without showing reasons, which Congress shall judge sufficient, or being present shall refuse to strike, the Congress shall proceed to nominate three persons out of each State, and the secretary of Congress shall strike in behalf of such party absent or refusing; and the judgment and sentence of the court to be appointed, in the manner before prescribed, shall be final and conclusive; and if any of the parties shall refuse to submit to the authority of such court, or to appear or defend their claim or cause, the court shall nevertheless proceed to pronounce sentence, or judgment, which shall in like manner be final and decisive, the judgment or sentence and other proceedings being in either case transmitted to Congress, and lodged among the acts of Congress for the security of the parties concerned: provided that every commissioner, before he sits in judgment, shall take an oath to be administered by one of the judges of the supreme or superior court of the State, where the cause shall be tried, 'well and truly to hear and determine the matter in question, according to the best of his judgment, without favor, affection or hope of reward': provided also, that no State shall be deprived of territory for the benefit of the United States.

All controversies concerning the private right of soil claimed under different grants of two or more States, whose jurisdictions as they may respect such lands, and the States which passed such grants are adjusted, the said grants or either of them being at the same time claimed to have originated antecedent to such settlement of jurisdiction, shall on the petition of either party to the Congress of the United States, be finally determined as near as may be in the same manner as is before prescribed for deciding disputes respecting territorial jurisdiction between different States.

The United States in Congress assembled shall also have the sole and exclusive right and power of regulating the alloy and value of coin struck by their own authority, or by that of the respective States—fixing the standards of weights and measures throughout the United States— regulating the trade and managing all affairs with the Indians, not members of any of the States, provided that the legislative right of any State within its own limits be not infringed or violated—establishing or regulating post offices from one State to another, throughout all the United States, and exacting such postage on the papers passing through the same as may be requisite to defray the expenses of the said office— appointing all officers of the land forces, in the service of the United States, excepting regimental officers—appointing all the officers of the naval forces, and commissioning all officers whatever in the service of the United States—making rules for the government and regulation of the said land and naval forces, and directing their operations.

The United States in Congress assembled shall have authority to appoint a committee, to sit in the recess of Congress, to be denominated 'A Committee of the States,' and to consist of one delegate from each State; and to appoint such other committees and civil officers as may be necessary for managing the general affairs of the United States under their direction—to appoint one of their members to preside, provided that no person be allowed to serve in the office of president more than one year in any term of three years; to ascertain the necessary sums of money to be raised for the service of the United States, and to appropriate and apply the same for defraying the public expenses—to borrow money, or emit bills on the credit of the United States, transmitting every half-year to the respective States an account of the sums of money so borrowed or emitted—to build and equip a navy—to agree upon the number of land forces, and to make requisitions from each State for its quota, in proportion to the number of white inhabitants in such State; which requisition shall be binding, and thereupon the legislature of each State shall appoint the regimental officers, raise the men and cloath, arm and equip them in a soldier-like manner, at the expense of the United States; and the officers and men so cloathed, armed and equipped shall march to the place appointed, and within the time agreed on by the United States in Congress assembled. But if the United States in Congress assembled shall, on consideration of circumstances judge proper that any State should not raise men, or should raise a smaller number of men than the quota thereof, such extra number shall be raised, officered, cloathed, armed and equipped in the same manner as the quota of each State, unless the legislature of such State shall judge that such extra number cannot be safely spread out in the same, in which case they shall raise, officer, cloath, arm and equip as many of such extra number as they judge can be safely spared. And the officers and men so cloathed, armed, and equipped, shall march to the place appointed, and within the time agreed on by the United States in Congress assembled.

The United States in Congress assembled shall never engage in a war, nor grant letters of marquee or reprisal in time of peace, nor enter into any treaties or alliances, nor coin money, nor regulate the value thereof, nor ascertain the sums and expenses necessary for the defense and welfare of the United States, or any of them, nor emit bills, nor borrow money on the credit of the United States, nor appropriate money, nor agree upon the number of vessels of war, to be built or purchased, or the number of land or sea forces to be raised, nor appoint a commander in chief of the army or navy, unless nine States assent to the same: nor shall a question on any other point, except for adjourning from day to day be determined, unless by the votes of the majority of the United States in Congress assembled.

The Congress of the United States shall have power to adjourn to any time within the year, and to any place within the United States, so that no period of adjournment be for a longer duration than the space of six months, and shall publish the journal of their proceedings monthly, except such parts thereof relating to treaties, alliances or military operations, as in their judgment require secrecy; and the yeas and nays of the delegates of each State on any question shall be entered on the journal, when it is desired by any delegates of a State, or any of them, at his or their request shall be furnished with a transcript of the said journal, except such parts as are above excepted, to lay before the legislatures of the several States.

Article X

The Committee of the States, or any nine of them, shall be authorized to execute, in the recess of Congress, such of the powers of Congress as the United States in Congress assembled, by the consent of the nine States, shall from time to time think expedient to vest them with; provided that no power be delegated to the said Committee, for the exercise of which, by the Articles of Confederation, the voice of nine States in the Congress of the United States assembled be requisite.

Article XI

Canada acceding to this confederation, and adjoining in the measures of the United States, shall be admitted into, and entitled to all the advantages of this Union; but no other colony shall be admitted into the same, unless such admission be agreed to by nine States.

Article XII

All bills of credit emitted, monies borrowed, and debts contracted by, or under the authority of Congress, before the assembling of the United States, in pursuance of the present confederation, shall be deemed and considered as a charge against the United States, for payment and satisfaction whereof the said United States, and the public faith are hereby solemnly pledged.

Article XIII

Every State shall abide by the determination of the United States in Congress assembled, on all questions which by this confederation are submitted to them. And the Articles of this Confederation shall be inviolably observed by every State, and the Union shall be perpetual; nor shall any alteration at any time hereafter be made in any of them; unless such alteration be agreed to in a Congress of the United States, and be afterwards confirmed by the legislatures of every State.

And Whereas it hath pleased the Great Governor of the World to incline the hearts of the legislatures we respectively represent in Congress, to approve of, and to authorize us to ratify the said Articles of Confederation and perpetual Union. Know Ye that we the undersigned delegates, by virtue of the power and authority to us given for that purpose, do by these presents, in the name and in behalf of our respective constituents, fully and entirely ratify and confirm each and every of the said Articles of Confederation and perpetual Union, and all and singular the matters and things therein contained: And we do further solemnly plight and engage the faith of our respective constituents, that they shall abide by the determinations of the United States in Congress assembled, on all questions, which by the said Confederation are submitted to them. And that the Articles thereof shall be inviolably observed by the States we respectively represent, and that the Union shall be perpetual. In Witness whereof, we have hereunto set our hands in Congress.

APPENDIX III

An Address to the People of the State of New York (1788)

BY THE HONORABLE JOHN JAY

Minister for Foreign Affairs to the United States in Congress Assembled

Friends and Fellow-citizens: The Convention concurred in opinion with the people, that a national government, competent to every national object, was indispensably necessary; and it was as plain to them, as it now is to all America, that the present Confederation does not provide for such a government. These points being agreed, they proceeded to consider how and in what manner such a government could be formed, as, on the one hand, should be sufficiently energetic to raise us from our prostrate and distressed situation, and, on the other, be perfectly consistent with the liberties of the people of every state. Like men to whom the experience of other ages and countries had taught wisdom, they not only determined that it should be erected by, and depend on, the people, but, remembering the many instances in which governments vested solely in one man, or one body of men, had degenerated into tyrannies, they judged it most prudent that the three great branches of power should be committed to different hands, and therefore that the executive should be separated from the legislative, and the judicial from both. Thus far the propriety of their work is easily seen and understood, and therefore is thus far almost universally approved; for no one man or thing under the sun ever yet pleased everybody.

The next question was, what particular powers should be given to these three branches. Here the different views and interests of the different states, as well as the different abstract opinions of their members on such points, interposed many difficulties. Here the business became complicated, and presented a wide field for investigation—too wide for every eye to take a quick and comprehensive view of it . . .

The question now before us naturally leads to three inquiries:

1. Whether it is probable that a better plan can be obtained
2. Whether, if attainable, it is likely to be in season
3. What would be our situation if, after rejecting this, all our efforts to obtain a better should prove fruitless

The men who formed this plan are Americans, who had long deserved and enjoyed our confidence, and who are as much interested in having a good government as any of us are or can be. They were appointed to that business at a time when the states had become very sensible of the derangement of our national affairs, and of the impossibility of retrieving them under the existing Confederation. Although well persuaded that nothing but a good national government could oppose and divert the tide of evils that was flowing in upon us, yet those gentlemen met in Convention with minds perfectly unprejudiced in favor of any particular plan. The minds of their constituents were at that time equally cool and dispassionate. All agreed in the necessity of doing something; but no one ventured to say decidedly what precisely ought to be done. Opinions were then fluctuating and unfixed; and whatever might have been the wishes of a few individuals, yet while the Convention deliberated, the people remained in silent suspense. Neither wedded to favorite systems of their own, nor influenced by popular ones abroad, the members were more desirous to receive light from, than to impress their private sentiments on, one another.

These circumstances naturally opened the door to that spirit of candor, of calm inquiry, of mutual accommodation, and mutual respect, which entered into the Convention with them, and regulated their debates and proceedings . . . They tell us, very honestly, that this plan is the result of accommodation. They do not hold it up as the best of all possible ones, but only as the best which they could unite in and agree to. If such men, appointed and meeting under such auspicious circumstances, and so sincerely disposed to conciliation, could go no farther in their endeavors to please every state and everybody, what reason have we, at present, to expect any system that would give more general satisfaction?

Suppose this plan to be rejected; what measures would you propose for obtaining a better? Some will answer, "Let us appoint another convention; and, as everything has been said and written that can well be said and written on the subject, they will be better informed than the former one was, and consequently be better able to make and agree upon a more eligible one."

Let those who are sanguine in their expectations of a better plan from a new convention, also reflect on the delays and risks to which it would expose us. Let them consider whether we ought, by continuing much longer in our present humiliating condition, to give other nations further time to perfect their restrictive systems of commerce, reconcile their own people to them, and to fence, and guard, and strengthen them by all those regulations and contrivances in which a jealous policy is ever fruitful. Let them consider whether we ought to give further opportunities to discord to alienate the hearts of our citizens from one another, and thereby encourage new Cromwells to bold exploits. Are we certain that our foreign creditors will continue patient, and ready to proportion their forbearance to our delays? Are we sure that our distresses, dissensions, and weakness, will neither invite hostility nor insult? If they should, how ill prepared shall we be for defense, without union, without government, without money, and without credit!

Consider, then, how weighty and how many considerations advise and persuade the people of America to remain in the safe and easy path of union; to continue to move and act, as they hitherto have done, as a band of brothers; and to have confidence in themselves and in one another; and, since all cannot see with the same eyes, at least to give the proposed Constitution a fair trial, and to mend it as time, occasion, and experience, may dictate. It would little become us to verify the predictions of those who ventured to prophesy that peace, instead of blessing us with happiness and tranquility, would serve only as the signal for factions, discord, and civil contentions, to rage in our land, and overwhelm it with misery and distress.

Let us also be mindful that the cause of freedom greatly depends on the use we make of the singular opportunities we enjoy of governing ourselves wisely; for, if the event should prove that the people of this country either cannot or will not govern themselves, who will hereafter be advocates for systems which, however charming in theory and prospect, are not reducible to practice? If the people of our nation, instead of consenting to be governed by laws of their own making, and rulers of their own choosing, should let licentiousness, disorder, and confusion, reign over them, the minds of men everywhere will insensibly become alienated from republican forms, and prepared to prefer and acquiesce in governments which, though less friendly to liberty, afford more peace and security.

Receive this address with the same candor with which it is written; and may the spirit of wisdom and patriotism direct and distinguish your councils and your conduct.

John Jay,
a Citizen of New York

Acknowledgments

GLENN

I will use another book for my regular list of acknowledgments. This time I just want to thank *you*. By reading this book you are taking a personal challenge to question with boldness and find the truth for yourself. It's your thirst to learn the *real* history of our founding and the *real* principles that this country stands for—and your enthusiasm for sharing that knowledge—that is the key to saving our Republic.

Laus Deo.

JOSHUA

Special thanks to . . .

All of the guys who went with me on the **WILMINGTON ROAD TRIP: DEREK REMPE**, one of my best friends, and a man who constantly inspires me to serve God more fully; **CHANDLER SCHMIDT**, for being my brother, the one I never had but always wanted, and for always being there; and **ZACH WATCHOUS**, for making me always desire to be a better leader.

Everyone in WILMINGTON who helped along the way: **ROBYN MORRIS**, for teaching me what true prayer is all about, and how deeply God loves us in all circumstances; **ALLEN WILLOUGHBY**, for showing me the power of the reckless, freely given, and unassuming love of God; and **DAVE HINMAN**, for opening up your home to a bunch of rascal college guys, and for being a true brother in Christ, a mentor, and a friend.

GUIN AND SUE BOGGS, for being my second set of parents, for loving me like I was your own son, and for constantly sharpening me and expecting nothing less of me but excellence.

JULIANNE BENZEL, for being the absolute best kind of U.S. History teacher there is, one whose love of history and her students inspires all who know her to be passionate about learning and truth.

SHAWN SPIESS, for being the best friend and the best mentor that anyone in any situation, in any place, in any circumstance, could ever possibly desire.

GLENN BECK, for being the same man in your office as you are on TV, for inspiring the better parts of our nature, and for seeking truth in a world that acts like it is irrelevant.